WIRELESS
HACKS™

Rob Flickenger

O'REILLY®

Beijing · Cambridge · Farnham · Köln · Paris · Sebastopol · Taipei · Tokyo

Wireless Hacks™

by Rob Flickenger

Copyright © 2003 O'Reilly & Associates, Inc. All rights reserved.
Printed in the United States of America.

Published by O'Reilly & Associates, Inc., 1005 Gravenstein Highway North,
Sebastopol, CA 95472.

O'Reilly & Associates books may be purchased for educational, business, or sales pro-
motional use. Online editions are also available for most titles (*safari.oreilly.com*). For
more information, contact our corporate/institutional sales department: (800) 998-9938
or *corporate@oreilly.com*.

Editor:	Rael Dornfest	**Production Editor:**	Mary Brady
Series Editor:	Rael Dornfest	**Cover Designer:**	Emma Colby
Executive Editor:	Dale Dougherty	**Interior Designer:**	David Futato

Printing History:

September 2003:   First Edition.

ISBN: 0-596-00559-8
[C]

Contents

Credits

About the Author

Rob Flickenger has been hacking as long as he can remember. He is the author of two other O'Reilly books: *Linux Server Hacks* and *Building Wireless Community Networks*, which is now in its second edition.

He recently served as sysadmin for the O'Reilly Network, and is currently working on promoting community wireless networking through efforts like NoCat (*http://nocat.net/*) and SeattleWireless (*http://seattlewireless.net/*).

Contributors

The following people contributed their hacks, writing, and inspiration to this book:

- By day, Schuyler Erle (*http://nocat.net/*) works as a software engineer for O'Reilly & Associates, Inc. By night, he hacks on Free Software and agitates for the cause of community networking. Schuyler is also chief architect of NoCatAuth, a leading open source captive portal application.

- Michael Erskine (*http://www.freeantennas.com*) works at Kaballero. Com.

- Based in the heart of Southern California's "Digital Coast," Dr. Trevor Marshall (*http://www.trevormarshall.com/*) offers a full spectrum of consulting services in technologies ranging from Wi-Fi Security and Internet Infrastructure through RF, Hardware, Software, and Audio/Video to Biomedical and Prepress. Previous speaking engagements have included COMDEX, Microprocessor Forums, and WLAN/Wi-Fi Security conferences in Paris, Boston, and Santa Clara.

- Terry Schmidt (*http://www.nycwireless.net/*) is the Vice President and Chief Technology Officer of Emenity, Inc. (*http://www.cloudnetworks. com/*) and is a leading expert on wireless networking technologies and applications. He has presented at major information technology conferences, including MacWorld, the O'Reilly Emerging Technologies Conference, and 802.11Planet.

- Roger Weeks (*http://nocat.net/*) has over ten years of experience in systems and network administration. Most recently he has been involved in building a wireless internet cooperative in Sonoma County, CA. In his spare time, he grows and sells organic herbs.

- Ron Wickersham (*http://www.alembic.com/*) is an inventor and the Chief Engineer at Alembic, Inc. where he designs guitar electronics. His hobbies involve everything interesting in the Universe including The Amateur Sky Survey and watering the flowers.

Acknowledgments

I'd like to thank my family and friends for their continuing support in giving me the encouragement (and occasionally, solitude) needed to complete my various little projects.

Many hacks in this book were inspired by conversations with countless hackers who willingly share their ideas with anyone who will listen. A few came from the weekly "hack night" sessions that SeattleWireless hosts to foster such cross-pollination of ideas. Without the free and enthusiastic exchange of ideas, this book wouldn't have been possible. Thank You to all of the brilliant hackers around the planet who know that the value of sharing one's ideas can greatly exceed the value of a keeping an idea to oneself.

Edd Dumbill, Casey Halverson, and Richard Lotz all provided technical review for the book. Ken Caruso and Matt Westervelt provided equipment, ideas, and valuable insight. Thank you, gentlemen!

And thanks everyone at O'Reilly who made this book a reality, and who continue to help relieve information pain in the world.

Foreword

As my wife likes to remind me, I'm an early adopter. I've bought piles of equipment that litter various shelves in the basement, home office, and work server closet that never quite met the promise that caused me to shell out the bucks in the first place.

Rob Flickenger is an early adopter's early adopter: before the technology has reached the fancy stage in which it's stuck in a box, wrapped in nice plastic clothing, and displayed to the masses, Rob has torn it open, decompiled its innards, and turned every part of it into something rich and strange.

Reading *Wireless Hacks* gives me a warm feeling inside, like holding my hands over the vacuum tube in a pre-transistor radio. The glow of this book illuminates Rob's intense interest in spreading knowledge about cool stuff in order to spread more knowledge about the world in general.

A large part of this book is devoted to extending access, whether it's by range, through antennas, signal strength, and other combinations of electromagnetic voodoo; or by price—introducing us to inexpensive alternatives to commercial gear or providing ways to take off-the-shelf items and, Julia Child-like out of the oven, produce serious production equipment; or by design, showing us ways to configure software to achieve better results.

Back in 1979, when I owned my first computer (an Ohio Scientific, Inc., C1P running a 6502 processor), I used to be a whiz with a soldering iron, assembling my own RS232C port and joystick circuitry. This book takes me back to those days when computing wasn't about fast chips, but it was about a lot of digital parts glued together with analog technology, such as wires and ports.

I guarantee that you don't need to master the art of hot dripping lead to make use of this book. The software tips and configuration advice for commercial gear is worth the price of admittance alone. But if you have ever—or even never—touched the electronic heart of a machine before, this book will reawaken that desire.

This book is the crystal radio of the 21st century, and Rob is the scratchy voice coming out of the receiver, carried over a long distances, without wires.

—Glenn Fleishman
August 15, 2003
Seattle, WA

Preface

Wireless networking technology has shown an explosive growth worldwide over the past few years, bucking the general downward economic trend in the telecommunications industry. What is it about wireless networking that makes it so alluring on a grand scale? Why did over 22 million Wi-Fi devices ship last year, with double that projected by some for this year? While marketing folk might tell you that the particular feature set and brand name of their product is driving demand, I believe the answer is much simpler: it's magic.

Right where you are sitting now, there could be dozens of wireless data networks slinging information to the far corners of the Earth. A neighbor orders food online while someone across the street is using voice chat to talk to relatives (for free!) in Hong Kong, all the while someone upstairs is downloading a new album from their favorite band's web site in San Francisco. The information flows all around you (and, indeed, even through you) without you seeing or hearing a thing. Make no mistake, wireless networking is probably the second most magical technology on the planet—just behind the Internet.

In hundreds of cities around the world, wireless networks are making ubiquitous connectivity more the rule than the exception, providing service (often free) to millions of users who suddenly need nothing more than a laptop and wireless card to get online. Wireless networking is getting people connected to each other more cheaply and easily than any other networking technology since the telephone.

Why Wireless Hacks?

The term *hacking* has a bad reputation in the popular press, where it used to refer to someone who breaks into systems or wreaks havoc with computers as their weapon. Among enthusiasts, on the other hand, the term *hack* refers to a "quick-n-dirty" solution to a problem, or to a clever way to get something done. The term *hacker* is taken very much as a compliment, referring to someone as being *creative*, and having the technical chops to get things done. O'Reilly's Hacks series is an attempt the reclaim the word, document the ways people are hacking (in a good way), and pass the hacker ethic of creative participation on to the uninitiated. Seeing how others approach systems and problems is often the quickest way to learn about a new technology.

Wireless Hacks is about getting the most out of your wireless networking hardware. In this book, you will find practical techniques for extending range, increasing throughput, managing wireless resources, and generally making your wireless networking vision a reality. Remember that reality is what you can get away with, and wireless hackers have found that they can get away with quite a lot using surprisingly little. This book will show you some of the best bits of their collected experience.

How to Use This Book

You can read this book from cover to cover if you like, but for the most part, each hack stands on its own. So feel free to browse, flipping around to whatever sections interest you most.

How This Book Is Organized

This book is divided into several subjects by chapter:

Chapter 1, *The Standards*
> Wireless technology has not only produced impressive improvements to communications, but also has produced an impressive list of acronyms. What is the difference between GPRS and GMRS? Which is fastest, 802.11, 802.11a, 802.11b, 802.11g, or 802.16? Exactly how do Wi-Fi and Bluetooth fit into all of this? This chapter will give you a good idea of what problems each technology is designed to solve, their relative strengths and weaknesses, and how to make the best possible use of each to solve your communication needs.

Chapter 2, *Bluetooth and Mobile Data*
> The last couple of years have brought millions of tiny battery-powered wireless devices to market. Some will get you an Internet connection just about anywhere with mobile phone service, while others keep your devices connected to the "last ten feet." This chapter demonstrates some uses for these technologies, which will keep your devices (and yourself) hyperconnected, without wires.

Chapter 3, *Network Monitoring*

Wireless networking can be a lot of fun, but when it breaks, trouble-shooting can be difficult without a good idea of what is really happening. This chapter will give you the tools you need to detect the presence of wireless networks, coordinate spectrum usage to avoid interference, and visualize network performance. It also covers a number of advanced data monitoring techniques to pinpoint networking issues and even get an idea of your users' online habits.

Chapter 4, *Hardware Hacks*

If it weren't for the hardware, there would be no such thing as wireless networks. This extensive chapter tells you how to push wireless hardware to the limits, extending range and increasing performance and efficiency. A large collection of microwave cables, connectors, antennas, and other components are presented, along with sources and recommendations on how best to use them. When that's not enough, you will find everything you need to know to build your own network access point from scratch.

Chapter 5, *Do-It-Yourself Antennas*

Since the first electrical spark was transmitted a few feet across a room more than 100 years ago, antenna design has been a fascination for wireless experimenters everywhere. This chapter presents several home-brew designs for wireless networking made by contributors from all over the world. These are practical, tested designs that can significantly extend the range of your wireless network.

Chapter 6, *Long Distance Links*

Having the equipment in place is one thing, but being able to make a wireless segment stretch for miles requires real-world experience. This chapter is a collection of techniques to help simplify the job of building long distance networks.

Chapter 7, *Wireless Security*

There has been a lot of press recently about the insecurity of wireless networks. In many cases, these alarmist reports are in fact absolutely true—the vast majority of wireless networks are either unintentionally left open, or worse, rely on unreliable methods for keeping them secure. This chapter explores the current standards for securing wireless networks, and suggests several strong methods for protecting yourself and your wireless users from abuse.

Conventions Used in This Book

The following is a list of the typographical conventions used in this book:

Italic

> Used to indicate new terms, URLs, filenames, file extensions, and directories, and to highlight comments in examples. For example, a path in the filesystem will appear as */usr/local*.

`Constant width`

> Used to show code examples, the contents of files, commands, or the output from commands.

`Constant width bold`

> Used in examples and tables to show commands or other text that should be typed literally.

`Constant width italic`

> Used in examples and tables to show text that should be replaced with user-supplied values.

Color

> The second color is used to indicate a cross-reference within the text.

↵

> A carriage return (↵) at the end of a line of code is used to denote an unnatural line break; that is, you should not enter these as two lines of code, but as one continuous line. Multiple lines are used in these cases due to page width constraints.

Menu symbols

> When looking at the menus for any application, you will see some symbols associated with keyboard shortcuts for a particular command. For example, to open a file, you would go to the File menu and select Open… (File → Open…). For Macintosh users, many menus have keyboard equivalents using the ⌘ symbol. The ⌘ symbol corresponds to the ⌘ key (also known as the "Command" key), located to the left and right of the spacebar on any Macintosh keyboard.

You should pay special attention to notes set apart from the text with the following icons.

 This is a tip, suggestion, or general note. It contains useful supplementary information about the topic at hand.

This is a warning or note of caution.

The thermometer icons, found next to each hack, indicate the relative complexity of the hack.

 beginner   moderate   expert

How to Contact Us

We have tested and verified the information in this book to the best of our ability, but you may find that features have changed (or even that we have made mistakes!). As a reader of this book, you can help us to improve future editions by sending us your feedback. Please let us know about any errors, inaccuracies, bugs, misleading or confusing statements, and typos that you find anywhere in this book.

Please also let us know what we can do to make this book more useful to you. We take your comments seriously and will try to incorporate reasonable suggestions into future editions. You can write to us at:

O'Reilly & Associates, Inc.
1005 Gravenstein Highway North
Sebastopol, CA 95472
(800) 998-9938 (in the U.S. or Canada)
(707) 829-0515 (international/local)
(707) 829-0104 (fax)

You can also send us messages electronically. To be put on the mailing list or to request a catalog, send email to:

info@oreilly.com

To ask technical questions or to comment on the book, send email to:

bookquestions@oreilly.com

The web site for *Wireless Hacks* lists examples, errata, and plans for future editions. You can find this page at:

http://www.oreilly.com/catalog/wirelesshks

For more information about this book and others, see the O'Reilly web site:

http://www.oreilly.com

Hack on! at:

http://hacks.oreilly.com

The Standards

Hacks #1–12

The mad rush to bring wireless products to market has left a slew of similar sounding yet often completely incompatible acronyms in its wake. 802.11b is the sequel to 802.11a, right? (Wrong.) If I just buy Wi-Fi, then everything will work together, right? (Unfortunately, no.) What is the difference between 802.11 a/b/g, 802.16, and 802.1x? How about GSM, GPRS, GMRS, and GPS? Where does Bluetooth fit into the picture?

Before we can jump into the more advanced hackery that is possible with wireless communications, it is important to understand what we have to work with. Remember that no technology is inherently "better" than any other; which one you should use depends on what you want to accomplish and the resources you have to work with. The goal of this chapter is to familiarize you with many of the popular wireless technologies available today, and to give you an idea of their relative strengths and weaknesses.

HACK #1 802.11: The Mother of All IEEE Wireless Ethernet

While definitely showing its age, the original 802.11 gear still has its uses.

The first wireless standard to be defined in the 802 wireless family was 802.11. It was approved by the IEEE in 1997, and defines three possible physical layers: Frequency Hopping Spread Spectrum (FHSS) at 2.4 GHz, Direct Sequence Spread Spectrum (DSSS) at 2.4 GHz, or Infrared. 802.11 could achieve data rates of 1 or 2 Mbps. 802.11 radios that use DSSS are interoperable with 802.11b and 802.11g radios at those speeds, while FHSS radios and Infrared obviously are not.

The original 802.11 devices are increasingly hard to come by, but can still be useful for point-to-point links with low bandwidth requirements.

Pros

- Very inexpensive (a few dollars or even free) when you can find them.
- DSSS cards are compatible with 802.11b/g.
- Infrared 802.11 cards (while rare) can offer interference-free wireless connections, particularly in noisy RF environments.
- Infrared also offers increased security due to significantly shorter range.

Cons

- No longer manufactured.
- Low data rate of 1 or 2 Mbps.
- FHSS radios are incompatible with everything else.

Recommendation

802.11 devices can still be useful, particularly if you find that you already have a few on hand. But the ever falling price of 802.11b and 802.11g gear makes the old 802.11 equipment less attractive each day. The FHSS and Infrared cards talk only to cards of the same era, so don't expect them to work outside of your own projects. Infrared requires an absolutely clean line of sight between devices and offers limited range, but it operates well away from the popular ISM and UNII bands. This means that it won't interfere with (or see interference from) other networking devices, which can be a huge advantage in some situations.

I probably wouldn't go out of my way to acquire 802.11 equipment, but you can still build a useful network if it's all you have to work with. They are probably best used for building point-to-point links, but might be better avoided altogether.

HACK #2 802.11a: The Betamax of the 802.11 Family

802.11a offers more channels, higher speed, and less interference than other protocols, but it still just isn't popular.

According to the specifications available from the IEEE (at *http://standards. ieee.org/getieee802/*), both 802.11a and 802.11b were ratified on September 16, 1999. Early on, 802.11a was widely touted as the "802.11b killer," as it not only provides significantly faster data rates (up to 54 Mbps raw, or about 27 Mbps actual data), but also operates in a completely different spectrum—the 5 GHz UNII band. It uses an encoding technique called Orthogonal Frequency Division Multiplexing (OFDM).

While the promises of higher speeds and freedom from interference with 2.4 GHz devices made 802.11a sound promising, it came to market much later than 802.11b. It also suffers from range problems: at the same power and gain, signals at 5 GHz appear to travel only half as far as signals at 2.4 GHz, presenting a real technical hurdle for designers and implementers. The rapid adoption of 802.11b only made matters worse, since users of 802.11b gear didn't have a clear upgrade path to 802.11a (as the two are not compatible). As a result, 802.11a still isn't nearly as ubiquitous or inexpensive as 802.11b, although client cards and dual-band access points (which essentially incorporate two radios, or a single radio with a dual-band chipset) are coming down in price.

Pros

- Very fast data rates: up to 54 Mbps (raw radio rate), with some vendors providing 72 Mbps or faster with proprietary extensions.
- Uses the much less cluttered (for now, in the U.S.) UNII band, at 5.8 GHz.

Cons

- As of this writing, 802.11a equipment is still more expensive on average than 802.11b or 802.11g.
- Most 802.11a client devices are add-on cards, and the technology is built into relatively few consumer devices (specifically laptops).
- 802.11a PCMCIA cards require a 32-bit CardBus slot, and won't work in older devices.
- Cards and APs with external antenna connectors are hard to find, making distance work difficult.
- Upgrading from 802.11b can be painful, as 5.8 GHz radiates very differently from 2.4 GHz, requiring a new site survey and likely more APs.
- Limited range compared to 802.11b and 802.11g, at the same power levels and gain.
- Internal 802.11a antennas tend to be quite directional, making them sometimes annoyingly sensitive to proper orientation for best results.

Recommendation

The Wi-Fi alliance (*http://www.weca.net/*) tried to call 802.11a "Wi-Fi5," but the name never stuck. These devices are also sometimes confusingly labeled "Wi-Fi," just like the completely incompatible 802.11b. Be sure to look for the specification's real name (802.11a) when purchasing gear.

802.11a can be significantly faster than 802.11b, but achieves roughly the same throughput as 802.11g (27 Mbps for 802.11a, compared to 20–25 Mbps for 802.11g). 802.11a would be ideal for creating point-to-point links, if devices with external antenna connectors were more readily available. Many people tout OFDM's ability to cope with reflections caused by obstacles (called *multipath*) as a good reason to use 802.11a, but 802.11g uses the same encoding while achieving greater range at the same power and gain. Some consider the shorter range of 802.11a to be a security advantage, but this can lead to a false sense of security. See the introduction to Chapter 6, as well as "Calculating the Link Budget" [Hack #81] for more details.

Keep in mind that the 54 Mbps data rate is the theoretical maximum, and frequently is only achieved when in very close proximity to the AP. The speed scales back sharply as your distance from the AP increases, and suffers dramatically when separated by a wall or other solid obstacle. It is a very good idea to perform a site survey complete with throughput testing to determine whether 802.11a is suitable for your intended location.

It is probably a bad idea to build an 802.11a-only network unless you are already committed to using only 802.11a gear. If you want to allow guests to use your network, it is a very good idea to at least incorporate a few dual-band APs (or perhaps a dedicated 802.11g AP), as guest users are more likely to bring 802.11b or 802.11g gear with them.

HACK #3   802.11b: The De Facto Standard

Many people continue to use 802.11b, the protocol of the Wi-Fi revolution.

Throughout this book, I mainly discuss 802.11b (also known as Wi-Fi, but then, so is 802.11a). It is the de facto wireless networking standard of the last few years, and for good reason. It offers excellent range and respectable throughput. (While the radio can send frames at up to 11 Mbps, protocol overhead puts the data rate at 5 to 6 Mbps, which is about on par with 10baseT-wired Ethernet.) It operates using DSSS at 2.4 GHz, and automatically selects the best data rate (either 1, 2, 5.5 or 11 Mbps), depending on available signal strength. Its greatest advantage at this point is its ubiquity: millions of 802.11b devices have shipped, and the cost of client and access point gear is not only phenomenally low, but also ships embedded in many laptop and handheld devices. Since it can move data at rates much faster than the average Internet connection, it is widely regarded as "good enough" for general use.

Pros

- Near universal ubiquity in standard consumer devices, add-on cards, and APs.

- Extreme popularity and pressure from 802.11a/g has led to massively discounted hardware. Cards less than $40 and APs less than $100 are common as of this writing.

- 802.11b "hot spots" are available at many coffee shops, restaurants, public parks, libraries, and airports, further increasing its popularity.

- With many people using and experimenting with it, 802.11b is arguably the most hackable (and customizable) wireless protocol on the planet.

Cons

- The 11 Mbps data rate of 802.11b will never get any faster, and is already surpassed by 802.11a and 802.11g.

- 802.11b's channel scheme allows only for three nonoverlapping channels, making for considerable contention in the 2.4 GHz ISM band.

- Standard 802.11b security features have been revealed to be less than effective. See "Dispel the Myth of Wireless Security" [Hack #87] and all of Chapter 7 for details.

Recommendation

While it is impossible to forecast the fickle weather patterns of the consumer marketplace, it is very likely that 802.11b has at least a few years left in it. Millions of devices have shipped, making it the most popular wireless networking protocol on the planet. Ironically, it will probably get a life extension from its competitor 802.11g, as the newer 802.11g equipment will work with existing 802.11b access points. This makes upgrades less of an immediate issue, and if there's anything that network administrators hate, it's upgrading the critical network devices.

Considering that average Internet speeds are still much slower than 802.11b, it is likely that 802.11b will be used as a mechanism for providing Internet access for some time yet. Backbone links and corporate networks may have an immediate need for the increased bandwidth of 802.11a and 802.11g, but for the average Internet user, 802.11b provides sufficient speed and a very simple mechanism for accessing networks. Even after three years of explosive growth, 802.11b continues to enjoy a lively general acceptance.

802.11g: Like 802.11b, only Faster

#4   Turbo charge your wireless network without leaving your 802.11b users in the cold.

At the time of this writing, the 802.11g specification has just been ratified by the IEEE. 802.11g uses the OFDM encoding of 802.11a in the 2.4 GHz band, and also falls back to DSSS to maintain backwards compatibility with 802.11b radios. This means that raw speeds of 54 Mbps (20 to 25 Mbps data) are achievable in the 2.4 GHz band, all while keeping backwards compatibility with existing 802.11b gear. This is a very promising technology—so promising, in fact, that the lack of ratification didn't stop some manufacturers from shipping gear that used the draft standard, even before it was ratified.

Pros

- Very high data rates of up to 54 Mbps.
- Backwards compatibility with the phenomenally popular 802.11b offers a simple upgrade path for existing users.
- 802.11g uses the same band as 802.11b, so existing antennas and feed lines can be reused.

Cons

- Slightly more expensive than 802.11b, but prices are expected to fall as more equipment ships.
- As it uses the 2.4 GHz ISM band, 802.11g will have to contend with many other devices, leading to more interference in crowded areas.

Recommendation

If you are building a network from scratch, strongly consider the benefits of 802.11g. It allows existing 802.11b users to continue to use the network, while providing a significant speed boost for 802.11g users. While it is a very new technology, reports from early adopters look very good. Apple has already decided to use 802.11g as its high speed standard in their new "Air-Port Extreme" line of wireless gear. Note that the WECA hasn't referred to 802.11g as "Wi-Fi" yet, but just give them time.

802.11g will likely be a massively popular technology, as it promises many of the advantages of 802.11a without significantly raising cost or breaking backwards compatibility. My advice is to keep watching 802.11g and roll it out if you can afford it. Since it offers many advantages with relatively few drawbacks, I believe it is poised to become the next massively ubiquitous wireless technology.

802.16: Long Distance Wireless Infrastructure

The long awaited Municipal Area Network protocol is on the way, but isn't here just yet.

Approved on December 6, 2001, 802.16 promises to be the answer to all of the shortcomings of long distance applications that people have encountered using 802.11 protocols. It should be pointed out that the 802.11 family was never intended to provide long distance, metropolitan-area coverage (although I'll show you some examples of people doing exactly that). The 802.16 specification is specifically designed for providing wireless infrastructure that will cover entire cities, with typical ranges measured in kilometers. It will use frequencies from 10 to 66 GHz to provide commercial quality services to stationary locations (i.e., buildings). In January 2003, a new extension (802.16a) was ratified, which will operate in the 2 to 11 GHz range. This should help significantly with line-of-sight requirements of the extremely short waves of 10 to 66 GHz. Realistically, actual equipment that implements 802.16 is just now coming to market, and will likely be priced well above the consumer-grade equipment of the 802.11 family.

Pros

- 802.16 is designed for long-range networking, likely providing ranges of 20 to 30 kilometers.
- Very high speed for fixed wireless, probably about 70 Mbps.

Cons

- Shorter wavelengths of 10 to 66 GHz are more susceptible to signal fade due to environmental conditions (such as rain).
- Many bands used by 802.16 and 802.16a are licensed spectrum.
- It's just not available yet.

Recommendation

It will be interesting to see the 802.16 MAN story as it evolves, but it's too early to tell how this technology will fare. Fujitsu is currently developing an 802.16a chipset that it expects to have ready sometime in 2004, and is currently targeting a price tag of about $300. 802.16 will certainly be a welcome technology for long distance point-to-multipoint applications, which are difficult to implement effectively using 802.11. But unfortunately, the hardware isn't available to play with yet.

Bluetooth: Cable Replacement for Devices

Bluetooth eliminates the need for cables that tether your tiny devices.

While the 802.11 protocols were designed to replace the ubiquitous CAT5 networking cable, Bluetooth aims to replace all of the *other* cables connected to your computer (with the sad exception of the power cable). Operating as a frequency hopper in the 2.4 GHz ISM band, it shares the same spectrum as 802.11b/g and many other devices. It is designed to create a so-called "Personal Area Network" for devices like cell phones, digital cameras, PDAs, headsets, keyboards and mice, and of course, computers. While it is possible to use Bluetooth for an actual Internet connection, it seems to be better suited for low bandwidth data and voice applications.

Pros

- Very low power requirements, making it ideal for small battery-powered devices such as handhelds, phones, and headsets.
- Simple interface and security model.
- Exceptional interoperability between devices.
- Built-in support for simultaneous data and voice traffic.

Cons

- Relatively low data throughput (about 720 Kbps maximum).
- Shares the 2.4 GHz band with many other devices, including 802.11b/g.
- Very limited range, by design.

Recommendation

Bluetooth uses an aggressive full duplex frequency–hopping scheme (changing channels up to 1,600 times per second) to attempt to avoid noise in the 2.4 GHz band. While this may be good for Bluetooth, high power frequency–hopping devices can cause considerable interference for other devices using the band. Fortunately, most Bluetooth products operate only at 1mW, keeping most interference limited to a very small area. Even when using Bluetooth alongside an 802.11b connection, the perceived interference turns out to be minimal, and most people don't even notice the difference with normal usage. If you are using 802.11a in the presence of Bluetooth devices, the two will not interfere with each other at all.

The 802.11 protocols and Bluetooth are complementary and solve very different problems. I will show you some cool things you can do with Bluetooth in Chapter 2, and much of the rest of this book will focus on fun with 802.11.

900 MHz: Low Speed, Better Coverage

HACK #7

Ubiquity is sometimes more important than speed. If you absolutely need to make a link that isn't possible with 802.11, then this older gear might be for you.

In the days before 802.11, a number of FCC Part 15 wireless networking products were competing in the marketplace. For example, Aironet, Inc. (before it was bought by Cisco) produced the Arlan networking series. The Arlan APs and bridges use 10baseT Ethernet, operate at 900 MHz, and have a data rate of 215 Kbps or 860 Kbps. They also made a number of complementary PCMCIA radio cards (the 655-900, 690-900, and PC1000, for example). These devices put out up to a whopping 1 Watt at 900 MHz. NCR had the WaveLAN 900 MHz line that included an ISA and PCMCIA card that would push 2 Mbps at 250mW. While the data rate can't compare to modern wireless networking gear, the higher power and lower frequency of this equipment offers significant advantages.

As the frequency of a signal increases, the apparent range it can cover at the same power and gain decreases. For example, a 100mW signal at 5.8 GHz appears to travel less than half the distance of a 100mW signal at 2.4 GHz, which appears to travel less than half that of a 100mW signal at 900 MHz. There is no limit to how far a signal can actually go, but its ability to rise above the background noise and be detected at a usable level is bounded by its power, frequency, and antenna gain. So to put it simply, all other variables being equal, lower frequency signals travel further than higher frequency signals. You can make higher frequency signals appear to travel further, but to do so you need to increase the power, antenna gain, or both.

Another curious property of radio is that the requirement of having line of sight between the devices becomes more important at higher frequencies, but is less critical at lower frequencies. Higher frequencies don't fare so well when there are obstacles between the ends of the radio link (particularly in urban and indoor settings). This property, combined with the advantage of greater range, means that 900 MHz equipment can be used in a variety of situations where 802.11b/g or 802.11a don't fare as well. It can penetrate foliage, buildings, and other obstacles better than its 802.11 counterparts. Of course, the big trade-off is throughput.

Pros

- Higher power and superior range.
- Equipment doesn't compete with the increasingly crowded 2.4 GHz ISM band, but must still tolerate 900 MHz phones, video cameras, baby monitors, and other devices.

Cons

- Low data throughput, from serial speeds of 9,600 bps up to 2 Mbps or so.
- Very little vendor interoperability.
- With the advent of 802.11 networking, 900 MHz gear has increasingly limited availability.
- Equipment can be quite expensive compared to 802.11 gear.

Recommendation

A number of manufacturers offer serial or Ethernet to 900 MHz bridges. While Ethernet is generally preferable, the serial devices are perfectly capable of supporting a PPP connection between two sites. If you need to create a long distance point-to-point link (particularly where clean line of sight just isn't possible) and can cope with limited data rates, then this equipment might be right for your project. Expect the hardware to be difficult to locate and a bit more expensive than the typical consumer grade 802.11b equivalent.

HACK #8 CDPD, 1xRTT, and GPRS: Cellular Data Networks

If you can't roll your own wireless, you might try one of these mobile phone carrier networks.

When it comes to data rates, most people are in agreement that faster is better. But current communications technology always involves a trade-off between speed, power, and range. 54 Mbps may be great if you can get it, but on a large scale, this can be difficult to maintain. The 802.11 protocols compensate for increased range by scaling back the data rate, but these devices simply aren't designed to serve hundreds of people scattered over many miles.

There are times when any data to the Internet is better than none at all, no matter how slow it might be. For example, you might need to log in to a remote machine or send a quick email while traveling, when Wi-Fi or even wired network access just isn't available. Or maybe you want to have an alternate communications channel into a wireless node in a remote place (say, on a mountaintop or deep in the woods) where telephone lines aren't even available. For these situations, you might consider exploiting the biggest advantage of the commercial mobile data networks: their ubiquity.

Mobile networks maybe be slow and relatively expensive, but you can't beat their coverage compared to current Wi-Fi networks. They can give you an IP address just about anywhere, but be warned that most mobile data services are not cheap. Most charge by the byte, and all charge for airtime while you are using it.

The type of data service you can use depends on the underlying wireless technology. Obviously, before choosing a technology, determine the coverage area of the mobile network in the place you intend to use it. The three leading mobile data services are described next, in decreasing order of availability in the U.S.

CDPD on TDMA

CDPD stands for *Cellular Digital Packet Data*. It works over the enormously popular *Time Division Multiple Access* (TDMA) mobile network, which is easily the most widely deployed mobile network in the U.S. CDPD "modems" typically use a serial port or PCMCIA slot and offer speeds of up to 19.2 Kbps (real world is typically closer to 9,600 bps).

It looks like TDMA operators are generally migrating to GSM, so it is probably unlikely that TDMA data services will ever be upgraded. In some areas, TDMA is being phased out altogether, making it difficult to obtain a CDPD account. But despite the relatively slow speed of CDPD, you can't beat its coverage. Virtually all of the populated regions of the U.S. are covered by TDMA.

1xRTT on CDMA

CDMA stands for *Code Division Multiple Access*: it is the second most popular mobile technology in the U.S. The original CDMA data services offered speeds of 9600 bps to 14.4 Kbps. A new upgrade called 1xRTT boasts speeds of up to 144 Kbps, but by many reports, real-world throughput is somewhere between 60 and 80 Kbps, occasionally bursting to 144 Kbps if you get lucky. If you think the 802.11 protocol names aren't confusing enough, you should really try following mobile phone technology. 1xRTT is also known in various circles as CDMA2000 Phase 1, or simply 95-C.

1xRTT is just the first phase of the CDMA2000 plan. A few communities are now trying the experimental 1xEV-DO technology, which can theoretically achieve 2 Mbps from fixed locations over CDMA. This technology hasn't yet been widely deployed. Also, we are told to expect 1xRTT Release A by the end of 2003. This is a software upgrade that promises 144 Kbps uploads and downloads of up to 300 Kbps.

GPRS on GSM

GPRS stands for *General Packet Radio Service*, and is the data service available on *Global System for Mobile communications* (GSM) networks. The original GSM data services offered only 9,600 bps throughput, but GPRS allows real-world speeds of 20 to 30 kbps. GPRS is a packet-based protocol, meaning that the GPRS radio transmits only when it actually has data to send. This can save on battery usage, and theoretically makes more efficient use of the network. A number of nifty gadgets such as the HipTop by Danger (*http://www.danger.com/*) use GPRS for connectivity.

Eventually, GPRS may be replaced by technologies like *Enhanced Data for Global Evolution* (EDGE—you have to ask yourself how they can use these acronyms with a straight face), which offers theoretical speeds of up to 384 Kbps over GSM. EDGE is still experimental, and hasn't yet been widely deployed. As of this writing, GSM coverage is increasing rapidly in the U.S. but still isn't as ubiquitous as CDMA or TDMA. Much of the rest of the world has a more thoroughly deployed GSM network.

If you find that you need simple wireless connectivity beyond what you can hope to provide with 802.11 technologies, commercial data networks are a viable alternative. They don't come cheap, but can be perfect for many low bandwidth applications.

HACK #9 FRS and GMRS: Super Walkie-Talkies

Use these high powered radios in places where mobile phones just don't cut it.

In the last couple of years, a number of manufacturers have come out with "high power" radios for general use, marketed as family or recreational communication devices and sold as impulse buy items at department stores. They claim a couple of miles range, operate on a chargeable battery pack or AA batteries, and most are surprisingly rugged and simple to use.

The two technologies behind these popular radios are *FRS* and *GMRS*. While sold in similar packaging and frequently sitting on shelves right next to each other, these two types of radios are quite different in capabilities and operating rules.

FRS

FRS stands for *Family Radio Service*, and was approved by the FCC for unlicensed use in 1996. It operates around 462 and 467 MHz, and is sometimes referred to as "UHF Citizens Band." It is *not* a Part 15 device like 802.11 radios, but is governed by FCC Part 95, *Personal Radio Services*. FRS radios share some channels with GMRS radios but are restricted to 500mW maximum power. Manufacturers typically claim two miles as the maximum range of FRS radios. FRS radios come with fixed antennas, and cannot be legally modified to accommodate antennas or amplifiers.

FRS channels 1 through 7 overlap with GMRS and can be used to communicate with GMRS radios. If you need to talk only to other FRS radios, use channels 8 through 14 to avoid possible interference with low band GMRS users. See Table 1-1 for the full list of FRS and GMRS frequencies.

GMRS

GMRS stands for *General Mobile Radio Service*, and is also known as "Class A Citizens Band." Its use is also covered by FCC Part 95, but requires a license to operate. As of this writing, a personal license costs $75 and can be obtained online at *http://wireless.fcc.gov/uls/*.

Handheld GMRS units can put out up to 5 Watts of power, although 4-Watt handhelds are more common. While fixed-base stations can use up to 15 Watts on most frequencies, they are restricted to 5 Watts when communicating on the FRS channels. Repeater stations are allowed and can transmit as high as 50 Watts. Both fixed-base stations and repeaters can only transmit on the lower "462" frequencies, while handhelds can operate on any GMRS frequency. Again, see Table 1-1 for the full list of FRS and GMRS frequencies. GMRS gear can include removable antennas, making it simple to use a handheld with a car mount or stationary antenna. Combined with the ability to use repeaters, GMRS can be used to communicate over considerable distances.

Table 1-1. FRS and GMRS frequencies

Lower frequency	Upper frequency	Purpose
462.550	467.550	GMRS "550"
462.5625	--	FRS channel 1, GMRS "5625"
462.575	467.575	GMRS "575"
462.5875	--	FRS channel 2, GMRS "5875"
462.600	467.600	GMRS "600"
462.6125	--	FRS channel 3, GMRS "6125"
462.625	467.625	GMRS "625"
462.6375	--	FRS channel 4, GMRS "6375"
462.650	467.650	GMRS "650"
462.6625	--	FRS channel 5, GMRS "6625"
462.675	467.675	GMRS "675"
462.6875	--	FRS channel 6, GMRS "6875"
462.700	467.700	GMRS "700"
462.7125	--	FRS channel 7, GMRS "7125"
462.725	467.725	GMRS "725"
467.5625	--	FRS channel 8

Table 1-1. FRS and GMRS frequencies (continued)

Lower frequency	Upper frequency	Purpose
467.5875	--	FRS channel 9
467.6125	--	FRS channel 10
467.6375	--	FRS channel 11
467.6625	--	FRS channel 12
467.6875	--	FRS channel 13
467.7125	--	FRS channel 14

Typically, handheld GMRS units use lower frequencies to communicate with each other when possible, and transmit on the upper frequencies (while listening 5 MHz lower) to talk to a repeater. This allows anyone listening on the "462" side to hear traffic both from handhelds as well as from anyone using the repeater. Always use the lower frequencies and the lowest power settings whenever possible to help avoid unnecessary interference with other GMRS users. Use repeaters only when you can't otherwise establish communications.

Extending Range

While higher power radios can help extend your range a little, the best method for increasing your range is to increase your altitude. UHF radios can reach significantly further when the antenna is high in the air, even with limited power. This is one reason why the Part 95 rules limit "small control stations" to antennas no more than 20 feet higher than the structure to which they are mounted. To make the best use of your FRS or GMRS radio, find high ground when transmitting. In some cases, this can push your available range out many, many miles. If you are using a GMRS radio, attaching it to a tall antenna can significantly improve your effective range.

While these radios are half duplex and allow only limited data transmissions, they are handy in a number of situations. For example, when fine tuning a long distance point-to-point 802.11 link, you may find them far more useful than mobile phones. Any time you are working far away from a city, particularly on hills and mountains, FRS and GMRS radios can work considerably better than a phone. But don't get any bright ideas about connecting a radio to a telephone patch; this is prohibited on both FRS and GMRS.

This writing is by no means authoritative on the labyrinthine FCC rulebook, but should give you an idea of what each technology is good for. If in doubt, see the rules for yourself online at *http://www.access.gpo.gov/nara/cfr/waisidx_00/47cfr95_00.html*. If you are looking for more information about FRS and GMRS, there is also a wealth of information available from the Personal Radio Steering Group at *http://www.provide.net/~prsg/rules.htm*.

802.1x: Port Security for Network Communications

Secure access to virtually any network port (wired or wireless) with 802.1x.

The 802.1x protocol is actually not a wireless protocol at all. It describes a method for port authentication that can be applied to nearly any network connection, whether wired or wireless.

Just when you thought you knew every IEEE spec relating to wireless, suddenly 802.1x appeared on the scene. The full title of 802.1x is "802.1x: Port Based Network Access Control." Interestingly enough, 802.1x wasn't originally designed for use in wireless networks; it is a generic solution to the problem of port security. Imagine a college campus with thousands of Ethernet jacks scattered throughout libraries, classrooms, and computer labs. At any time, someone could bring their laptop on campus, sit down at an unoccupied jack, plug in, and instantly gain unlimited access to the campus network. If network abuse by the general public were common, it might be desirable to enforce a policy of port access control that permitted only students and faculty to use the network.

This is where 802.1x fits in. Before any network access (to Layer 2 or above) is permitted, the client (the *supplicant*, in 802.1x parlance) must authenticate itself. When first connected, the supplicant can only exchange data with a component called the *authenticator*. This in turn checks credentials with a central data source (the *Authentication Server*), typically a RADIUS server or other existing user database. If all goes well, the authenticator notifies the supplicant that access is granted (along with some other optional data) and the client can go about its merry way. The various encryption methods employed are not defined in particular, but an extensible framework for encryption is provided—the *Extensible Authentication Protocol*, or EAP.

802.1x is widely regarded by the popular press as "the fix" for the problems of authentication in wireless networks. For example, the "other data" that is sent back to the supplicant could contain WEP keys that are dynamically assigned per session and are automatically renewed every so often, making most data collection attacks against WEP futile. Unfortunately, 802.1x has been found to be susceptible to certain session hijacking, denial of service, and man-in-the-middle attacks when used with wireless networks, making the use of 802.1x as the "ultimate" security tool a questionable proposition.

As of this writing, 802.1x drivers for Windows XP and 2000 are available, and many access points (notably Cisco and Proxim) support some flavor of 802.1x. There is also an open source 802.1x supplicant implementation project available at *http://www.open1x.org/*. It is possible to use the Host AP driver to provide authenticator services to a RADIUS server or other authentication server via the backend.

Unfortunately, the popular press tends to abbreviate 802.11a/b/g as 802.11x, which looks a lot like 802.1x—but don't be fooled. While it has an application in wireless networks, 802.1x actually has nothing to do with wireless networking. For a good discussion of 802.1x security methods and problems online, take a look at *http://www.sans.org/rr/wireless/802.11.php*.

H A C K   HPNA and Powerline Ethernet
#11   These nontraditional networking protocols can save you a ton of effort.

While not wireless networking protocols per se, both HPNA and Powerline Ethernet are finding their way into many people's network scheme. Like wireless, they both provide network functionality without requiring the installation of CAT5 cable. But rather than use wireless, they use other common media for their physical connection.

HPNA

HPNA stands for *Home Phone Networking Alliance*. It provides networking capabilities over existing CAT3 cable, and can share the same wire as a standard telephone line (even if you are using DSL on the same line). HPNA can reach about 1,000 feet over CAT3. The original HPNA 1.0 products can communicate at about 1.3 Mbps, while the newer HPNA 2.0 standard allows for speeds of up to 32 Mbps (although devices operating at 10 Mbps are more common). Some consumer grade routers, such as 2Wire Home-Portal 100W, incorporate Ethernet, HPNA, and 802.11b in one unit.

Pros

- Instant networking in any building with existing telephone wiring.
- Very simple installation; just plug it in and you're done.
- Fairly inexpensive.

Cons

- HPNA isn't nearly as popular as Ethernet or Wireless, so it can sometimes be hard to find in retail stores.
- HPNA 1.0 is much slower than wireless, but HPNA 2.0 approaches speeds of 802.11b.
- Every HPNA device uses the telephone line as a shared medium, making it less efficient than a network switch as more devices are added.

Recommendation

HPNA can be ideal for adding access points to additional locations in a house or building that doesn't have CAT5 Ethernet laid to each room. Dedicated Ethernet is better for speed and reliability, but HPNA can make your job much easier. If you need to add additional access points to a building for greater coverage, or you want to shoot "through" a building by adding a device with external antennas on opposite walls, then HPNA can save a great deal of effort when tying it all together.

Powerline Ethernet

Powerline Ethernet uses AC power lines as a physical medium for network traffic. Powerline devices are about as simple as they come; simply plug in a CAT5 cable to one side of the device, plug the other end into any wall outlet, and you should be up and running. Some devices support encryption on the devices, but this is hardly ever necessary. Powerline Ethernet won't cross a power transformer, so your network signal usually stops at the end of your house wiring.

Siemens, Linksys, and NetGear all make popular Powerline adapters that should interoperate well with each other. They advertise speeds of up to 14 Mbps, but actual data rates of 5 or 6 Mbps are typical. As with HPNA, Powerline is a shared medium, much like a networking hub. More devices means more possible collisions and lower throughput.

Pros

- Very simple installation, with virtually no configuration needed.
- Data speeds comparable to 802.11b.
- Ethernet bridges mean no configuration at all on the computer side.

Cons

- Slightly expensive as of this writing (typically $100 per device, with at least two devices required).

Recommendation

Much like HPNA, Powerline Ethernet can be ideal in situations where CAT5 wiring just isn't practical. This can make installation much simpler whenever you have an AC outlet handy but can't quite get to a telephone line or CAT5 cable. There is no configuration needed in most cases, as the Powerline bridge acts just like a network hub to your Ethernet devices.

While CAT5 is usually preferred over line-sharing protocols such as HPNA and Powerline, these devices can save you a tremendous amount of installation time and effort. If you can cope with the slower data rates and slightly higher cost (compared to Ethernet), then these devices might be a perfect component for your wireless networking project.

HACK #12   BSS Versus IBSS

BSS/Master/AP/Infrastructure/IBSS/Ad-Hoc/Peer-to-Peer: these all refer to 802.11b operating modes, but what does it all mean?

802.11b (see "802.11b: The De Facto Standard" [Hack #3]) defines two possible (and mutually exclusive) radio modes that stations can use to intercommunicate. Those modes are *BSS* and *IBSS*.

BSS stands for *Basic Service Set*. In this operating mode, one station (the *BSS master*, usually a piece of hardware called an *access point*) acts as a gateway between the wireless and a wired (likely Ethernet) backbone. Before gaining access to the wired network, wireless clients (also called *BSS clients*) must first establish communications with an access point within range. Once the AP has authenticated the wireless client, it allows packets to flow between the client and the attached wired network, either routing traffic at Layer 3, or acting as a true Layer 2 bridge. A related term, *Extended Service Set* (ESS), refers to a physical subnet that contains more than one access point (AP). In this sort of arrangement, the APs can communicate with each other to allow authenticated clients to "roam" between them, handing off IP information as the clients move about. Note that (as of this writing) there are no APs that allow roaming across networks separated by a router.

IBSS (*Independent Basic Service Set*) is frequently referred to as Ad-Hoc or Peer-to-Peer mode. In this mode, no hardware AP is required. Any network node that is within range of any other can communicate if both nodes agree on a few basic parameters. If one of those peers also has a wired connection to another network, it can provide access to that network.

Note that an 802.11b radio must be set to work in either BSS or IBSS mode, but cannot work in both simultaneously. Also, BSS Masters (that is, APs) cannot speak to each other over the air without using WDS or some other tricky mechanism. Both BSS and IBSS support shared-key WEP encryption, for what it's worth (see "Dispel the Myth of Wireless Security" [Hack #87] and the rest of Chapter 7).

Generally speaking, most 802.11b networks consist of one or more BSS Master devices (like a hardware access point, or a general purpose computer running the Host AP driver as seen in "Getting Started with Host AP" [Hack #57]) and several BSS clients (laptops, handhelds, etc.). Ad-Hoc networks, on the other hand, are handy for setting up a point-to-point connection between two fixed devices, or if a couple of laptops need to exchange files and there is no other wireless network present.

In the early days of 802.11b, many manufacturers implemented their own version of Ad-Hoc mode, sometimes referred to as Peer-to-Peer or Ad-Hoc Demo mode. Such devices could only communicate with each other and weren't compatible with true IBSS mode. Recent firmware updates have helped IBSS mode interoperability quite a bit, but not all cards can communicate with each other when speaking IBSS. Generally, any client device can talk to any access point regardless of the manufacturer, provided that both are certified to speak 802.11b.

Bluetooth and Mobile Data
Hacks #13–19

There is much talk in the communications industry of providing "last mile" connectivity. Think of Bluetooth as providing connectivity for the last 10 feet. Bluetooth excels as a handy cable replacement technology, helping to eliminate the need for cumbersome wires that you might find on headsets, remote controls, PDAs, and other small devices. Bluetooth aims to end the days of needing to carry a three-foot piece of cable with obscure connectors on either end everywhere you go, just to interface to your laptop. You can use Bluetooth-enabled devices to talk to a laptop or a desktop, or even have them talk to each other to exchange data almost effortlessly. There are also a number of Bluetooth-enabled input devices on the market, such as mice and keyboards. While it does increase one's dependency on batteries, Bluetooth can go a long way toward cutting down on the rat's nest of cables that comes with personal computing. This chapter demonstrates some nifty directions people are taking with Bluetooth.

Also presented in this chapter are a couple of hacks about how to interface with mobile data networks [Hack #8]. These networks are particularly handy to use when Wi-Fi or other connectivity just isn't available. Devices that combine Bluetooth, mobile data networks, on-board storage, audio capability, and even video cameras are just coming to market. These advanced devices are just the beginning of the inevitable convergence of consumer products with general purpose computers and the Internet, creating an unprecedented level of connectivity for the average user. Here are some hacks that push this concept of hyperconnectivity quite far.

Remote Control OS X with a Sony Ericsson Phone

HACK
#13

Use your phone as a remote control for presentations or iTunes, or for about anything you can script with AppleScript.

The Salling Clicker is one of the niftiest applications for Bluetooth that I've seen. It effectively turns a Sony Ericsson mobile phone into a full color, programmable remote for OS X. You can launch apps, control presentations, and even use it as a general purpose mouse. It works with many Sony Ericsson phones, including the T39m, R520m, T68, T68i, and T610. It is available online on VersionTracker, or directly from *http://homepage.mac.com/jonassalling/Shareware/Clicker/*.

The app will install itself as a new control panel and automatically launch. Click on the tiny phone in the menu bar (Figure 2-1), select *Open Salling Clicker Preferences...* and click *Select Device*. Make sure Bluetooth is enabled in OS X and that your phone is on and somewhere near your computer.

Figure 2-1. The Clicker's menu bar icon.

Select your phone from the list and save the changes. You can now use your phone to steer OS X as well as to publish custom menus to the phone itself. Under the *Phone Menu* tab, you can create custom menus of whatever you like and publish them to your phone. Control OS X by navigating these menus on the phone and selecting what you want to do, such as launch an app or skip to the next track in iTunes. Some phones (like T68/T68i) will even allow you to use the phone as a mouse, making it possible to control any application. Just select *System → Mouse mode*, and you can use the tiny stick on the phone as a pointer.

Since Bluetooth's range is limited to 30 feet or less, it is possible to signal Clicker to take action when your phone moves in and out of range. You can control this functionality by looking under the *Proximity Sensor* tab (Figure 2-2). For example, you might want Clicker to pause iTunes and turn on the screensaver whenever you leave your machine. The interface is very simple: just drag the actions you want it to perform into the relevant boxes, and away you go.

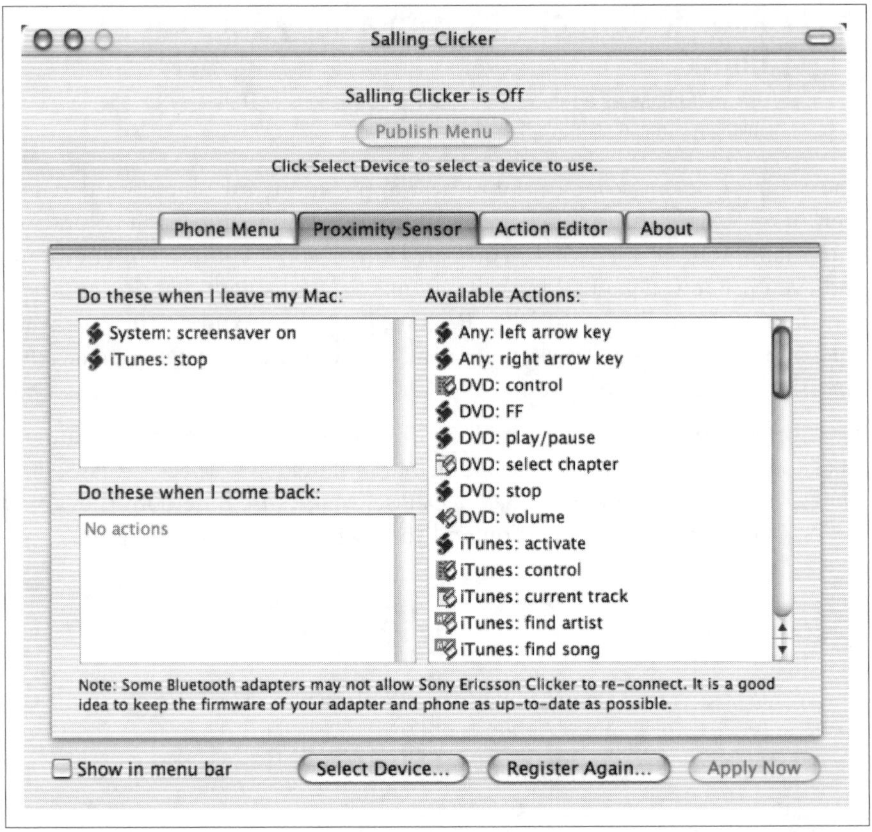

Figure 2-2. *You can assign any action you like to the Proximity Sensor.*

If the built-in actions don't do everything you need, you can always create your own. The actions are just AppleScript snippets, so anything that you can do with AppleScript can be triggered with the phone. You can edit existing actions or create your own under the *Action Editor* tab (Figure 2-3) in the Clicker control panel.

Clicker comes with handy actions for remotely controlling slideshows in PowerPoint or Keynote, but since it can simulate any keystroke, it can be used with just about any application. It is particularly handy when making presentations, since you are virtually guaranteed to have your phone with you (and it is likely to be charged). I bought an infrared USB remote control ages ago specifically for this purpose, but many times I don't have it with me, and when I do, there is no guarantee that the batteries are charged, since I don't use it very often. On the other hand, my phone is *always* with me, and I charge it just about every night. In my opinion, any application that takes advantage of my own habits and laziness is worth investigating.

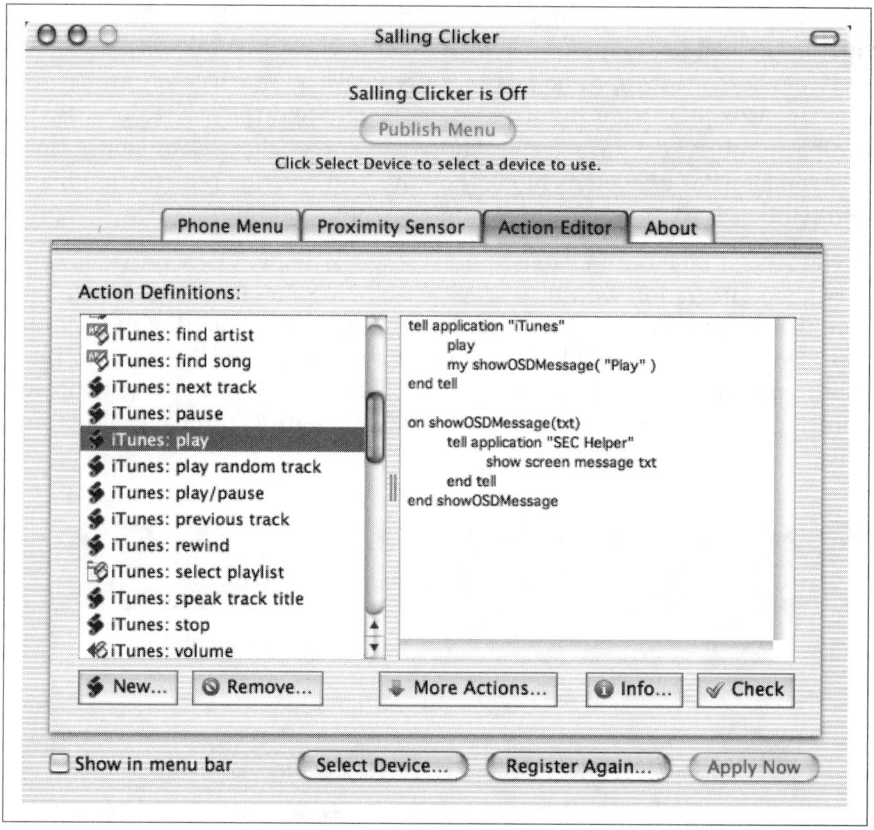

Figure 2-3. *If the built-in actions aren't functional enough for you, write your own.*

Most people think of voice or data applications when they think of Bluetooth, but Clicker is a clever app that transcends the traditional "cable replacement" idea. If you own a Sony Ericsson phone and use OS X, you will probably find all sorts of novel uses for this software. Particularly since it is easy to use and is fully scriptable, Clicker is an application that just screams "hack me!"

HACK #14 SMS with a Real Keyboard

Stop fiddling around with your phone's keypad and use your laptop for text messaging.

Short Message Service (SMS) is better known as text messaging for mobile devices. It has proven to be surprisingly popular in many parts of the world (particularly Japan, the Philippines, and much of Europe), but for one reason or another has been less than enthusiastically received in the U.S. Part of the barrier to entry for many people is the sometimes painful text entry interface on most mobile phones. The demand for tiny phones has squeezed out virtually all hope of a usable integrated keyboard. While predictive text technologies like *T9* have helped make typing require fewer keystrokes, the interface is still far from intuitive. Many people find themselves obsessively hitting number keys in a feeble effort to express themselves, most times mistyping one or two letters along the way. And entering punctuation marks and symbols is so inconvenient that most people don't bother.

If you have a Bluetooth-enabled phone, there is hope. OS X provides some very good integration with these devices and SMS. In order to get started, be sure that Bluetooth is enabled and that your phone is paired with your laptop as you normally would. When you launch the Address Book with Bluetooth enabled, you will notice an extra Bluetooth button at the top left corner of the window (Figure 2-4). Click this button to enable Bluetooth integration in the Address Book.

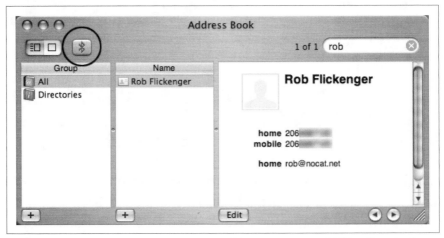

Figure 2-4. Click the Bluetooth button in the Address Book to enable the phone book's Bluetooth integration.

Having Bluetooth enabled turns on a number of useful features. In addition to being able to simply dial the number directly from an Address Book entry, you can also send an SMS message. Click the label to the left of the number you want to message (Figure 2-5) and select *SMS Message*. This opens a small textbox for you to type in your message. Lo and behold, you can use your standard keyboard to enter SMS messages!

The Address Book also gives you possibly the most useful Caller ID implementation there is. When your phone rings, Address Book will pop up a window with the name and phone number of the person calling (Figure 2-6). You can choose whether to answer the call, send them straight to voice mail, or send them an SMS message.

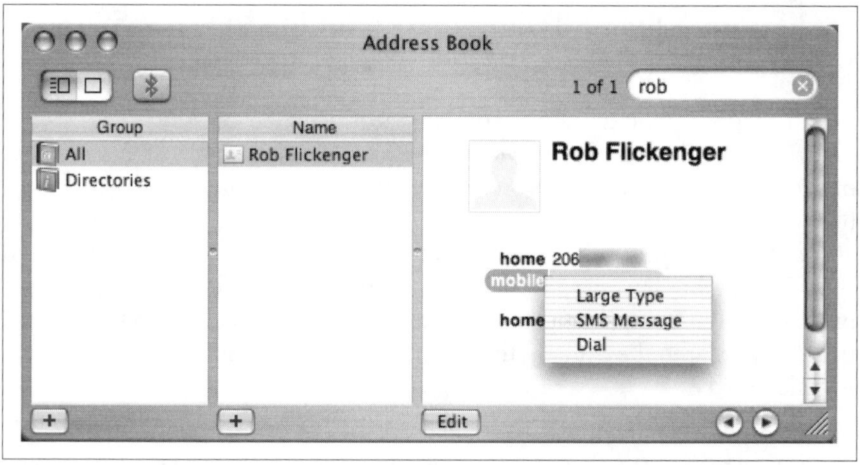

Figure 2-5. Clicking on a number in your Address Book lets you dial it or send an SMS message from the keyboard.

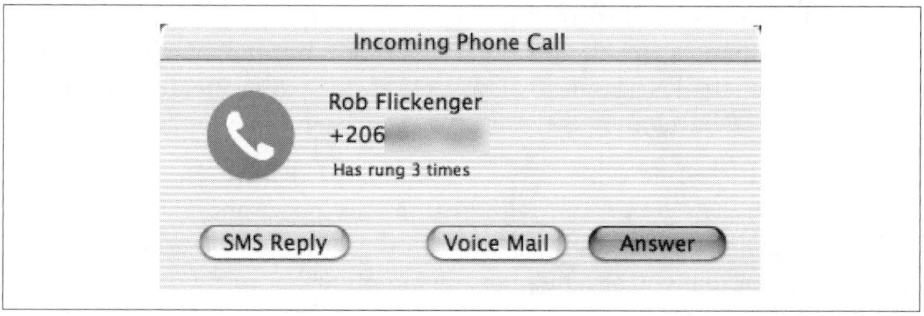

Figure 2-6. Send an incoming call straight to voice mail, or type in an SMS reply.

Clicking *SMS Reply* sends the call to voice mail, but also opens a window allowing you to enter an SMS message. As long as the Address Book app is open, incoming SMS messages will be automatically displayed, and will allow you to reply via SMS as well. While not nearly as portable as SMS on a mobile phone, using a regular keyboard with SMS can help you be more expressive much more quickly.

Incidentally, one very good application for SMS messaging is in situations where mobile phone coverage is flaky on one side (or both sides) of the conversation. In areas where mobile voice calls drop out frequently or aren't even possible, SMS messages will automatically be retried until they get through. This can be ideal for squeezing in a quick message to a friend when you can't otherwise establish a phone call. A low bandwidth message that gets through no matter what can be infinitely more useful than a high bandwidth message that just never gets there. SMS, for all of its faults, can be the ideal communications medium in many situations.

Photo Blog Automatically with the Nokia 3650

#15   Instantly publish your photos from the road, without even logging in.

To me, digital photography is something of a mixed blessing. The instant gratification of being able to view your photos immediately is many times offset by two small details: you need to have your camera with you and it has to be charged. My camera is much too large and fragile to carry with me all of the time, and I'd hate to have yet another device to keep track of and plug in at night. This means that I end up with lots of "event-style" photos, but relatively few impromptu snapshots of daily life. All too often, by the time I run to grab the camera, the moment has passed, and the perfect photo is gone forever.

A number of manufacturers have realized that there is a device that people habitually carry with them and nearly always keep well charged: their cell phones. Nokia has managed to merge a whole slew of nifty technologies into their 3650 phone, including Bluetooth, GPRS, GSM, and of course, a digital camera. This leads to all sorts of fascinating possibilities. Not only is it simple to upload photos to a laptop using Bluetooth, but the interface for sending photos via email is also dead simple. As if IM spam weren't bad enough, mankind is now developing the ability to spam each other with video.

Rather than throw photo bits at your friends and relatives, it is much more efficient to publish your photo album to a web page, and IM your friends and family the link to it. With a little bit of scripting fu, it is straightforward to have a script that will accept an email and publish it to a web page.

The Code

First, you need to have your script accept email. This is easily done with a procmail recipe. Add this to your *.procmailrc* on your mail server:

```
:0
* ^TO yoursecretaddress@yourdomain.com
| /home/username/bin/phonecam.sh
```

Of course, change *yoursecretaddress@yourdomain.com* to the email address that your photo server will use, and fix the path to the following script to point to a real directory. Keep this address private, because any images sent to it will automatically be published! If you're not running procmail on your mail server, consult your friendly neighborhood sysadmin for assistance.

Next, save the following code to a file called *phonecam.sh* in the directory you specified in your *.procmailrc*. You can download the original from *http://freenetworks.org/~mattw/badsoftware/phonecam/* (this copy has been edited slightly for size). Edit the variables at the top to suit your system.

```
#!/bin/sh
#phonecam.sh
filepath="/home/username/public_html/phonecam"
imgdir="img"
html="html"
time=`date +%s`
baseref="http://yoursite.com/~username/phonecam"
title="Phonecam v.3"
arcdate=`date +%D |sed '''s/\//./g'''`
perpage="16"

umask 062

if [ ! -f $filepath/count ]; then
  echo "0" > $filepath/count
fi

if [ ! -f $filepath/arc.txt ]; then
  touch $filepath/arc.txt
fi

if [ ! -d $filepath/archive ]; then
  mkdir $filepath/archive
fi

if [ ! -d $filepath/$html ]; then
  mkdir $filepath/$html
fi

if [ ! -d $filepath/$imgdir ]; then
  mkdir $filepath/$imgdir
fi

count=`head -1 $filepath/count`

mkdir ~/.$$
cd ~/.$$
munpack

for i in *.jpg; do
  a=`basename $i .jpg`
  mv $i $filepath/$imgdir/$time.jpg
  convert -resize 320x240 \
    $filepath/$imgdir/$time.jpg $filepath/$imgdir/$time.thumb.jpg

  convert -resize 150x90 $filepath/$imgdir/$time.jpg $filepath/latest.jpg

  # make the new page
  cat $filepath/new.txt > $filepath/new.tmp
  echo "<a href=\"$baseref/$html/$time.html\">
    <img src=\"$baseref/$imgdir/$time.thumb.jpg\"
    width=\"320\" height=\"240\" border=0></a>"
      > $filepath/new.txt
```

```
    cat $filepath/new.tmp >> $filepath/new.txt
    rm $filepath/new.tmp

    # make the individual photo page
    echo "<html>
    <head><title>$title</title></head><body bgcolor=000000>
    <center><img src=\"$baseref/$imgdir/$time.jpg\" border=1></center><p>"
      > $filepath/$html/$time.html

    cat $a.desc >> $filepath/$html/$time.html

    echo "</body></html>" >> $filepath/$html/$time.html

    count=`expr $count + 1`
done

echo $count > $filepath/count

if [ $count = 1 ]; then
  echo "There is 1 image in the queue" > $filepath/notify
else
  echo "There are $count images in the queue" > $filepath/notify
fi

if [ $count = $perpage ]; then
  echo "<html><head><title>$title</title></head><body bgcolor=000000>
<center>"
    > $filepath/archive/$time.html

  cat $filepath/index.txt >> $filepath/archive/$time.html
  cp $filepath/new.txt $filepath/index.txt
  rm $filepath/count
  rm $filepath/new.txt
  cat $filepath/arc.txt > $filepath/arc.tmp
  echo "<li><a href=\"$baseref/archive/$time.html\">$arcdate</a></li>"
    >> $filepath/arcn.txt

  cat $filepath/arc.tmp >> $filepath/arcn.txt
  rm $filepath/arc.tmp
  mv $filepath/arcn.txt $filepath/arc.txt

  echo "There are no new images in the queue" > $filepath/notify
fi

rm -rf ~/.$$
```

In addition to this script, you need a copy of *munpack* (to decode mime attachments) and *convert* (part of the Image Magick suite). These tools are available in all standard Linux distributions.

Finally, create an *index.shtml* file in your web server's document root that contains a line like this:

```
<!--#include virtual="index.txt"-->
```

For a more advanced example of what you can do with the *index.shtml* file, take a look at the example available at *http://freenetworks.org/~mattw/ badsoftware/phonecam/index.shtml.txt*.

Running the Hack

With all of the above in place, simply send a photo via email to your secret photo email address. The script automatically decodes the email, creates a thumbnail, and puts the photo into a queue. When the queue accumulates *perpage* photos, it rotates in the page full of photos, and moves the old page into an archive. You can always access the latest photo at *http://server/ ~yourname/phonecam/latest.jpg*, and see the entire pending queue at *http:// server/~yourname/phonecam/new.txt*. The script manages the queue and archives without any intervention, and will even post an optional description of your photos. Just add a text body to the email and it will be inserted as the photo's description.

This script could probably be simplified and improved, but this simple shell script should run on just about any server. It creates a simple but powerful archiving web interface that is easily integrated into a weblog or other existing web page. And it pushes the instant gratification of digital photos even further, into the realm of instant publication.

See Also

- Matt Westervelt's phonecam project (*http://freenetworks.org/~mattw/ badsoftware/phonecam/*)
- Image Magick (*http://www.imagemagick.org/*)

Using Bluetooth with Linux
Get Bluetooth up and running quickly under Linux 2.4.

As you might expect, getting Bluetooth to work under Linux takes a little more work than other operating systems. First, it should be noted that there are actually three distinct Bluetooth protocol stacks for Linux: Affix, OpenBT, and BlueZ, each with varying support for different Bluetooth adapters, and each with somewhat distinct means of configuration. Since BlueZ has been crowned as the "official" Linux Bluetooth stack, that's the one we'll focus on here.

First, make sure you have a supported Bluetooth adapter. You can find a reasonably current list of BlueZ-supported hardware at *http://www.holtmann.org/ linux/bluetooth/devices.html*.

Next, you'll need to make sure that your kernel has Bluetooth support enabled. Kernels shipped with both the Red Hat 9.0 and Debian "Sarge" distributions already include Bluetooth support. You can test your kernel for Bluetooth supports by running modprobe rfcomm as root. If the modprobe fails, you'll need to rebuild your kernel.

In the event of a failure, build and install a fresh copy of the Linux kernel at Version 2.4.21 or better (or 2.4.20 with the -mh6 patch). When you configure the kernel, select all of the options under "Bluetooth support" to be built as separate modules. However, be sure that the "USB Bluetooth support" option under "USB support" is disabled—this compiles in UART support the OpenBT protocol stack, which will interfere with the BlueZ stack. Newer versions of the kernel disable this last option for you automatically, if BlueZ is selected.

One additional note: if you are running a newer Toshiba or Sony laptop and want to use the built-in Bluetooth adapter, you will need to enable the Toshiba- or Sony-specific kernel options under the "Processor type and features" and "Character devices" sections. You will also need special user-space utilities to enable the Bluetooth adapters on these laptops; these utilities are beyond the scope of this book, but more information about them can be found on the BlueZ-supported device listing referred to earlier in this section.

Next, add the following lines to your */etc/modules.conf*:

```
alias net-pf-31 bluez
alias bt-proto-0 l2cap
alias bt-proto-2 sco
alias bt-proto-3 rfcomm
alias bt-proto-4 bnep
alias tty-ldisc-15 hci_uart
alias bluetooth off
```

Run /sbin/depmod -a as root.

These options tell the kernel which modules to load when Bluetooth support is requested. The last option, -- alias bluetooth off, is included to tell modprobe not to load the OpenBT UART module, in case it was installed by accident.

You also need the BlueZ userspace utilities. Again, Red Hat 9.0 comes with these tools installed. You can get the source code, as well as RPMs and *.debs*, from the BlueZ homepage at *http://bluez.sourceforge.net*. Be sure to build and/or install the bluez-libs, bluez-utils, bluez-sdp, and bluez-hcidump packages. You may be able to simply run apt-get from Debian, except that Debian refers to "bluez-libs" as "libbluetooth1" and offers "libsdp2" as a separate package.

This next bit is for UART-based (that is, non-USB) devices only, so if you're running a USB Bluetooth adapter, you can skip it. Serial-style devices, which include serial dongles and PCMCIA cards, need to be explicitly "attached" to the Bluetooth host controller interface, using the *hciattach* utility. When you connect the device, the appropriate kernel driver may be loaded automatically, leaving a log entry in */var/log/messages*. If you're using a UART-based device, you may see a reference to a */dev/ttySn* serial device, where *n* is some integer. In any event, you can try attaching the device to the Bluetooth host controller device by running /sbin/hciattach /dev/ttySn any from the command line. Like any good Unix utility, you know that *hciattach* worked if it returns without printing anything. If it doesn't work, make sure you have the right device and check the manpage for other options.

Assuming that the *hciattach* command *did* work, you will want to add a reference to this device to your */etc/bluetooth/uart* file, so that the device can be appropriately attached to the Bluetooth host controller interface at boot time. If this file doesn't exist, create it. Add a single line to this file that reads "/dev/ttySn any", replacing "n" with the appropriate serial device number. If you're using a USB adapter, of course you don't need to bother with this step.

Now that you have everything installed, plug in your Bluetooth adapter and try running /etc/rc.d/init.d/bluetooth start as root. In Debian, start Bluetooth with /etc/init.d/bluez-utils start; /etc/init.d/bluez-sdp start. You should see some appropriate status messages in your */var/log/ messages*. If your install of BlueZ didn't include the */etc/rc.d/init.d/bluetooth* script, you can copy a suitable version from the *scripts/* subdirectory of the bluez-utils package. Assuming everything works, you may wish to add the Bluetooth script to the appropriate *rc.d* directory for your default runlevel with the *chkconfig* utility or via a manual symlink.

Now run hciconfig from the command line. You should see something like:

```
hci0:   Type: USB
        BD Address: 00:11:22:33:44:55 ACL MTU: 192:8   SCO MTU: 64:8
        UP RUNNING PSCAN ISCAN
        RX bytes:99 acl:0 sco:0 events:13 errors:0
        TX bytes:296 acl:0 sco:0 commands:12 errors:0
```

If you don't see anything like this, make sure that hcid is running, and that there aren't any error messages in */var/log/messages*. The BD Address shown is the unique Bluetooth identifier for your adapter, much like an Ethernet MAC address.

Now bring another Bluetooth device within range of your computer, and make sure that the device is visible to Bluetooth scans. Then run hcitool scan from the command line. It may take up to 15 or 20 seconds to complete its scan, and then it should display something like:

```
$ hcitool scan
Scanning ...
        00:99:88:77:66:55       Nokia3650
```

You can now test the device to see which services it supports, using *sdptool browse 00:99:88:77:66:55*. You should see a lengthy list of supported services, providing information that can be used to configure access to those services.

—Schuyler Erle

HACK #17 Bluetooth to GPRS in Linux

Use your Bluetooth phone as a modem when Wi-Fi isn't available.

No doubt the novelty of being able to scan for nearby Bluetooth devices from your Linux machine will wear off all too soon, and you'll be wanting to actually *do* things with your shiny new Bluetooth connection. Being able to use your cell phone as a modem from all those places you can't pull in a Wi-Fi signal would be pretty cool, wouldn't it?

Bluetooth supports a number of "profiles," which define the way that Bluetooth devices can communicate with each other. In this case, we want to make use of the Dial-up Networking (DUN) profile, which relies on a protocol called RFCOMM to emulate a serial link between two devices. You can use RFCOMM to connect your Linux box to your phone, and then run *pppd* over the link to get access to the Internet. This works using GPRS, or even an ordinary Internet dial-up.

Assuming you've got Bluetooth working **[Hack #16]**, you should be able to bring your phone within range of your computer and scan for it using *hcitool*. We'll presume that you've done this, and that *hcitool* reports a BD address for your phone of *00:11:22:33:44:55*.

You can also use *sdptool* to verify that there's a device in range that supports the DUN profile:

```
$ sdptool search DUN
Inquiring ...
Searching for DUN on 00:11:22:33:44:55 ...
Service Name: Dial-up Networking
Service RecHandle: 0x10001
Service Class ID List:
  "Dialup Networking" (0x1103)
  "Generic Networking" (0x1201)
Protocol Descriptor List:
  "L2CAP" (0x0100)
  "RFCOMM" (0x0003)
    Channel: 1
```

Note this channel number, because you'll need it later. As you can see, *hci-tool* and *sdptool* offer a lot of other useful Bluetooth diagnostic functions, which you can read more about on their respective manpages.

Before you can actually connect to the phone, however, you may need to set up what's referred to as *device pairing* between your Linux box and your phone, so that your phone knows to allow your computer access to its services, and possibly vice versa. Your computer's PIN can be found in */etc/bluetooth/pin*, and you will want to alter this to a unique value that only you know.

Most phones have a Bluetooth PIN that you can configure within the phone itself. BlueZ comes with a little Python utility called *bluepin* that pops up a GTk+ dialog to ask for your phone's PIN as needed; this utility apparently doesn't work out of the box requires in some Linux distributions. More to the point, who wants to be asked for your phone's PIN every time you use the thing, anyway? The following Perl script can be saved to */etc/bluetooth/pindb*, and you can use it store PINs for multiple Bluetooth devices:

```
#!/usr/bin/perl
while ( ) {
    print "PIN:$1\n" if /^$ARGV[1]\s+(\w+)/o;
}
__DATA__
# Your Bluetooth PINs can go here, in BD address / PIN pairs,
# one to a line, separated by whitespace.
#
# ## etc.

00:11:22:33:44:55        11111
```

Make sure that */etc/bluetooth/pindb* is owned by root and chmod 0700—you don't want ordinary users being able to look up your Bluetooth device PINs. The options section of your */etc/bluetooth/hcid.conf* should accordingly look something like this:

```
options {
        autoinit yes;
        security auto;
        pairing multi;
        pin_helper /etc/bluetooth/pindb;
}
```

This ensures that HCI devices are configured at boot, that pairing is allowed, and that *hcid* will ask *pindb* for your PINs on a per-device basis. Be sure to restart *hcid* by running /etc/rc.d/init.d/bluetooth restart if you made any changes to your */etc/bluetooth/hcid.conf*.

Now that your computer is set up for pairing, you'll have to set up your phone similarly, for which you'll need to refer to your user's manual. This set-up process often requires that the phone can scan for your computer's Bluetooth adapter, so be sure that your computer is within range with a working Bluetooth adapter. The interface will probably come up as "BlueZ (0)", or something similar, unless you changed the "name" option in your *hcid.conf*. You probably want to set up the pairing on the phone as "trusted," or the moral equivalent, so that the phone doesn't ask you to verify the connection each time you try to dial out from your Linux box.

Now that I've shown that there's a device in range that offers dial-up networking, and set up pairing with it, the next step is to bind an RFCOMM interface to that device. First, make sure that there are RFCOMM entries in your */dev* directory, using ls -l /dev/rfcomm*. If ls reports "No such file or directory", you can trivially create 64 RFCOMM device entries by switching to the superuser and doing the following:

```
# for n in `seq 0 63`; do mknod -m660 /dev/rfcomm$n c 216 $n; done
# chown root:uucp /dev/rfcomm*
```

If you're running Debian, you probably want to chown your RFCOMM devices to group *dialout*, instead of *uucp*.

Now, as the superuser, bind */dev/rfcomm0* to your phone on the channel reported for DUN by *sdptool* earlier, using the *rfcomm* utility from bluez-utils:

```
# rfcomm bind /dev/rfcomm0 00:11:22:33:44:55:66 1
```

You'll know that the device was bound successfully if, like any good Unix utility, *rfcomm* just returns silently. You can demonstrate that it did actually work, however, by running *rfcomm* without any arguments:

```
# rfcomm
rfcomm0: 00:11:22:33:44:55 channel 1 clean
```

Now you can pretty much just treat this serial device as if it were an ordinary modem. Just to prove it, try running minicom as root, and switch the serial device to */dev/rfcomm0*. When the terminal loads, type **AT** and press Enter. If the phone responds OK, then congratulations are in order—you're talking to your cell phone over a Bluetooth connection.

Before going any further, you may want to add the following to your */etc/bluetooth/rfcomm.conf*, so that the RFCOMM device is configured by default when Bluetooth loads:

```
rfcomm0 {
        # Automatically bind the device at startup
        bind yes;
        device 00:11:22:33:44:55;
        channel 1;
        comment "My Phone";
}
```

If you're running bluez-utils 2.3 or earlier on a non-Debian-based distro, you may need to add `rfcomm bind all` to the `start( )` section of your */etc/rc.d/init.d/ bluetooth* for this to work right.

From here, it's just a short hop to getting your computer on the Net. Put the following into */etc/ppp/peers/gprs*:

```
/dev/rfcomm0

connect '/usr/sbin/chat -v -f /etc/ppp/peers/gprs.chat'
noauth
defaultroute
usepeerdns
lcp-echo-interval 65535
debug
```

Then save the following as */etc/ppp/peers/gprs.chat*:

```
TIMEOUT      15
ECHO         ON
HANGUP       ON
''           AT
OK           ATZ
OK           ATD*99#
```

Alternately, if you prefer using *wvdial*, try adding the following to your */etc/ wvdial.conf*:

```
[Dialer gprs]
Modem       = /dev/rfcomm0
Phone       = *99#
Username    = foo
Password    = bar
```

Note that while European providers give you a username and password, in the U.S. you still need to supply dummy values to satisfy *wvdial*. Consult your network provider's web site for details about what values you may need to use. Your GPRS is actually already authenticated by your very presence on the cellular network, so you don't have to re-auth just to use PPP. The "phone number" listed is the standard GPRS dial-up number, which may work for you right off the bat if your phone is configured properly. Most GSM phones support multiple GPRS access points, however—so, if the default for your phone doesn't work for you, try going into minicom and typing **AT+CGDCONT?** followed by a carriage return. Your phone should respond with a list of available Packet Data Protocol (PDP) contexts. Pick the one that seems the most appropriate, and then set your GPRS phone number in */etc/wvdial.conf* to *99***n#, replacing *n* with the number of the PDP profile you want to use. Failing that, try contacting your service provider for advice!

You can test this setup as root by running either pppd call gprs or wvdial gprs, depending on your setup, and watching */var/log/messages* in another window. The only hitch with this setup is that it doesn't set up your nameservers in */etc/resolv.conf* by default. The way around this on Red Hat is to store the following in */etc/sysconfig/network-scripts/ifcfg-ppp0* (or *ppp1*, *ppp2*, etc. as you prefer):

```
# comment out CHATSCRIPT and uncomment WVDIALSECT if you're using wvdial
DEVICE=ppp0
MODEMPORT=/dev/rfcomm0
CHATSCRIPT=/etc/ppp/peers/gprs.chat
# WVDIALSECT=gprs
```

This way you can just use ifup ppp0 and ifdown ppp0 to bring the link up and down. To get the identical result on Debian, use the *pppd* configuration just shown, and add the following to your */etc/network/interfaces*:

```
iface ppp0 inet ppp
    provider gprs
```

If you're not using a Red Hat– or Debian-like distribution, you can always just add the following additional lines to your */etc/ppp/peers/gprs* to make DNS work right, and use pppd call gprs and killall pppd to bring the link up and down:

```
welcome 'cp -b /etc/ppp/resolv.conf /etc/resolv.conf'
disconnect 'mv /etc/resolv.conf~ /etc/resolv.conf'
```

That's just about all you need to know to get online from anywhere you can get GSM service. Just don't expect blistering speeds from it: as of this writing, GPRS ranges in speed from under 5k/s to just over 20k/s, depending on your service—not exactly high speed by modern standards, but amazing where you would otherwise have nothing at all.

As a little bonus, here's a short *iptables* script to let you share that GPRS with anyone in Wi-Fi range, which could be stored as or called from */etc/ppp/ip-up.local*:

```
# Enable IP forwarding and rp_filter (to kill IP spoof attempts).
echo "1" > /proc/sys/net/ipv4/ip_forward
echo "1" > /proc/sys/net/ipv4/conf/all/rp_filter

# Load relevant kernel modules, if necessary.
for i in ip_tables ipt_MASQUERADE iptable_nat
    ip_conntrack ip_conntrack_ftp ip_conntrack_irc \
    ip_nat_irc ip_nat_ftp; do
    modprobe $i 2>/dev/null;
done

# Masquerade anything that's not from a PPP interface
# (e.g. ethernet, Wi-Fi, etc.)
iptables -t nat -A POSTROUTING -o ppp+ -j MASQUERADE
```

But what, you ask, about regular dial-up connections? How about faxes? Well, it turns out that you're in luck: simply replace the GPRS access number with any regular phone number of your choice and (on most phones) you get a 9,600 baud data connection to that line. Configuring *efax* or *mgetty-sendfax* to use Bluetooth to fax from a GSM phone in this manner is therefore left as an exercise for the reader.

—Schuyler Erle

HACK #18 Bluetooth File Transfers in Linux

Exchange data freely between your Bluetooth device and your Linux box.

Getting on the Net [Hack #17] from anywhere your cell phone works is pretty darn cool, but your phone probably has other features. Maybe someone messaged you a photo from their family barbecue that you want to copy over to your laptop. Or maybe you just want to install some applications on your shiny new phone.

The heart of file transfer over Bluetooth is called the *Object Exchange*, or OBEX, protocol, a binary file transfer protocol run over not merely Bluetooth, but also Infrared and even generic TCP/IP. The OpenOBEX project at *http://openobex.sf.net/* offers the most ubiquitous open source implementation of the protocol. You can get packages for *libopenobex* and *openobex-apps* from the *sid* distribution, and Red Hat packages for *openobex* can be had from the SourceForge site or on *rpmfind.net*. Bluetooth actually supports two different OBEX profiles for transferring files: OBEX Push, which is primarily used for dumping individual files to a Bluetooth device, and OBEX File Transfer, which supports a richer set of file exchange operations.

Unfortunately, the present state of the art in Bluetooth file transfer using Linux is still in considerable flux. The *openobex-apps* package contains an *obex_test* application, which offers one very rudimentary way of sending files to your Bluetooth devices. First, you need to figure out which Bluetooth channel your phone or other device uses for OBEX File Transfer; to do this, type:

```
# sdptool search FTRN
Inquiring ...
Searching for FTRN on 00:11:22:33:44:55 ...
Service Name: OBEX File Transfer
Service RecHandle: 0x10003
Service Class ID List:
  "OBEX File Transfer" (0x1106)
Protocol Descriptor List:
  "L2CAP" (0x0100)
  "RFCOMM" (0x0003)
    Channel: 10
  "OBEX" (0x0008)
```

Now you can try connecting to the device with *obex_test*, using the -b option (for Bluetooth), the BD address of the device, and the FTRN channel number:

```
$ obex_test -b 00:11:22:33:44:55 10
Using Bluetooth RFCOMM transport
OBEX Interactive test client/server.
> c
Connect OK!
Version: 0x10. Flags: 0x00
> x
PUSH filename> /home/sderle/images/image.jpg
name=/home/sderle/images/image.gif, size=7294
Going to send /home/sderle/images/image.gif(opt21.gif), 7294 bytes
Filling stream!
```

obex_test proceeds to display some progress messages, followed by a confirmation:

```
Made some progress...
Made some progress...
Made some progress...
Filling stream!
PUT successful!
```

The file should appear on your device. Similarly, *obex_test* can receive files sent from your device, if you configure your computer's Bluetooth interface to answer to OBEX Push requests, again using *sdptool* with the same channel your device uses for OBEX Push:

```
$ sdptool add --channel=10 OPUSH
$ obex_test -b 00:11:22:33:44:55 10
Using Bluetooth RFCOMM transport
OBEX Interactive test client/server.
> s
```

obex_test should print a blank line and then pause. Now send a file from your phone via Bluetooth. You'll see a ton of status messages, and then *obex_test* will report that it's finished. You should be able to find your file in */tmp*.

The problem with *obex_test*, other than a total lack of documentation, is that it's entirely driven by terminal-based user interaction. What if we want to script file transfers or be able to receive files automatically? Another, probably easier way of getting files from your computer to your phone involves a little app called *ussp-push*, which you can get from *http://www. unrooted.net/hacking/ussp-push.tgz*. *ussp-push* is based on some code from the Affix stack, but actually relies on OpenOBEX. Also, it doesn't compile at present right out of the box, so we'll use Perl to tweak it so that it compiles properly with modern versions of OpenOBEX:

```
# tar xfz ussp-push.tgz
# cd ussp-push
# perl -pi -e 's/custfunc\.userdata/custfunc.customdata/g' obex_main.c
```

```
# make
...
# cp ussp-push /usr/local/bin
```

ussp-push relies on having an RFCOMM serial device bound to the Bluetooth channel your device uses for OBEX Push, so we'll first need to fire up *sdptool* again, and then use *rfcomm* to bind the device to the listed channel:

```
# sdptool search OPUSH
Inquiring ...
Searching for OPUSH on 00:11:22:33:44:55 ...
Service Name: OBEX Object Push
Service RecHandle: 0x10004
Service Class ID List:
  "OBEX Object Push" (0x1105)
Protocol Descriptor List:
  "L2CAP" (0x0100)
  "RFCOMM" (0x0003)
    Channel: 9
  "OBEX" (0x0008)

# rfcomm bind /dev/rfcomm1 00:11:22:33:44:55 9
```

Now you can use *ussp-push* to send files to your device.

```
$ ussp-push /dev/rfcomm1 /home/sderle/images/image.jpg image.jpg
```

ussp-push takes three arguments: an RFCOMM device, a local file to push, and the name of the file to save it as on the remote side. When you run *ussp-push*, you'll see an avalanche of progress info, hopefully concluding with the file appearing on your phone. If you create an entry for the new RFCOMM device in */etc/bluetooth/rfcomm.conf*, you can have the device bound on boot. Save the following wrapper script as *btpush*, and save it somewhere handy (such as your *~/bin* directory). You can then use it to trivially send files directly to your phone:

```
#!/bin/bash

# btpush - send files to a Bluetooth device using ussp-push
# just run it as: btpush <file>

ussp-push /dev/rfcomm1 $1 `basename $1`
```

If you get permissions issues when running *ussp-push*, make sure your */dev/rfcomm** devices are group-writeable, and are owned by a group that you're a member of.

Similarly, you can receive files using another small app called *obexserver*, which you can fetch from *http://www.frasunek.com/sources/unix/obexserver.c*. *obexserver* needs to be built together with *openobex-apps*. Once you've built *openobex-apps*, do the following from within the top-level source directory:

```
# cd src
# wget http://www.frasunek.com/sources/unix/obexserver.c
```

```
# gcc -o obexserver obexserver.c libmisc.a -lopenobex
# cp obexserver /usr/local/bin
```

To receive files, first set up OBEX Push service on your computer by running sdptool add --channel=10 OPUSH, changing the channel as necessary to match the one your device uses for OBEX Push. Now you can just run *obexserver* without arguments, and send a file from your phone. *obexserver* will receive the file, store it in */tmp*, and exit.

Being able send files from phone to computer and back is nice, but having to send and receive files individually doesn't present the absolutely most convenient interface. Fortunately, if your Bluetooth device is running the SymbianOS or EPOC operating system—this includes Series 60 phones and the Ericsson P800—you can actually mount your device's filesystem on your computer via NFS. The package that performs this minor miracle is called p3nfs, and it's available at *http://www.koeniglich.de/p3nfs.html*. The source distribution comes with binaries to run on your phone, in case you don't have a cross-compiler (which is likely). The phone application is called *nfsapp*, and you can find the appropriate binary version for your phone in the *bin/* subdirectory, with a *.sis* extension. Use one of the methods just described to send the appropriate SIS file to your phone and install it there. Next, build and install p3nfsd in the usual way. If you installed the RPM provided by *koeniglich.de*, you can find the SIS files in */usr/share/doc/ p3nfs-[version]*.

You'll want to create a mount point in your filesystem for the NFS share; p3nfs uses */mnt/psion* by default. Also, p3nfs needs its own RFCOMM device, so you'll need set one up. If you're running a Nokia phone, you'll probably want to bind to channel 4; otherwise, you may be using channel 3.

```
# mkdir /mnt/phone
# rfcomm bind /dev/rfcomm2 00:11:22:33:44:55 4
```

Now, start *nfsapp* on your phone. Don't worry if you pick the wrong channel at first—when you run *nfsapp* on your phone, it will tell you which channel it's listening to. If you told *rfcomm* to bind to the wrong one, just run rfcomm unbind /dev/rfcomm2 and try the right channel. At first, *nfsapp* defaults to listening to the infrared port—click the joystick or press the p key to cycle between IR, Bluetooth, and TCP transport. Once you select Bluetooth, *nfsapp* gives you 30 seconds to start p3nfs on your computer. Assuming everything else is configured correctly, you should be able to start p3nfsd as follows:

```
# p3nfsd -series60 -tty /dev/rfcomm2 -dir /mnt/phone -user sderle
p3nfsd: version 5.13a, using /dev/rfcomm2 (115200), mounting on /mnt/phone
p3nfsd: to stop the server do "ls /mnt/phone/exit". (pid 3274)
```

p3nfsd will probably take a few seconds to finish mounting. A quick look at *lsmod* will verify that, in fact, it's using your kernel's NFS support. You'll want to replace `-series60` with `-UIQ` or another option if you're not running a Series 60 phone—run p3nfsd without any options for a list. You'll want to alter the `-tty`, `-dir`, and `-user` options as appropriate. The `-user` option isn't strictly necessary, but p3nfsd mounts the share with user-only read and execute permissions, so if you don't use it, you'll need to be root to browse the share. Now you should be able to `cd` into */mnt/phone*, and do all the things you're accustomed to doing in a Unix-like NFS mount. You'll need to `ls /mnt/phone/exit` to unmount the share, which is a little weird. Otherwise, p3nfsd unmounts after a few minutes of inactivity—you can control the timeout using the `-timeout` option.

By this point, you've got several options for exchanging data between Bluetooth devices. Obviously, you can easily reuse these techniques to exchange files between two Bluetooth-equipped Linux machines as well, and, in fact, these same methods work pretty well for infrared file transfers, with a little tweaking, but that's beyond the scope of this hack. One last thing: if you want your new RFCOMM devices to be there the next time you boot, don't forget to add entries for them to */etc/bluetooth/rfcomm.conf*. Now start installing those applications!

—Schuyler Erle

HACK #19 Controlling XMMS with Bluetooth

Use your Bluetooth device to control your music remotely under Linux.

If you have a mobile Bluetooth device that you'd like to use to control XMMS in Linux, you may be in luck. There are actually a couple of applications out there that use a WAP-like serial interface to Ericsson's T-series phones (including the T68i and the T39m) to configure them for use as XMMS remote controls.

The first of the two is a standalone Ruby-based application called *bluexmms*, which is available from *http://linuxbrit.co.uk/bluexmms/*. Make sure your phone is paired (**[Hack #16]**) with the Bluetooth interface on your computer. Install *bluexmms*, and then use *rfcomm* to bind an RFCOMM device to channel 2 on the T68i, which is (oddly) the T68's "generic telephony" service.

Next, run `bluexmms /dev/rfcomm1` on your device, substituting the name of the RFCOMM device you just created. You should now be able to go to *Accessories/XMMS Remote* on your phone's menu, and voila!

A second, but very similar approach, involves an XMMS plugin called *btexmms*, which can be downloaded from *http://www.lyola.com/bte/*. Build and install the plugin, and create an RFCOMM device on channel 2, as just described. Then, go into the XMMS preferences menu, and under *Effects →* *General Plugins*, enable and configure the BTE Control plugin. Set the device to whatever RFCOMM device you created for this purpose, and save your changes. Now you should be able to access the remote control from *Accessories/XMMS Remote*, as described above.

If you don't have an Ericsson T-series phone, you might try Bemused, which runs on SymbianOS devices, like the Nokia 3650/7650 and the Ericsson P800. Unlike the T68 apps just listed, which rely on the computer to establish a connection to the phone, Bemused instead uses a client that initiates the connection from your phone to a server running on your computer.

You can get the Bemused server and client from *http://www.compsoc.man.ac.uk/~ashley/bemused/*. First, unpack *bemused.zip* and upload and install the *.sis* file on your phone. Then download *bemusedlinuxserver.tar.gz*, and build and install it on your computer. You'll need to advertise Bluetooth serial port services on your laptop by running `sdptool add --channel=10 SP`, and then edit and configure */etc/bemused.conf* appropriately. The Bemused README suggests using Bluetooth channel 10 on your computer, but any unused channel will do. Start X11, if you haven't already. Run `bemusedserverlinux` from the command line. At this point, you should be able to fire up the Bemused application on your phone and have the full power of XMMS at your fingertips, from clear across the room.

If you don't have one of these devices, don't fret—nearly every Bluetooth device these days implements some kind of serial communications layer. Using examples from the projects just listed, you can probably create an XMMS remote control for your own phone or PDA. The hackability quotient of Bluetooth for this particular kind of application is pretty high.

Clearly, if you've made it this far, you're probably thinking that, with a wireless remote control for XMMS, you could plug a dedicated MP3 server running Linux into the hi-fi amplifier in your living room and never need a monitor or a keyboard for it. Or maybe you're considering plugging a low-power FM transmitter into your sound card, so you can listen to your music collection from any radio in the house. And you're absolutely right. With Bluetooth, you can do all of this, and probably more. Let the rockin' out commence!

—Schuyler Erle

## CHAPTER THREE

Network Monitoring

Hacks #20–42

Perhaps the most difficult task in wireless networking is trying to visualize what is really going on. Radio waves are invisible and undetectable to humans without the aid of sophisticated tools, such as a spectrum analyzer. Such devices aren't cheap, ranging from several hundreds to tens of thousands of dollars, depending on its capabilities. Obviously, such devices are well beyond the reach of the average networking aficionado. And even if they weren't, a spectrum only gives you a visualization of what is going on at the physical radio layer, and doesn't give you any indication of what is happening with the actual network data.

Fortunately, every radio networking device can not only transmit data, but can listen as well. Combined with sophisticated (and generally free) software, this can turn an average laptop or handheld into a powerful monitoring tool. In this chapter, I'll show you how to use standard hardware to detect wireless networks and clients, generate statistics on their usage, and gather valuable insight into how your network is being used by sifting through the deluge of available radio information. Using these tools can help you coordinate networking efforts with people in your local vicinity to make the most efficient possible use of the available radio spectrum.

HACK #20 Find All Available Wireless Networks

Locate all wireless networks in range without installing any additional software.

So, you've got a laptop. You've got a wireless card. The card might even be built into your laptop. You know there are wireless networks in your area. How do you find them? You might even have an external antenna connected to your wireless card, hoping to establish a longer distance connection. How do you find that network a half-mile away?

If you are connected to a wireless network already, you could download a tool like NetStumbler [Hack #21], but this requires a network connection and you don't have one yet.

All of the major operating systems have integrated software that allows you to discover wireless networks and obtain some status information about the currently connected network.

Windows XP

If a wireless access point is in range of your wireless card, Windows XP by default will attempt to automatically connect to the access point. It will inform you using a pop up above the task bar, which says, "One or more wireless connections are available."

Clicking on the network icon opens a window titled "Wireless Network Connection," as shown in Figure 3-1.

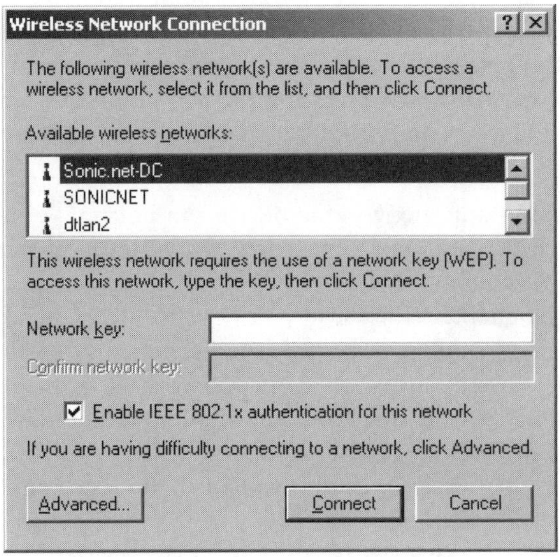

Figure 3-1. Available networks under Windows XP.

This window lists any wireless networks that are in range of your wireless card. In this example, there are three within range. The window also shows you that the selected wireless network requires the use of a WEP key [Hack #86] in order to join the network.

In order to join this network, you would need to type in the WEP key and then confirm the key by retyping. Once done, you would click on *Connect*.

The window will close, and the network icon in the task bar should say "Wireless Network Connection (network name)". The icon also displays the wireless network speed and signal strength.

As shown in Figure 3-1, if you have difficulty connecting to any of the listed networks, you can click on the *Advanced* button, which opens a Wireless Networks window (Figure 3-2).

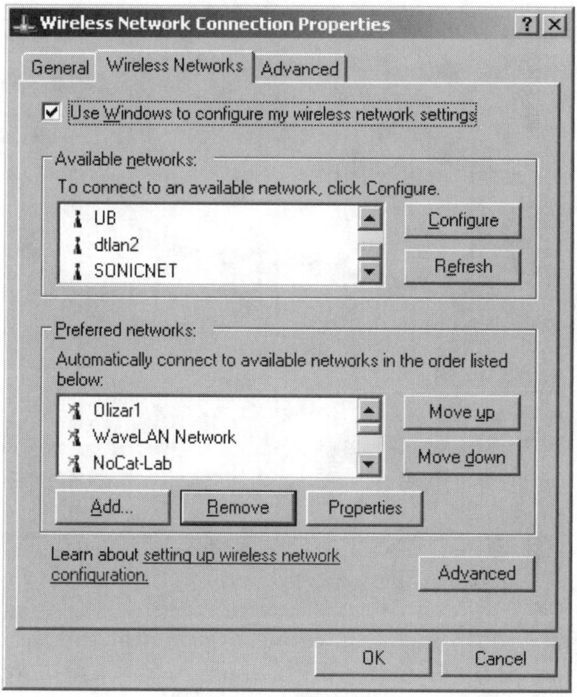

Figure 3-2. Advanced wireless network options.

This window again shows the available wireless networks. It also shows a list of "preferred networks" that can be added by the user. This is important to know if your wireless access point does not broadcast the SSID, saving you from repeatedly having to type in the name of the otherwise-invisible network and, indeed, needing to remember its name in the first place. Many access points have the ability to disable SSID broadcast as a security feature (so-called "closed" networks). This means that you need to know the SSID so you can add a preferred network (assuming, of course, that you aren't using a passive monitor like Kismet **[Hack #31]** or KisMac **[Hack #24]**).

At the top of this window is the checkbox: *Use Windows to configure my wireless network settings*. If this box is checked, Windows will automatically attempt to connect to any wireless networks listed in your preferred networks. If no preferred networks are available, it will provide you with a list of available wireless networks as shown above.

To get status on the wireless network to which you are currently connected, right-click on the network icon in the task bar and select *Status*. A typical status screen is shown in Figure 3-3.

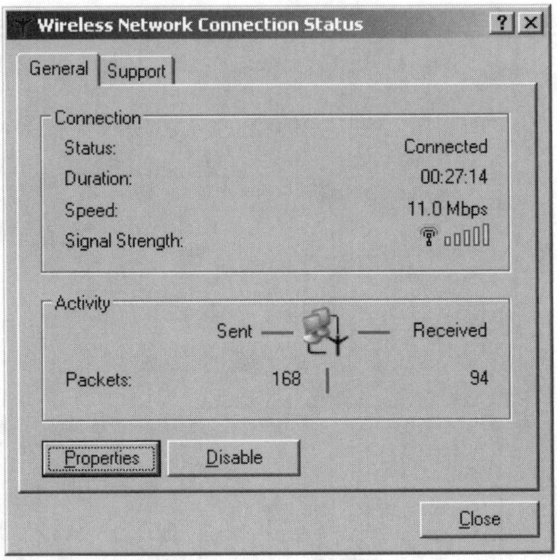

Figure 3-3. Status details about the connected network.

While this gives you some basic connection information, it doesn't show you actual signal strength in dB, which would be very useful for testing wireless connections. You also do not get any information on signal-to-noise ratio. Clicking on the *Support* tab gives you IP addressing information for this wireless card.

Mac OS X

For Apple notebooks with a built-in AirPort card, all wireless configuration is handled through the System Preferences (*System Preferences → Network*), as shown in Figure 3-4.

You will likely have two available network cards. Click the *Show* pull-down menu for a choice of adapters, including *Built-in Ethernet* and *AirPort*. Select *AirPort*. To get to the wireless network settings, select the *AirPort* tab.

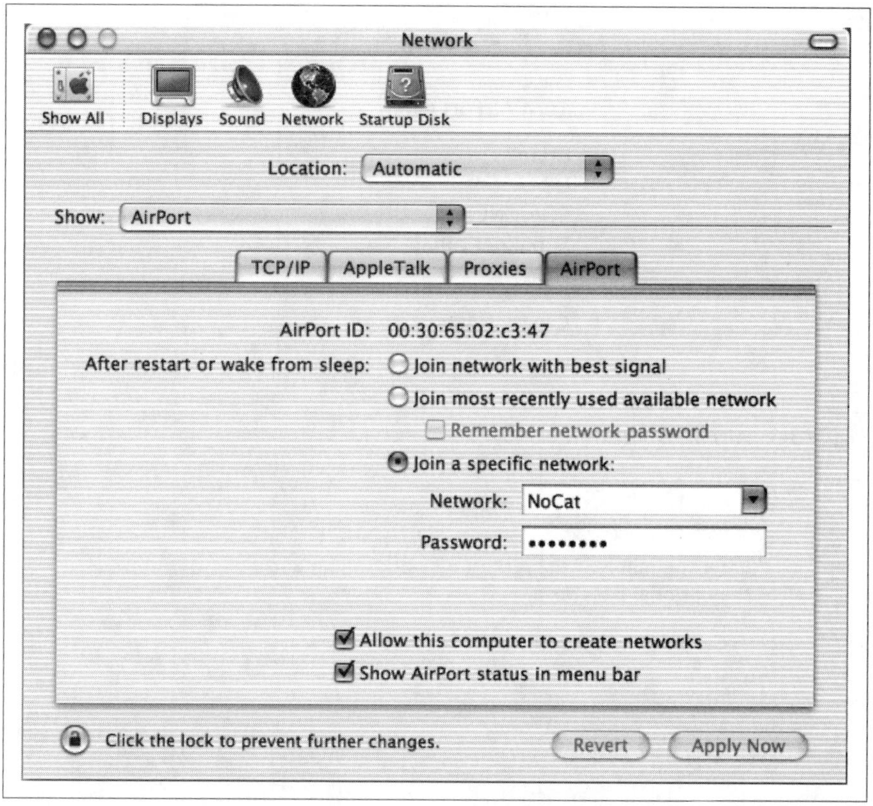

Figure 3-4. AirPort configuration.

I'll come back to some of this later. Right now, you should be mostly concerned with the *Show AirPort status in menu bar* setting, which should be checked. Once you check this box and close the configuration window, you'll see a new icon in the menu bar (Figure 3-5). The first thing you'll want to do is click the menu bar icon and select the option to turn on the AirPort card.

Once the AirPort card is on, you'll be able to see a list of available networks; you can select any of these. If a password (WEP key) is required for the selected network, you'll be prompted for it.

To connect to a network that is not listed, click on *Other....* You will be presented with the *Closed Network* box, as shown in Figure 3-6.

Here you can enter the network name (SSID) of the wireless network you want to join and the password (WEP key), if one is required. This is how you can join networks that do not broadcast their SSID.

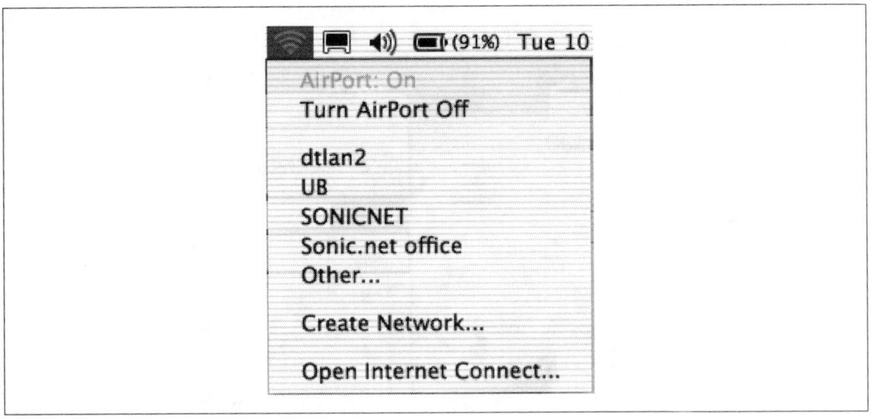

Figure 3-5. AirPort configuration.

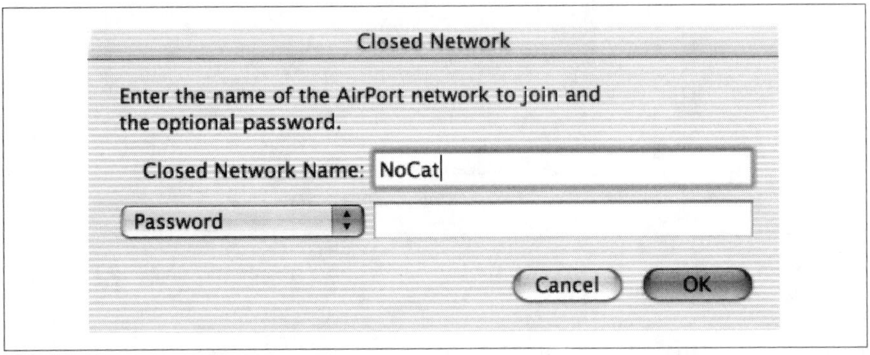

Figure 3-6. Specifying the ESSID for a "closed" network.

Once you've either selected an available network or entered information for another network not listed, you'll see which network is currently connected by using the AirPort menu bar (Figure 3-7).

The AirPort software offers a signal strength meter, though it is rather limited in its granularity. Click the AirPort icon in the menu bar and select *Internet Connect*; you'll see a window similar to that shown in Figure 3-8.

Combined with the lack of a connector for external antennas, this severely limits the AirPort wireless card as a useful tool for testing wireless network connections. For more advanced diagnostics, you might want to take a look at MacStumbler **[Hack #22]**.

Linux

Using wireless networking cards in Linux can require a good deal of work, depending on your particular Linux distribution. We're not going to cover that here. This assumes you have PCMCIA support for your wireless card,

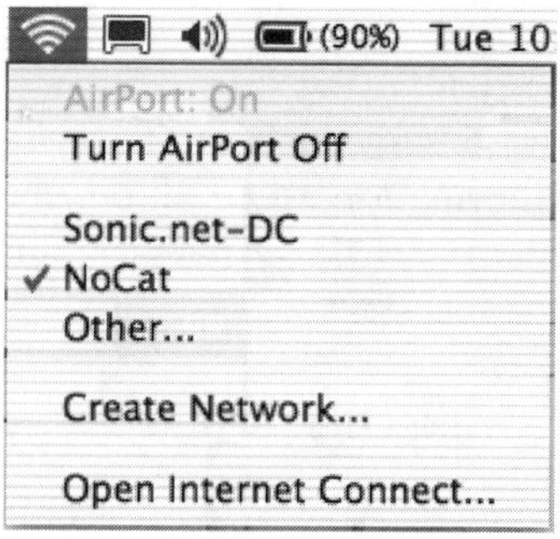

Figure 3-7. You can quickly tell which network you are on, and easily choose between all available networks.

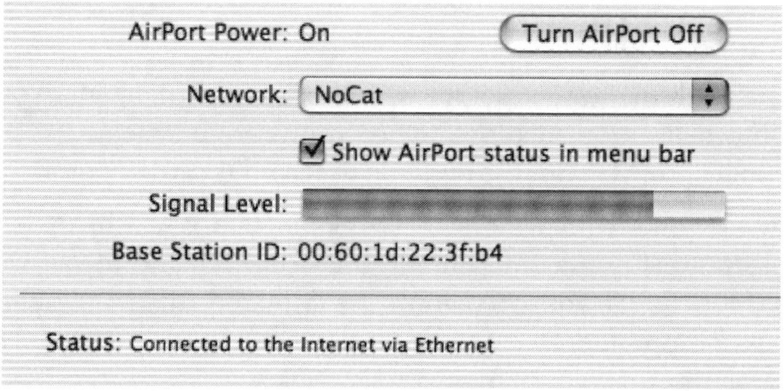

Figure 3-8. Apple's simple status screen leaves much to the imagination.

the Wireless Extensions in your kernel, and the Wireless Tools package installed. Both the Wireless Tools and kernel patches for the Wireless Extension can be found at *http://www.hpl.hp.com/personal/Jean_Tourrilhes/Linux/ Tools.html*. The v.14 Wireless Extensions are included in the 2.4.20 kernel, and v.16 are included in the 2.4.21 kernel.

The Wireless Tools package does come with many distributions. It provides four command-line tools:

iwconfig
> Allows you to manipulate the basic wireless parameters

iwlist
> Allows you to list addresses, frequencies, bit-rates, and more

iwspy
> Allows you to get per node link quality

iwpriv
> Allows you to manipulate the Wireless Extensions specific to a driver

iwlist is the tool you need at the command line to show you available wireless networks. To enable scanning, use this:

```
# iwlist wlan0 scanning
```

This gives you detailed information about all detected networks and is supported in the newer versions of the Wireless Extensions/Tools. You'll see output similar to the following:

```
wlan0    Scan completed :
         Cell 01 - Address: 00:02:6F:01:76:31
                   ESSID:"NoCat "
                   Mode:Master
                   Frequency:2.462GHz
                   Quality:0/92 Signal level:-50 dBm Noise level:-100 dBm
                   Encryption key:off
                   Bit Rate:1Mb/s
                   Bit Rate:2Mb/s
                   Bit Rate:5.5Mb/s
                   Bit Rate:11Mb/s
```

If there are multiple access points visible from your machine, you receive detailed information on each one. Once you've found the access point you need to connect to, you can use *iwconfig* to tell your card about it.

Anyone who works with wireless networks in Linux will likely be looking for a more powerful link state monitoring tool. Be sure to take a look at Wavemon [Hack #33] if you need more functionality than the simple command-line tools provide.

—*Roger Weeks*

HACK #21 Network Discovery Using NetStumbler
Find all available wireless networks with this infamous monitoring tool.

Once you've tried using the wireless client software included with any of the major operating systems, you'll quickly realize the major shortcomings of these utilities. Most tools don't give a detailed measurement of signal strength and won't even indicate when multiple networks are using the same channel.

NetStumbler (*http://www.stumbler.net/*) is an excellent (and free) utility that will give you a great deal of detail about all of the wireless networks in range, including their ESSID, whether they use WEP, the channels they use, and more. As of this writing, the current version is 0.30, and the author is working on Version 0.4. Installation is easy and quick, and for everything that NetStumbler does, the software package is remarkably small.

NetStumbler does not support all wireless network cards. You'll want to check the README before installing to make sure you've got a compatible wireless card. Supported cards include all cards using the Hermes chipset (Lucent/Orinoco/Avaya/Agere/Proxim cards). As of Version 0.30, the software also supports native NDIS 5.1 drivers in Windows XP, allowing it to support Cisco Aironet and some Prism-based cards.

When you launch NetStumbler for the first time, you're going to want to set some options. Click on *View* and select *Options*. You'll see the *Options* dialog as shown in Figure 3-9.

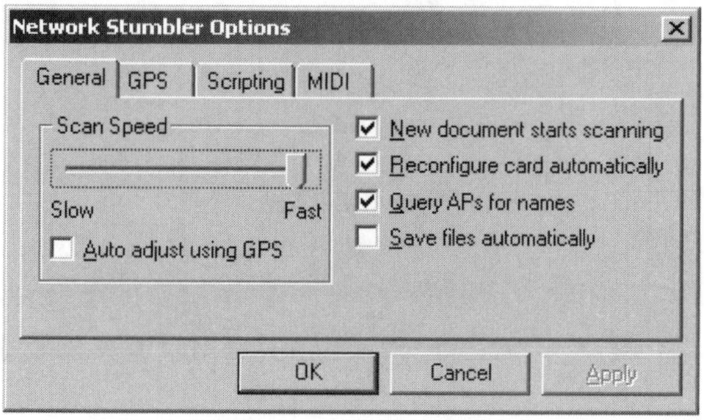

Figure 3-9. NetStumbler Options.

There are a couple of very important options here that you must select to get the best performance out of NetStumbler. You will probably want to set the scan speed to Fast. You'll get more frequent and more accurate updates of wireless networks with this setting. Also, if you are using Windows 2000 or Windows XP, you should definitely check the "Reconfigure card automatically" option. If you don't check this, NetStumbler will find whatever wireless network your card is currently associated with, but no other networks.

One of NetStumbler's coolest features is the ability to give you MIDI feedback for signal strength. This is great for finding the best possible signal between two points, such as when you are trying to align antennas on a long distance shot [Hack #82]. When the signal strength rises, so does the pitch of the tone that NetStumbler plays. This makes tuning an antenna similar to pointing a satellite dish; just move the antenna around until you hear the highest pitch tone. Choose a MIDI channel and patch sounds under the *MIDI* tab of the *Options* screen (Figure 3-10). You'll need a MIDI-capable sound card to use this option.

With your options properly set, you're ready to discover wireless networks. Assuming your wireless card is installed, NetStumbler will immediately start

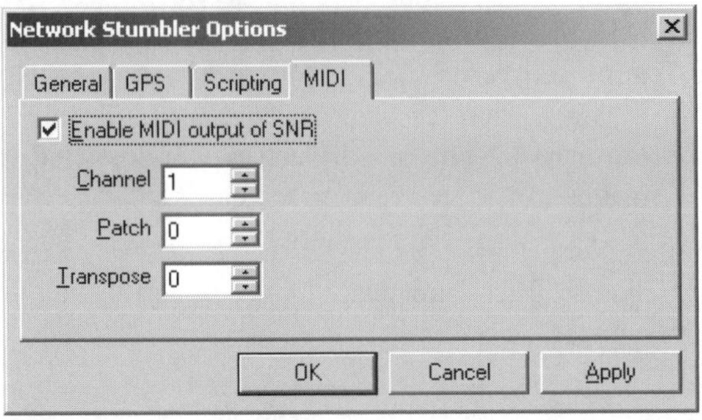

Figure 3-10. MIDI output options.

scanning. If you've got the MIDI option turned on, you'll get a LOT of audio feedback, particularly if you have multiple networks in your area. Figure 3-11 shows a typical NetStumbler session.

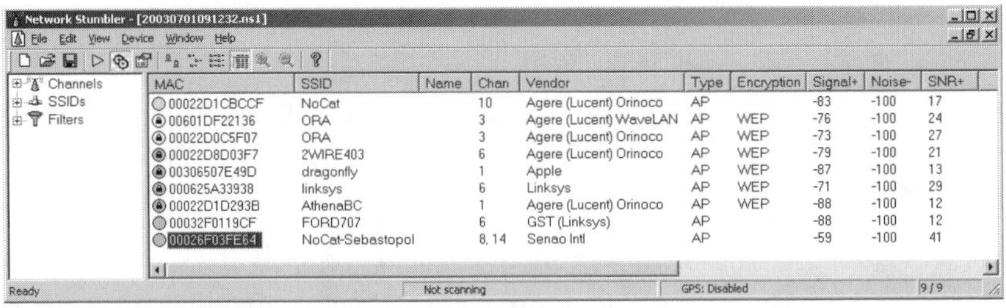

Figure 3-11. NetStumbler showing many detected networks.

NetStumbler shows the most active links by color. Green indicates a strong signal, yellow is marginal, and red is almost unusable. Grey means the wireless network is not in reach. The lock symbol shown in many of the link buttons indicates that the network is using WEP.

You can see at a glance all of the wireless networks that NetStumbler has found, along with their signal strength, SNR, and noise. You can also see which vendor chipset the wireless network is using. This can be particularly handy when you are looking for a specific network in a populated area.

To use NetStumbler for fine-tuning a wireless link, start up NetStumbler and make sure that it has found the network on the other end of the point-to-point link. Once it has done so, you'll start hearing the MIDI tones as it reports signal strength. A higher tone indicates better signal strength. Turn up your speaker volume, and then concentrate on pointing the antenna. You'll know it's pointed as accurately it can be when NetStumbler is generating the highest MIDI tone.

A second option to visualize signal strength is available by drilling down through the navigational menus on the lefthand side of the NetStumbler screen. Click on the plus sign next to "SSIDs". You'll see something similar to Figure 3-12 by clicking on the plus sign next to it. You'll see all of the MAC addresses associated with that SSID. Click on the MAC address to see a graphical representation of signal strength to this wireless network. As you can see in Figure 3-13, this is a very handy visual tool. Again, you can use this to tell you when a directional antenna is placed properly. You can also use it in a corporate environment to determine best placement location for an access point.

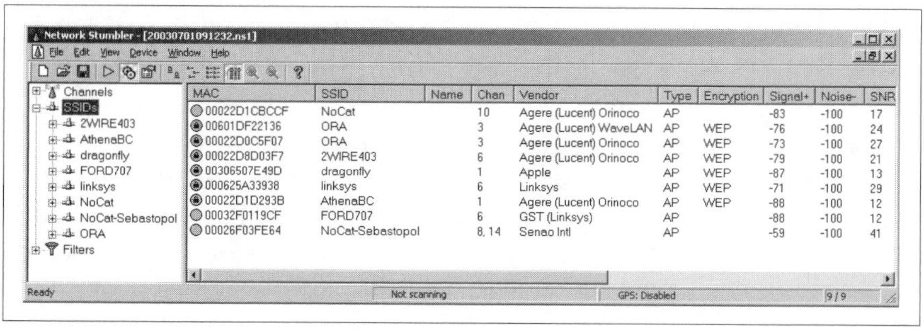

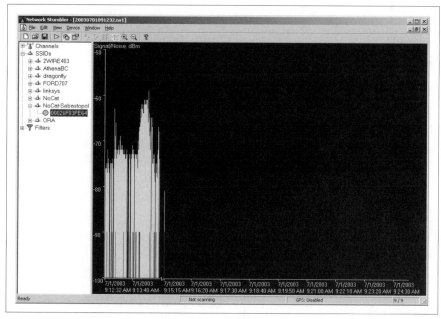

Figure 3-12. Viewing networks by SSID.

Figure 3-13. The visual meter shows signal strength over time.

NetStumbler will also interface with a GPS system connected to your PC. You can choose your GPS system from a list in the *View → Options* dialog. Once you have told NetStumbler about your GPS unit, the main screen not only shows details of the wireless network, but also shows the latitude and longitude of the wireless network.

A note regarding support for wireless cards: as mentioned at the beginning of the hack, the author of NetStumbler includes NDIS 5.1 driver support for Cisco and some Prism cards if you are running Windows XP.

In order to make this work, you'll need to click on the *Device* menu. There will be two drivers listed. You must select the driver labeled *NDIS 5.1* in order to make NetStumbler work with Prism or Cisco cards. I've successfully tested this with the Senao/Engenius 200mW high power cards, and it works well.

NetStumbler is an active network scanner that sends out probe requests and watches for responses to those probes; as such, it won't detect so-called "closed" networks. To accomplish this, you need a passive monitoring tool such as Kismet **[Hack #31]** or KisMAC **[Hack #24]**. But for many situations, NetStumbler is a small, powerful tool for detecting and monitoring the majority of wireless networks.

—*Roger Weeks*

HACK #22 Network Detection on Mac OS X

Find out everything you ever wanted to know about the networks available in your area.

If you are simply looking for any available network, you can usually get by with the built-in AirPort client. But if you are building your own network, or troubleshooting someone else's, you need much more detail than the standard clients provide. In particular, knowing which networks are in range and which channels they are using can be invaluable when determining where to put your own equipment. Here are two very easy-to-use survey tools for OS X that give you a far better idea of what's really going on.

MacStumbler

Sharing nothing but a name with the very popular NetStumbler **[Hack #21]**, *MacStumbler* (*http://www.macstumbler.com/*) is probably the most popular network scanner for OS X. It is simple to use, and provides the details that you are most likely interested in: available networks, the channels they use, and their received signal strength. It also displays received noise, whether WEP is enabled, and a bunch of other useful details. See Figure 3-14.

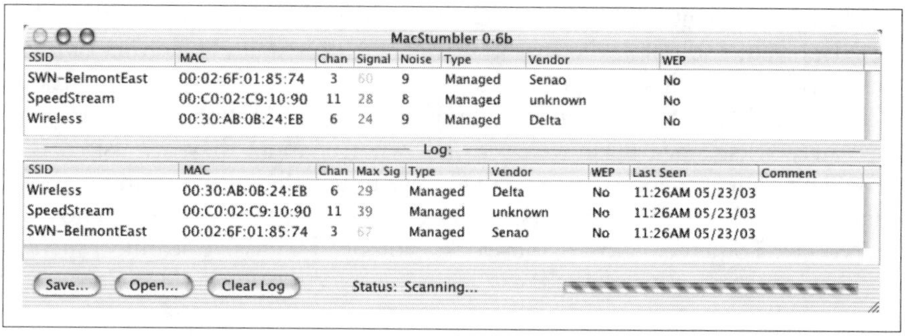

Figure 3-14. MacStumbler's main screen.

Like many OS X apps, MacStumbler is capable of text-to-speech, so it will even speak the ESSIDs of networks that it finds as they appear. Although it is still in beta, I have found MacStumbler to be a very reliable tool. It currently supports network scanning using only the built-in AirPort card.

iStumbler

Another popular network discovery tool is iStumbler (*http://homepage.mac. com/alfwatt/istumbler/*). This tool is even simpler than MacStumbler, in that there is really nothing to configure. Just fire it up and it will find all available networks for you, complete with a real-time signal and noise meter.

As you can see in Figure 3-15, there are plans for GPS support in the next release, but as of v0.6b and at the time of this writing, the Coordinates field is meaningless. Like MacStumbler, iStumbler supports scanning only when using the built-in AirPort card.

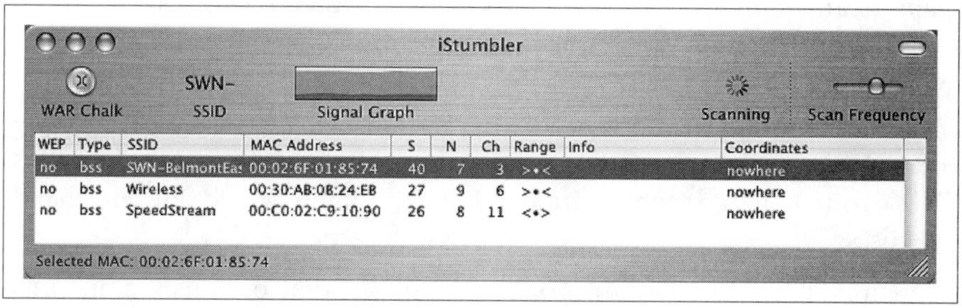

Figure 3-15. iStumbler's simple, brushed metal interface.

These tools will both find all available networks quickly, and will keep historical logs if you need to monitor wireless networks over time. If you need to find all available networks in range, either of these tools are ideal.

MacStumbler and iStumbler work by actively sending out probe requests to all available access points. The access points respond to the probes (as they would for any legitimate wireless client), and this information is then collected, sorted, and displayed by the scanners. Unfortunately, neither of these tools will find "closed" networks, since they don't respond to probe requests. This is an unfortunate side effect for people who choose to hide their networks. Since it isn't easy to tell what channel they are using, it is very likely that someone nearby will choose to use the same (or an adjacent) channel for their own network. This causes undesirable interference for everybody. To detect "closed" networks, you need a passive scanner, such as KisMAC [Hack #24] or Kismet [Hack #31].

Detecting Networks Using Handheld PCs

HACK
#23   Easily monitor wireless networks while walking around.

If you have a handheld PC, you know how convenient it is. What you may not realize is that it makes an excellent wireless testing device. If your handheld has a Compact Flash or PC card slot, you can use a wireless card in these slots.

If you have a Sharp Zaurus or Compaq iPAQ running Linux, then you're in luck. Kismet [Hack #31] runs well on these machines, giving you the most powerful and tiny network monitoring tool there is. When compiling Kismet for a handheld platform, be sure to include the handheld optimizations. See the Kismet documentation for details.

For Pocket PC 3.0 and 2002 users, the author of NetStumbler has written a miniature version just for Pocket PCs: *MiniStumbler*.

MiniStumbler can be downloaded from *http://www.stumbler.net/*. As of this writing, the current version is 0.3.23. MiniStumbler supports Hermes chipset cards only (the Lucent/Orinoco/Agere/Avaya/Proxim strain). There is currently no support for Prism or Cisco cards.

To install MiniStumbler, just copy the proper file for your Pocket PC processor architecture from your host PC over to the Pocket PC. There is no setup routine. Supported processor architectures include ARM, MIPS, and SH3. Check your system documentation if you don't know which one your handheld uses.

As with NetStumbler [Hack #21], you'll want to set some options the first time you launch it. There are two menus at the bottom that you'll want to check out. The first is Opt, as shown in Figure 3-16. Make sure that *Reconfigure card automatically* and *Get AP Names* are both checked.

Notably missing from MiniStumbler is MIDI support for audio feedback. However, you can still set the scanning speed, by clicking on the *Spd* menu, as shown in Figure 3-17. Generally, you want to set it to the fastest possible speed.

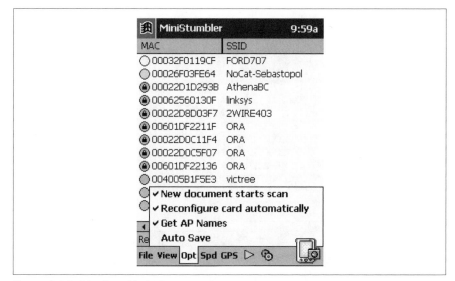

Figure 3-16. MiniStumbler's Opt menu.

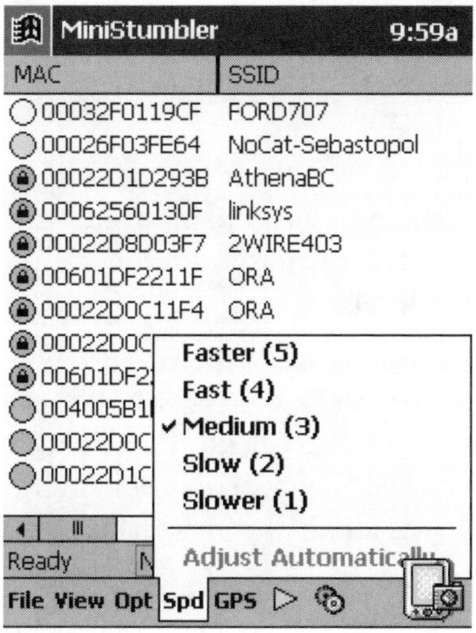

Figure 3-17. MiniStumbler scanning speed.

With MiniStumbler's options properly configured, you're ready to discover wireless networks. As long as your wireless card is installed, MiniStumbler will immediately start scanning for networks. A typical scanning session looks something like Figure 3-18.

If you've ever used NetStumbler, you should be right at home. The data is displayed in exactly the same way, using the same color scheme for the

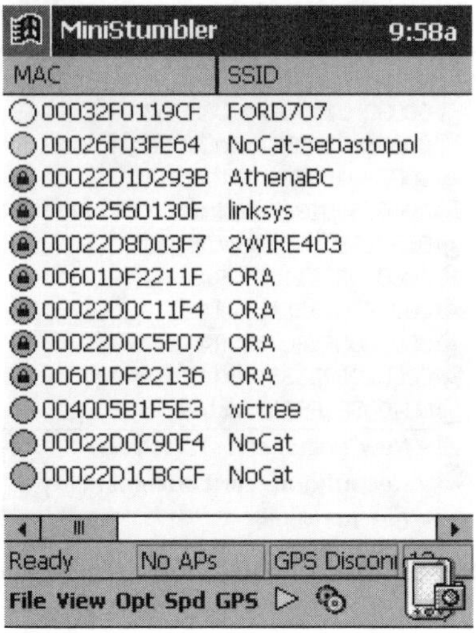

Figure 3-18. MiniStumbler in action.

networks it has detected (green, yellow, or red to indicate signal strength, grey for networks out of range, and a tiny lock icon for networks using WEP). If you need to pause the scanning process, simply click on the green triangle in the bottom menu.

While the tiny screen on a Pocket PC is wonderfully portable, it makes viewing large amounts of data sometimes painful. In order to see all of the data in MiniStumbler, you have to scroll to the right. This includes signal strength, SNR, and noise levels.

MiniStumbler does not support any of the visualization views in NetStumbler, so you can't get a graph of wireless signal over time. However, there is support for location logging using a GPS. Click on the *GPS* menu (Figure 3-19) and select the COM port attached to your GPS. MiniStumbler will then show latitude and longitude locations for all of your wireless networks as it finds them.

Obviously, a GPS can only effectively be used for outdoor network detection. But the extreme portability of Pocket PCs make them ideal for performing informal site surveys, checking for unauthorized access points, or establishing the coverage area of your wireless network. MiniStumbler may be missing many of the handy features of NetStumbler and Kismet, but it is simple to use and far better than the system client for finding networks.

—*Roger Weeks*

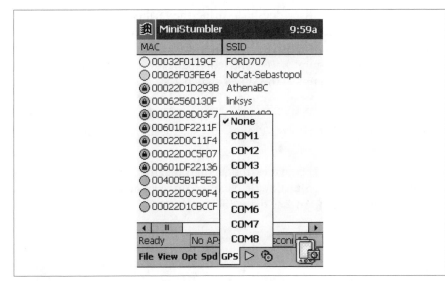

Figure 3-19. Select the port to which your GPS is attached.

Passive Scanning with KisMAC

Glean detailed network information with this passive scanner for OS X.

KisMAC (*http://www.binaervarianz.de/projekte/programmieren/kismac/*) is another OS X tool that shares a name with the popular monitoring tool Kismet **[Hack #31]**. This is a much more advanced network discovery and monitoring tool than either MacStumbler or iStumbler **[Hack #22]**.

As stated earlier, active scanners work by sending out probe requests to all available access points. Since these scanners rely on responses to active probing, it is possible for network administrators to detect the presence of tools like MacStumbler and iStumbler (as well as NetStumbler **[Hack #21]**, miniStumbler **[Hack #23]**, or any other tool that makes use of active network probes).

KisMAC is a *passive* network scanner. Rather than send out active probe requests, it instructs the wireless card to tune to a channel, listen for a short time, then tune to the next channel, listen for a while, and so on. In this way, it is possible to not only detect networks without announcing your presence, but also find networks that don't respond to probe requests—namely, "closed" networks (APs that have beaconing disabled). But that's not all. Passive monitors have access to every frame that the radio can hear while tuned to a particular channel. This means that you can not only detect access points, but also the wireless clients of those APs.

The standard AirPort driver doesn't provide the facility for passive monitoring, so KisMAC uses the open source Viha AirPort driver (*http://www.dopesquad.net/security/*). It swaps the Viha driver for your existing AirPort driver when the program starts, and automatically reinstalls the standard driver on exit. To accomplish this driver switcheroo, you have to provide your administrative password when you start KisMAC. Note that while KisMAC is running, your regular wireless connection is unavailable. KisMAC also supplies drivers for Orinoco/Avaya/Proxim cards, as well as Prism II–based wireless cards.

KisMAC's main screen provides much of the same information as MacStumbler or iStumbler. But double-clicking any available network shows a wealth of new information (see Figure 3-20).

Property	Setting		#	Client	Vendor	Signal	sent Bytes	recv. Bytes	Last Seen
SSID	SWN–BelmontEast		0	FF:FF:FF:FF:FF:FF	Broadcas	0	0B	8.10KB	
BSSID	00:02:6F:01:85:74		1	00:02:6F:01:85:74	Senao	34	8.34KB	0B	2003-05-23 1
Vendor	Senao		2	00:30:65:03:E7:8A	Apple	0	0B	2.70KB	
First Seen	2003-05-23 12:13:5C		3	00:40:63:C0:AA:4B	unknown	34	3.34KB	386B	2003-05-23 1
Last Seen	2003-05-23 12:14:4C		4	00:40:96:41:83:AB	Cisco	0	0B	78B	
			5	00:02:2D:69:0D:23	Proxim	0	0B	248B	
Channel	2		6	00:02:2D:3B:56:50	Proxim	12	386B	580B	2003-05-23 1
Signal	34								
MaxSignal	40								
Type	managed								
WEP	disabled								
Packets	154								
Weak Packets	0								
Data Packets	21								
Bytes	12.52KB								
Key									
LastIV	00:00:00								
Latitude	0.000000N								
Longitude	0.000000E								

Figure 3-20. Wireless network details in KisMAC.

One interesting side effect of passive scanning is that channel detection isn't 100 percent reliable. Since 802.11b channels overlap, it is sometimes difficult for a passive scanner to know for certain which channel an access point is tuned to, and it can be one off from time to time. The AP in Figure 3-21 is actually set to channel 3, although it is reported as channel 2.

KisMAC allows you to specify which channels you would like to scan on. This can help if you are trying to find access points that are using the same channel as your own. See Figure 3-21.

KisMAC has a slew of nifty features, including GPS support, raw frame injection (for Prism II and Orinoco cards), and even a real-time relative

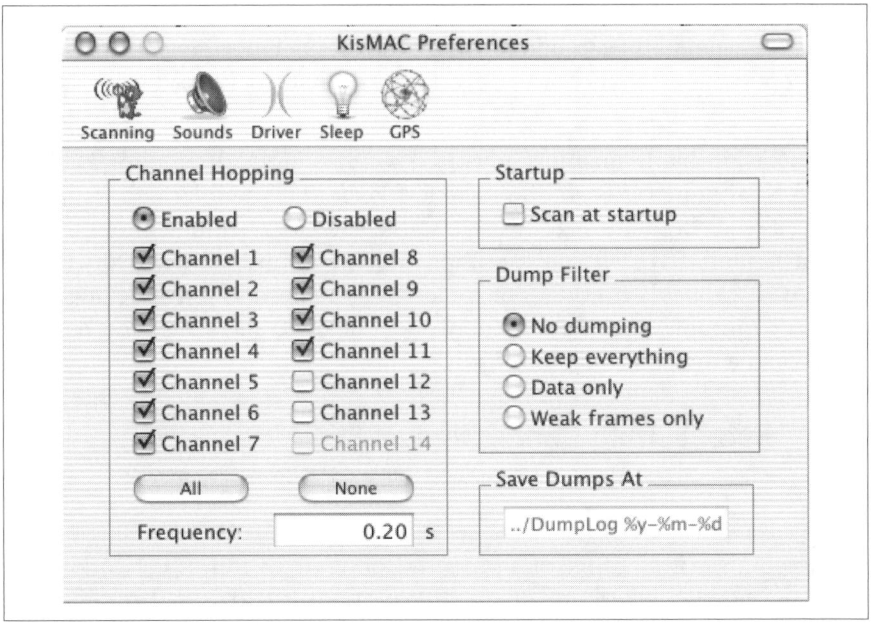

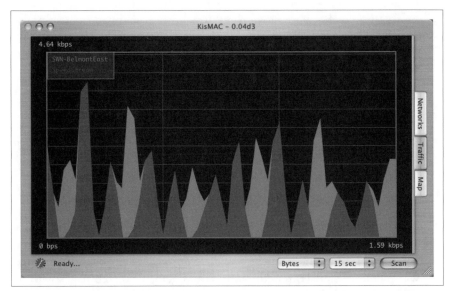

Figure 3-21. You can select only the channels you need to scan in KisMAC.

traffic graph (Figure 3-22). If it detects a WEP network, it can use a number of advanced techniques to try to guess the password. And yes, it can even read discovered ESSIDs aloud.

Figure 3-22. Show the relative traffic of all detected networks, without transmitting a single bit.

Perhaps the most powerful feature of all is KisMAC's ability to log raw 802.11 frames to a standard pcap dump. Check the "Keep Everything" or the "Data Only" option in preferences to save a dump file that can be read by tools such as Ethereal [Hack #39].

KisMAC is probably the most advanced wireless network monitor available for OS X, although it is still quite beta. I keep MacStumbler and iStumbler handy, as they both are slightly more stable and can operate without removing the AirPort driver. If you are simply looking for available networks, then KisMAC is probably overkill. But sometimes you need as much detail as you can get to troubleshoot difficult network problems, and when you do, KisMAC can be the right tool for the job.

HACK #25   Establishing Connectivity

What to do first when you just can't get your wireless connection working.

As ethereal as wireless networks seem to be, they work surprisingly well. Once you are within range of a properly configured wireless network, there is usually very little work required on the part of the end user. Typically, you simply open your laptop and it all "just works."

Except, of course, when it doesn't. If you are having trouble getting online, it's time to practice your troubleshooting skills. Here are some simple steps that should help you to quickly pinpoint the source of the trouble.

Is your wireless card installed and turned on? Many laptops have the ability to disable the wireless card, either through software or a physical switch. Is your card plugged in (all the way!), is it turned on, and does it have all of the proper drivers installed? This is the troubleshooting equivalent of "is it plugged in," but is certainly worth checking first.

Are you in range of an AP? When in doubt, always check your signal meter. Do you have enough signal strength to talk to the AP? You could simply be out of range. If your client software shows noise levels, check them as well to be sure that you have a high signal-to-noise ratio. It is always possible that a neighbor has just started microwaving a burrito, or maybe they just answered their 2.4 GHz phone.

Are you associated with the proper network? This step sounds silly, but is becoming more important to check every day. For example, I live in an apartment building in a busy part of Seattle. I once sat down at my laptop and tried to log into my local file server, only to find that it was unreachable. I thought I was having connectivity problems, but there was plenty of signal strength, and I could get out to web pages with no problem. I plugged in the console to my file server and everything seemed fine. Puzzled, I decided to try to ping my laptop from the file server. It was then that I realized that my laptop was using a strange IP address, not even in the same network that I use for my home. How could it possibly be able to get to web pages if it is using the wrong network numbers?

Then it dawned on me that earlier that day, I had set my laptop to use the network with the strongest signal, regardless of the ESSID. It turns out that a neighbor had just installed an access point, and I was associated with it instead! Since my neighbor and I are both running open networks, my laptop dutifully associated and started using my neighbor's DSL line. Of course my home machines were unreachable; they are all on a private network behind my router.

So the moral of the story is: be sure that you know which network you are talking to.

Do you have an IP address? From the command line in Linux, BSD, or OS X, run ifconfig -a. Look for an *inet* address associated with your wireless device.

In Windows NT, 2000, or XP, run ipconfig /all from a command shell. You should see an IP address associated with your wireless device.

In Windows 95/98, run winipcfg. Select your wireless card from the drop-down box, and your IP address will be displayed.

If your IP is listed as 0.0.0.0, is missing, or starts with 169, then you have no IP address. That means that you don't have a DHCP lease. Be absolutely sure that your WEP settings are correct, and if you are using MAC address filtering, be sure that the MAC address of your wireless card matches the list in your AP.

If all of your wireless settings are correct and you have plenty of signal, then for some reason you simply haven't received a DHCP lease. This can happen for a variety of reasons. Is your card configured to request DHCP? Is the DHCP server up and running on your network? If you are serving a large number of clients, have you run out of DHCP leases? If in doubt, this level of troubleshooting is best done with the help of your network administrator. If you are the network admin, try using a traffic sniffer like *tcpdump* [Hack #37] or Ethereal [Hack #38]. Can you see traffic from the AP? What happens when your machine requests a DHCP lease? A good sniffer can help find the source of the problem very quickly.

If you absolutely need to get onto a network that isn't offering DHCP leases, and you have access to a sniffer, you can always "camp." This is *not* recommended except in the most dire of emergencies, but it wouldn't be a hack if I didn't tell you how, would it? Using a sniffer on a busy network, you can quickly discern the network layout, including the IP range being used and the likely default gateway. Pick an IP address in that range and assign it statically. Then define your default router, and you should be all set. This is highly discouraged as it is difficult to tell if you are "sharing" an IP address with another machine on the network, which could cause problems for both of you. Also, any self-respecting network admin who figures out what you are doing will likely bring his wrath down upon your head. But if they are so self-respecting, be sure to inquire why his DHCP server didn't work in the first place.

Before continuing on to the remaining troubleshooting steps, it is a good idea to disable any encrypted tunnels or proxies that you might be running, in order to establish basic connectivity without too many variables getting in the way.

Can you ping the default gateway's IP address? The first hop on the way to the Internet is your default gateway. Can you ping it?

In Linux, BSD, or OS X, run `netstat -rn`. Look for the Destination *default* or *0.0.0.0*. This is your default gateway.

In Windows NT, 2000, or XP, run `ipconfig /all` from a command shell. Your default gateway will be listed there.

In Windows 95/98, run `winipcfg`. Select your wireless card from the drop-down box, and the default gateway will be displayed.

Try to ping the IP address listed. An unreachable gateway by itself doesn't necessarily indicate a problem, as not all routers respond to ping requests. However, if you can't reach the gateway, and you can't get out to the rest of the Internet, then make sure that the gateway is up. If you aren't the network admin, then you had better find her.

Can you ping an IP on the Internet? This step is important and frequently overlooked. Try to ping any popular IP on the Internet. For example, 216.239.33.99 is listed as the IP address of *www.google.com*. You should memorize one IP address that is guaranteed to be up and try to ping it. A successful ping here establishes basic connectivity to the rest of the Internet. If you have been successful in all tests so far, but can't ping an Internet IP, then traffic isn't getting beyond your default gateway or it isn't coming back. See the section "Using traceroute," next.

Can you ping www.google.com? This is an important but separate step from the previous step. If you can ping 216.239.33.99, but attempts to ping *www.google.com* take a long time and eventually fail, then it is very likely that your routing is fine, but DNS name resolution isn't working. Check the DNS servers that your DHCP server handed to you.

In Linux, BSD, or OS X, try cat /etc/resolv.conf. There should be one or more *nameserver* lines listed with an IP address.

In Windows NT, 2000, or XP, run ipconfig /all from a command shell. Your DNS Servers will be listed there.

In Windows 95/98, run winipcfg. Select your wireless card from the drop-down box, and the DNS servers will be displayed.

If you have no DNS servers listed, then your DHCP server didn't hand one out. Assign one manually, or better yet, fix your DHCP server. If you have DNS servers listed but you can't resolve DNS names, then something is probably wrong with your DNS configuration. At this point, contact your network admin, as here there be dragons.

Can you browse to www.google.com? This is, of course, an obvious test, which may have been what started you troubleshooting in the first place. If this test works, then you have some sort of connectivity to the Internet. But it is always worth trying as part of your regular routine, particularly if you are using a public access point. Many public networks run a captive portal (such as NoCatAuth **[Hack #89]**) that prohibits most network connectivity before logging into a web page. This can be very confusing, particularly if you are able to perform many of these tests but can't establish an SSH connection or check your email, for example. Always try to browse to a popular web page if you are having trouble connecting to a public network, because you might find yourself redirected to instructions on how to gain further network access.

This can also turn up unexpected problems with intervening transparent proxies, such as squid. It may also indicate that there is a manual proxy that you are supposed to use for Internet traffic. If you can ping and resolve hostnames, but you can't browse to web sites, check with your network admin to see if there is a proxy server somewhere on the network and that it is functioning properly.

Using traceroute

One very handy tool for finding the source of network problems is *traceroute*. While not completely infallible, it can help to pinpoint exactly where communications are breaking down. It is best used when you can reach some machines (for example, your default gateway) but not others.

traceroute attempts to contact every machine along the route between your local computer and the ultimate destination, and reports on the average amount of time it takes to contact each one. Not all routers will allow *traceroute* traffic to pass through it, but it is worth trying if you are having network troubles.

Under Linux, BSD, or OS X, run traceroute -n 208.201.239.36

In any version of Windows, from the command shell, run:

```
tracert -n 208.201.239.36
```

Of course, you can use any Internet IP address you like. You should see something like the following:

```
traceroute to 208.201.239.36 (208.201.239.36), 30 hops max, 40 byte packets
 1 10.15.6.1 4.802 ms 4.411 ms 4.886 ms
 2 216.254.17.1 11.341 ms 11.202 ms 10.797 ms
 3 206.191.168.200 14.212 ms 25.894 ms 11.811 ms
 4 206.191.168.220 14.362 ms 13.564 ms 23.587 ms
 5 206.253.192.194 13.046 ms 13.244 ms 13.595 ms
 6 157.130.191.113 147.823 ms 16.747 ms 17.827 ms
 7 152.63.106.190 19.723 ms 156.864 ms 23.545 ms
 8 152.63.106.233 22.393 ms 32.006 ms 18.52 ms
 9 152.63.2.134 14.93 ms 115.795 ms 34.949 ms
10 152.63.1.34 35.249 ms 139.869 ms 32.841 ms
11 152.63.54.130 38.268 ms 148.991 ms 33.852 ms
12 152.63.55.70 33.457 ms 49.736 ms 90.575 ms
13 152.63.51.125 34.17 ms 32.661 ms 32.978 ms
14 157.130.203.234 53.416 ms 67.974 ms 35.621 ms
15 64.142.0.1 41.108 ms 60.794 ms 92.63 ms
16 208.201.224.30 40.331 ms 54.544 ms 144.794 ms
17 208.201.239.36 49.154 ms 36.918 ms 124.526 ms
```

This shows the IP address of each intervening hop on the way to the destination, and the approximate amount of time it took to reach each hop. It makes three attempts to contact each hop, and reports the timing of each to help establish something of an average. If you are absolutely sure that name resolution is working properly, you can omit the –n switch, which will cause *traceroute* to look up the name of each hop along the way as well.

Connectivity problems are indicated by the presence of stars in the IP address field. For example, here is a *traceroute* to a nonexistent IP address:

```
rob@caligula:~$ traceroute -n 192.168.1.1
traceroute to 192.168.1.1 (192.168.1.1), 30 hops max, 40 byte packets
 1 10.15.6.1 4.795 ms 4.586 ms 4.3 ms
 2 216.254.17.1 169.344 ms 17.067 ms 15.115 ms
 3 206.191.168.200 15.13 ms 24.71 ms 16.03 ms
 4 * * *
^C
```

The router at 206.191.168.200 likely realized that 192.168.1.1 is a nonroutable IP address, and is silently discarding packets with that destination. If there are connectivity problems between any two points along a *traceroute*, you will see stars in the IP field, or very large response times at each hop. Generally, anything in excess of a couple of hundred milliseconds means that you should probably try your call again later.

In my experience, it is hardly ever necessary to go through this entire check-list to establish connectivity. But when it is necessary, it is important to remember to go slow, eliminate variables as you go, and try to fix things so that the same problem doesn't happen again. For really tough connectivity issues that these steps won't solve, you'll need more powerful measures. A powerful protocol analyzer like tcpdump or Ethereal can quickly bring the trickiest of network problems to light.

HACK #26 Quickly Poll Wireless Clients with ping

A quick and dirty method for determining who is on your local subnet.

This is a simple, quick hack, but useful in many circumstances. Suppose you are associated with a wireless network, and are curious about who else is also using the network. You could fire up a network sniffer (like Ethereal [Hack #38] or *tcpdump* [Hack #37]), or manually scan for associated clients (using nmap [Hack #40]), although that might be construed as antisocial. You're not so much interested in what people are doing, just how many people are online.

It is simple to find clients on your local network using the ubiquitous *ping* utility. Simply ping the broadcast address of your network, and see who responds.

You can find the broadcast address by running *ifconfig* like so:

```
rob@florian:~$ ifconfig eth0
eth0   Link encap:Ethernet HWaddr 00:40:63:C0:AA:4B
       inet addr:10.15.6.1 Bcast:10.15.6.255 Mask:255.255.255.0
       UP BROADCAST RUNNING MULTICAST MTU:1500 Metric:1
       RX packets:13425489 errors:0 dropped:33 overruns:0 frame:0
       TX packets:19603221 errors:1118 dropped:0 overruns:0 carrier:0
       collisions:0 txqueuelen:100
       RX bytes:3073225705 (2930.8 Mb) TX bytes:1301320438 (1241.0 Mb)
       Interrupt:10 Base address:0xe800
```

There it is, the *Bcast* address. This is the broadcast address for your local subnet, which every machine is listening to. In Mac OS X and BSD, it is simply listed as the broadcast address:

```
rob@caligula:~$ ifconfig en1
en1: flags=8863<UP,BROADCAST,SMART,RUNNING,SIMPLEX,MULTICAST> mtu 1500
     inet6 fe80::230:65ff:fe03:e78a%en1 prefixlen 64 scopeid 0x5
     inet 10.15.6.49 netmask 0xffffff00 broadcast 10.15.6.255
     ether 00:30:65:03:e7:8a
     media: autoselect status: active
     supported media: autoselect
```

Most (but not all) machines will respond to a ping sent to this address. But simply running ping won't always leave enough time for the clients to respond between echo requests. Run ping with a long wait time (say, 60 seconds) between requests, and be sure to send at least one ping:

```
rob@florian:~$ ping -c3 -i60 10.15.6.255
PING 10.15.6.255 (10.15.6.255): 56 octets data
64 octets from 10.15.6.1: icmp_seq=0 ttl=255 time=0.3 ms
64 octets from 10.15.6.72: icmp_seq=0 ttl=64 time=0.4 ms (DUP!)
64 octets from 10.15.6.61: icmp_seq=0 ttl=64 time=0.7 ms (DUP!)
64 octets from 10.15.6.65: icmp_seq=0 ttl=64 time=0.9 ms (DUP!)
64 octets from 10.15.6.64: icmp_seq=0 ttl=64 time=1.7 ms (DUP!)
64 octets from 10.15.6.66: icmp_seq=0 ttl=64 time=2.0 ms (DUP!)
64 octets from 10.15.6.69: icmp_seq=0 ttl=64 time=10.9 ms (DUP!)
64 octets from 10.15.6.68: icmp_seq=0 ttl=64 time=38.0 ms (DUP!)
^C
--- 10.15.6.255 ping statistics ---
1 packets transmitted, 1 packets received, +7 duplicates, 0% packet loss
round-trip min/avg/max = 0.3/6.9/38.0 ms
```

After duplicates (those suffixed with DUP!) stop arriving, feel free to hit Control-C to kill the running ping, or wait 60 seconds for another try. This gives you a quick, rough idea of how many machines are connected to the local subnet.

Note that not all machines answer to broadcast ping requests, and some block ICMP traffic (ping's protocol) altogether. Still, in terms of ease, speed, and ubiquity, you can't beat the results of the broadcast ping.

If you are curious about what kinds of wireless cards people are using, you might try looking up their serial numbers online [Hack #27].

HACK #27   Finding Radio Manufacturers by MAC Address

Find out what sort of radio cards and laptops are in use on your local network.

If you just joined us from the last hack [Hack #26], you might be wondering about who is using your wireless network. Sure, you have their IP addresses, and their MAC addresses are easily found with a simple arp -an. But what kind of computers are they using?

The IEEE maintains the database of *Organizationally Unique Identifiers* (OUI). These are the first 24 bits of the MAC address, parceled out to vendors who manufacture Ethernet devices. If you know the first three bytes of a MAC address, you can look up the device's manufacturer directly from the IEEE. There is a searchable database on the Web at *http://standards.ieee.org/regauth/oui/index.shtml*. Note that to use this service, you need to specify the OUI separated by hyphens, not colons (e.g., 00-02-2d, not 00:02:2d.).

The Code

Of course, this is handy for the occasional query, but what if you want to instantly see the manufacturer of all devices on your local subnet? Just after performing a broadcast ping [Hack #26], try this bit of Perl:

```perl
#!/usr/bin/perl

my %cards;
my %ips;

open(ARP,"arp -an|") || die "Couldn't open arp table: $!\n";

print "Looking up OUIs.";
while(<ARP>) {
 chomp;
 my $addr = $_;
 my $ip = $_;
 $addr =~ s/.* ([\d\w]+:[\d\w]+:[\d\w]+):.*/$1/;
 $addr =~ s/\b([\d\w])\b/0$1/g;
 $addr =~ s/:/-/g;
 next unless $addr =~ /..-..-../;

 $ip =~ s/.*?(\d+\.\d+\.\d+\.\d+).*/$1/;
 print ".";
 $cards{$addr}||=`curl -sd 'x=$addr' http://standards.ieee.org/cgi-bin/↵
ouisearch`;
 ($cards{$addr} =~ /Sorry!/) && ($cards{$addr} = "Unknown OUI: $addr");
 $ips{$ip} = $addr;
}
print "\n";
for(keys(%ips)) {
 $cards{$ips{$_}} =~ s/.*.hex.\s+([\w\s\,\.]+)\n.*/$1/s;
 print "$_ -> $cards{$ips{$_}}\n";
}
```

This script works well on Linux, Mac OS X, and BSD. It requires only Perl and the *curl* network utility (*http://curl.sourceforge.net/*), and it assumes that the *arp* utility is in your PATH. For efficiency's sake, it queries only the IEEE once for each OUI it encounters.

Running the Hack

Save the code to a file called *machines.pl* and invoke it from the command line, producing output somewhat like the following:

```
rob@florian:~$ perl machines.pl
Looking up OUIs.........
10.15.6.98 -> Compaq Computer Corporation
10.15.6.44 -> Aironet Wireless Communication
10.15.6.64 -> Aironet Wireless Communication
10.15.6.49 -> APPLE COMPUTER, INC.
```

```
10.15.6.75 -> Netgear, Inc.
10.15.6.87 -> APPLE COMPUTER, INC.
10.15.6.62 -> Senao International Co., Ltd.
```

This node has a Compaq card, two Cisco Aironet cards, two Apple Air-Ports, a Netgear, and a Senao card associated with it. This quickly gives you some idea of the demographic of your wireless users; plotted over time, it might show some interesting trends.

Some vendors are not listed in the OUI database, but the vast majority are. Some vendors are listed under the name of a subsidiary company (frequently from Taiwan), which can be misleading. But for an informal poll of just who is using your wireless network, this script can be quite illuminating.

Rendezvous Service Advertisements in Linux

#28   Let your users know what services are available on your network, even if you aren't running OS X.

Since I'm running a node on SeattleWireless (as well as a streaming jukebox that I'm developing), I'd like to let people know what local services are available. Sure, most visitors just jump straight to their favorite web site or check their email (or their popularity) when they hit my node, but perhaps they'd like to enjoy some local content at a whopping 11 Mbps?

This is one reason why I love multicast DNS service (*http://www. multicastdns.org/*) advertisements (and Rendezvous, in particular). My Linux Jukebox and Wiki are now announcing themselves like an old-time barker at the county fair. Wireless users at the cafe across the street (or anywhere within a block or so) can find my local services any time just by looking at available Rendezvous sites (Figure 3-23). As if that weren't enough, my streamer is even advertising itself as a *daap* stream, so iTunes 4 users can see that it's available from inside iTunes.

Figure 3-23. Users can easily find advertised services using a Rendezvous-enabled browser.

To advertise Rendezvous services, you need a multicast DNS advertiser. I think Apple's own Posix implementation is more than adequate. (Download it after a free registration on Apple's site at *http://www.opensource.apple.com/projects/rendezvous/source/Rendezvous.tar.gz.*) The application you're after is *mDNSProxyResponderPosix*, in the *mDNSPosix/* directory. It builds cleanly and without so much as a warning under Linux 2.4.20. Once it's built, install it somewhere handy (such as */usr/local/bin*, for example).

Next, figure out which services you want to advertise. They don't even have to be local services, since the Proxy server will obligingly hand out whatever IP addresses you care to throw at it, local or not. I'm advertising my local Wiki, the Jukebox, and the NoCat web site, just for fun.

The *mDNSProxyResponderPosix* program expects the following arguments:

```
mDNSProxyResponderPosix [IP] [Host] [Title] [Service type] [Port] [Optional
text]
```

The first argument is the IP address you'd like to advertise. The second should be a simple name that will be resolved as a *.local* address in multicast DNS. The Service title should be enclosed in double quotes, and should be a descriptive name for what is being advertised.

The Service type field is a little tricky. It takes the form:

```
_service._transport.
```

where *service* is a well-known IANA service name (i.e., something out of */etc/services*) and *transport* is the actual transport (such as _tcp. or _udp.). The Port argument is simply the port number, and the optional text field supplies additional information to the application receiving the advertisements (more on this later).

For example, here's how I advertise my local music jukebox:

```
$ mDNSProxyResponderPosix 10.15.6.1 muzik "Music Jukebox" _http._tcp. 80 &
```

This creates a *muzik.local* address that resolves to 10.15.6.1. It is an HTTP service, running on tcp port 80. Also notice the & at the end of the line. This is necessary because *mDNSProxyResponderPosix* doesn't auto-daemonize (hey, it's just example code, after all). As it listens on UDP port 5353, it doesn't need any special privileges to run, so I recommend running it as a nonprivileged user.

This is all well and good for the jukebox, but what if you need to go to a particular URL? For example, to get to my Wiki, you need to go to *http://florian.local/wiki*, not just *http://florian.local/*. This is where the optional text field at the end comes in. Safari accepts a path= argument in this field that gets appended to the URL line. For example:

```
$ mDNSProxyResponderPosix 10.15.6.1 florian "About this node" _http._tcp.80⏎
path=/wiki &
```

And there you have it. Incidentally, if you're using VirtualHosts in Apache, you'll have to tell Apache to respond to the name you're advertising (*florian. local* in the above example.) This is done easily with the *ServerAlias* directive from within your <VirtualHost> stanza:

```
ServerName florian.rob.swn
ServerAlias florian.local
```

What about advertising nonlocal services, like other web sites? Just specify their IP address as normal:

```
$ mDNSProxyResponderPosix 216.218.203.211 nocat "NoCatNet" _http._tcp. 80 &
```

Finally, since we have music available, it would be nice to advertise directly to iTunes' sharing feature. Since iTunes is simply expecting advertisements to the *daap* service (as opposed to HTTP), this is a piece of cake:

```
$ mDNSProxyResponderPosix 10.15.6.1 squeal "http://muzik.rob.swn/" ↵
_daap._tcp. 80
```

Unfortunately, you can't play the stream directly from the "shared" play list, as Apple uses a proprietary protocol to handle the streaming. So, since I can't easily stream directly to the user (yet), I do the next best thing: just spam the user with the relevant URL. If the user is curious enough to browse to the URL that automagically pops up in their iTunes playlist, they'll be presented with my streamer.

Of course, *mDNSProxyResponderPosix* isn't nearly as efficient as it could be. After all, you're starting a separate instance for each service you want to advertise, and there is not even a simple configuration file. But keep in mind that this application is just example code from Apple, and in due time more sophisticated multicast DNS advertisement tools will come along. The full source (as well as the complete spec, and some other great documents) are available, just waiting for someone to write the killer Linux/BSD/Windows Rendezvous app.

H A C K   Advertising Arbitrary Rendezvous Services in
#29   OS X

Rendezvous isn't just for web pages and iChat. Use this OS X app to advertise whatever you like.

While you can certainly use *mDNSProxyResponder* [Hack #28] to advertise arbitrary Rendezvous services from the command line, OS X has a number of pretty Aqua apps that will also do this for you. My favorite is a freeware app called Rendezvous Beacon, available at *http://www.chaoticsoftware.com/ ProductPages/RendezvousBeacon.html*. It incorporates all of the functionality of *mDNSProxyResponder* inside a simple, well-organized interface (Figure 3-24).

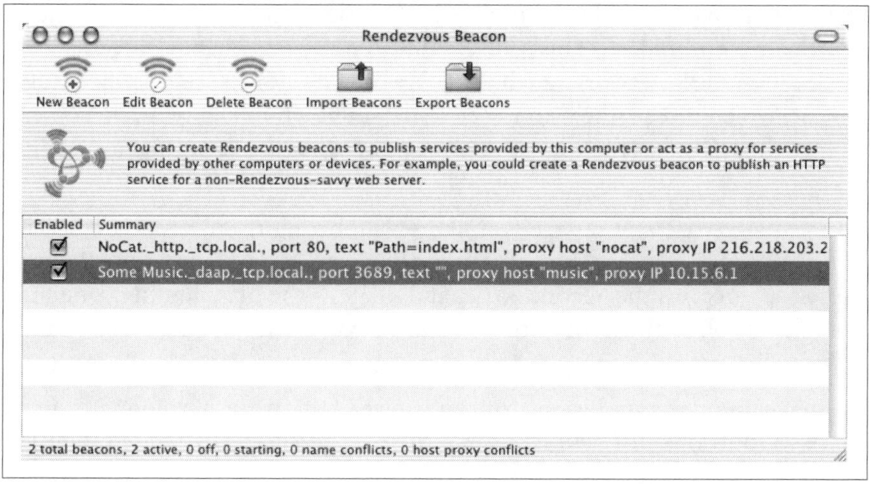

Figure 3-24. Rendezvous Beacon's main screen.

Turing beacons on and off is as simple as clicking a checkbox. You can add as many beacons as you like, to whatever service, protocol, and port you need. Like *mDNSProxyResponder*, it will even allow you to advertise services that aren't local to your machine or network, as shown in Figure 3-25.

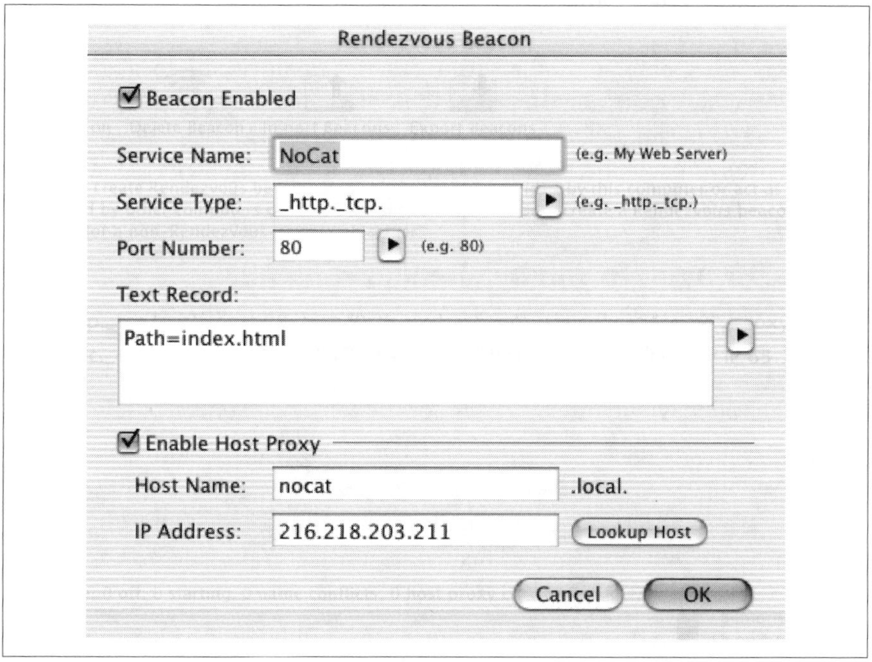

Figure 3-25. Advertise Rendezvous services that reside on other networks entirely.

In this example, I'm advertising the NoCat web site as the local multicast DNS name *nocat.local*. This causes any Rendezvous-enabled browsers on the local wireless network (such as Safari or Camino) to see a service called NoCat, which directs them to the IP address shown in Figure 3-25. You can change the URL that the user lands on by changing the Path= line in the *Text Record* box.

You can advertise any service you like by supplying the appropriate Service Type and Port Number. For example, to advertise an iTunes DAAP share, use _daap._tcp. as the Service Type, and 3689 as the port number. The little triangle button to the right of these fields provides a cheat sheet for common services and ports.

To make Rendezvous Beacon run whenever you are using your machine, simply add it to your *Login Items* in *System Preferences*. If you are interested in advertising Rendezvous services, I highly recommend trying out this nifty free app.

Another quick and easy method for advertising web pages with Rendezvous is to use *mod_proxy*, part of the Apache installation on every OS X box. Add an entry like the following to your */private/etc/httpd/httpd.conf*:

```
<IfModule mod_rendezvous_apple.c>
  RegisterResource "Muzik on Caligula" "/Music/"
</IfModule>
```

This registers a path with the given description for your local machine. Restart Apache by clicking Stop and then Start under *System Preferences* → *Sharing* → *Personal Web Sharing*. Unfortunately, *mod_rendezvous* doesn't support proxy like the previous method does, but it can make it easy to publish local paths without any additional software.

HACK #30 "Brought to you by" Rendezvous Ad Redirector

Spam your fellow Rendezvous users with sponsored links.

Note that you may only use this hack for the forces of Good.

In "Rendezvous Service Advertisements in Linux" [Hack #28] and "Advertising Arbitrary Rendezvous Services in OS X" [Hack #29], we saw how simple it is to advertise arbitrary services using Rendezvous in any Posix operating system, Mac OS X, or even Windows. This makes it easy to provide easy reference links to every user on your wireless network.

Wouldn't it be nice to give those same users a public service announcement en route to their destination, to let them know who was kind enough to provide the link? You could even give them more information about yourself or the network you provide before they head out to the Internet. This is easily achieved with a simple application of Apache magic.

In the *httpd.conf* on your web server, create a new *VirtualHost* entry like this:

```
<VirtualHost *>
  ServerName adserver.local
  DocumentRoot /home/rob/ads/
</VirtualHost>
```

You can, of course, call the server anything you want, and put the *DocumentRoot* wherever is convenient. Restart your Apache for the change to take effect. Just be sure that the *ServerName* ends in *.local*.

Now create as many *html* files in *DocumentRoot* as you like, using this as a template:

```
<html>
<head>
    <meta http-equiv="Refresh" content="5;http://freenetworks.org" />
</head>
<body>

<h1>This Rendezvous link brought to you by: me!</h1>

Redirecting you automatically in five seconds...
</body>
</html>
```

The URL at the end of the Refresh line will be the users' final destination, and the number at the beginning specifies the number of seconds to wait before redirecting. The body of the HTML can contain whatever message you want the users to see before the redirect takes effect.

Finally, advertise *adserver.local* (or whatever you used in your *VirtualHost* entry) as a proxy service using one of the methods described in Hack #28 or Hack #29. In the text field of the Rendezvous advertisement, specify the HTML file you just created. For example, I save the above HTML file to /*home/rob/ads/freenetworks.html*, and specify *path=/freenetworks.html* as the text field.

Now users who share my wireless network see a Rendezvous advertisement called *FreeNetworks*, and are presented with the previous HTML when they browse to the site. Five seconds later, they are redirected automatically to the real *http://freenetworks.org/*, and are left to go about their merry way. This sort of service is ideal for permanent services on public access wireless nodes, to give users an idea of who is providing Internet access.

Detecting Networks with Kismet

#31 Troubleshoot network problems with one of the most advanced wireless monitoring tools available.

Unlike simple beacon scanners such as NetStumbler **[Hack #21]** and Mac-Stumbler **[Hack #22]**, Kismet is one of the most advanced diagnostic tools available for wireless networking. It is a completely passive network scanner, capable of detecting traffic from APs and wireless *clients* alike (including NetStumbler clients). It finds "closed" networks by monitoring the traffic sent from its users, and logs all raw 802.11 frames in standard pcap format for later use with specialized diagnostic and analysis tools—as you'll see in "Tracking 802.11 Frames in Ethereal" **[Hack #39]**. If you have a machine with multiple wireless cards, Kismet even splits the work of network scanning across all of them, making a scanner capable of simultaneously tracking all 802.11 traffic in range. These are just a few of the incredible features of this piece of free software.

Of course, with all of this power comes a fair amount of complexity. For starters, you need an 802.11b card capable of entering RF Monitoring mode. Some of these cards are Prism-based (such as the Senao/EnGenius, Linksys, or D-Link cards), some are Lucent/Orinoco/Proxim/Avaya, and some are Cisco Aironet. Kismet also works with ar5k-based 802.11a cards. I was able to get Kismet running well on an iBook with an internal AirPort card (an Orinoco derivative) under Debian. The following explains what I had to do to make it work.

Installation

Download Kismet from *http://www.kismetwireless.net/*. Unpack the source tree and navigate into it. If you want to use Kismet's dump files with Ethereal (*highly* recommended), you need a copy of the Ethereal source tree. Configure Kismet with a line like this:

```
./configure --with-ethereal=../ethereal-0.9.12/
```

Of course, substitute the full path to your Ethereal sources. Now you should be able to build Kismet with a standard:

```
make; make dep; make install
```

Depending on your platform and wireless card, you may also need to install a driver capable of setting up RF Monitor mode. For the AirPort on my iBook, I used the precompiled kernel and modules available at *http://www.macunix.net:443/ibook.html*.

Next, create a user that Kismet will assume when it isn't running as root. You can also use your own UID if you wish. Kismet needs to run as root initially, but will drop its privileges to this UID as soon as it begins capturing data.

Now edit */usr/local/etc/kismet.conf* to suit your system. At the very least, set the source= line to match your hardware. For the iBook, I set it to source=orinoco,eth1,Airport. The format for this line is *driver,device,description*. See the comments in the file for supported drivers.

If you want Kismet to be able to read the SSID of detected networks aloud, also download and install the Festival text to speech package. Kismet will play sound effects if you wish; by default, it expects */usr/bin/play* to be installed (part of the Sox sound utility), but any command-line audio player will work. All of the audio and other display parameters are configured in */usr/local/etc/kismet_ui.conf*.

Running Kismet

Before you launch Kismet, you need to put your wireless card into RF monitoring mode. You can do this easily by running kismet_monitor as root. Note that once in RF monitoring mode, your card is no longer able to associate with a wireless network, so you should use Ethernet (or another wireless card) if you need a network connection.

Now you can start Kismet by simply running kismet under your normal UID. This should present you with a screen that looks something like Figure 3-26.

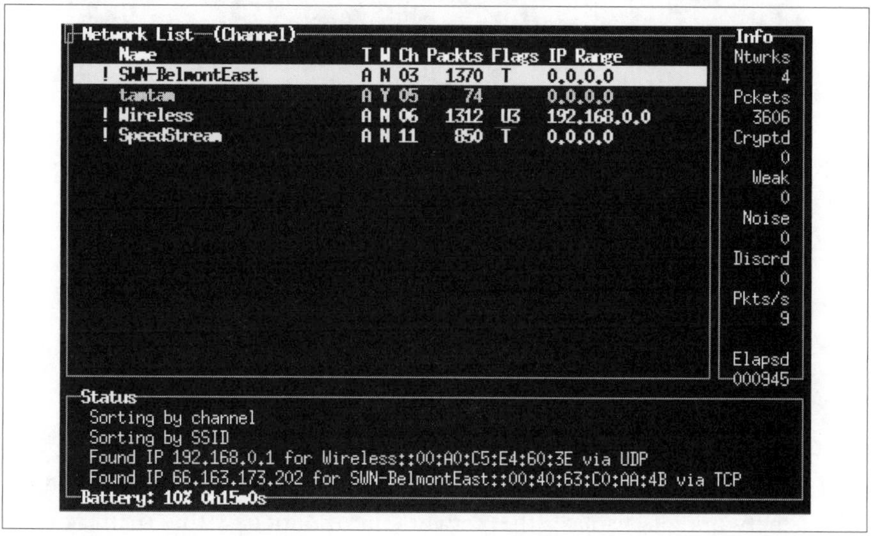

Figure 3-26. Kismet's main screen.

I say that it will look something like this figure, because more likely than not you will see only one network, if any. This is because you need to manually tell your card to start hopping between channels. From another xterm, run kismet_hopper -p as root. This makes your card skip between channels in an efficient manner. Naturally, the skip pattern is completely configurable to your tastes. See man kismet_hopper for details.

Once *kismet_hopper* is up and running, you should see the main screen spring to life with all sorts of information. By default, Kismet initially sorts the network list based on the last time it saw traffic from each network. This list constantly changes, making it impossible to select one network for more detailed operations. Change the sort order by hitting s at any time, followed by the desired sort order (for example, to sort on SSID, hit ss). You can now use the arrow keys to select a particular network for further inspection. Hit h at any time to see the keystroke help, and q to close any pop-up window.

Now that a couple of networks are listed, you can get more information on any one of them by selecting it and hitting i. Figure 3-27 shows the network information screen.

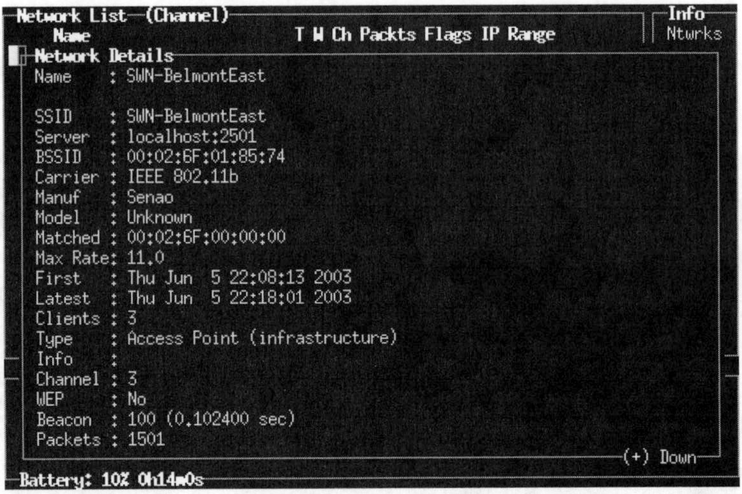

```
┌Network List─(Channel)───────────────────────────────────────┐Info┐
│     Name                    T W Ch Packts Flags IP Range     ║ Ntwrks │
│┌Network Details─────────────────────────────────────────────────────┐
│ │ Name    : SWN-BelmontEast                                          │
│ │                                                                    │
│ │ SSID    : SWN-BelmontEast                                          │
│ │ Server  : localhost:2501                                           │
│ │ BSSID   : 00:02:6F:01:85:74                                        │
│ │ Carrier : IEEE 802.11b                                             │
│ │ Manuf   : Senao                                                    │
│ │ Model   : Unknown                                                  │
│ │ Matched : 00:02:6F:00:00:00                                        │
│ │ Max Rate: 11.0                                                     │
│ │ First   : Thu Jun  5 22:08:13 2003                                 │
│ │ Latest  : Thu Jun  5 22:18:01 2003                                 │
│ │ Clients : 3                                                        │
│ │ Type    : Access Point (infrastructure)                            │
│─│ Info    :                                                          │─│
│─│ Channel : 3                                                        │─│
│ │ WEP     : No                                                       │
│ │ Beacon  : 100 (0.102400 sec)                                       │
│ │ Packets : 1501                                                     │
│ │                                                    ─(+) Down─       │
│└Battery: 10% 0h14m0s─────────────────────────────────────────────────┘
```

Figure 3-27. Detailed network information.

In addition to standard access points, Kismet displays Ad-Hoc networks, as well as so-called "closed" networks. If there are no clients actively using a closed network, it displays the network information with a name of <no ssid>. Once a client associates with the closed network, this information is updated with the proper SSID.

Kismet also tracks a great deal of information about wireless clients. For example, to see the associated clients of a particular AP, hit c from the main screen. This is illustrated in Figure 3-28.

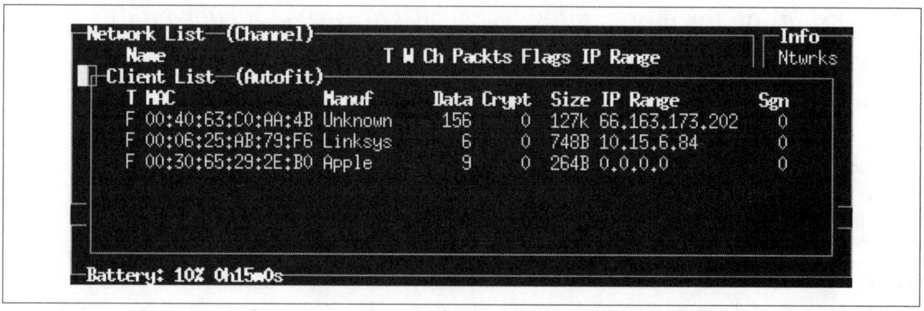

```
┌Network List──(Channel)─────────────────────────────────────────┐┌Info──┐
│ Name                        T W Ch Packts Flags IP Range        ││ Ntwrks│
│┌Client List──(Autofit)─────────────────────────────────────────┐│
││ T MAC                  Manuf       Data Crypt  Size IP Range    Sgn │
││ F 00:40:63:C0:AA:4B Unknown         156     0  127k 66.163.173.202  0 │
││ F 00:06:25:AB:79:F6 Linksys           6     0  748B 10.15.6.84       0 │
││ F 00:30:65:29:2E:B0 Apple             9     0  264B 0.0.0.0          0 │
│                                                                  │
│                                                                  │
│                                                                  │
│                                                                  │
│                                                                  │
│┌Battery: 10% 0h15m0s─────────────────────────────────────────────┘
```

Figure 3-28. View associated clients for a particular wireless network.

Kismet attempts to guess the IP network in use based on the traffic it sees. It also keeps statistics about how much traffic each client is generating, making it easy to discover who is hogging all of the bandwidth.

If you find that you are missing packets while monitoring a particular wireless network, this is probably because you are still scanning for networks. To focus on a specific channel, kill *kismet_hopper* and set your channel manually. In Linux, this is accomplished with a command such as:

```
# iwpriv eth1 monitor 2 6
```

eth1 is set to monitor mode, and the last number specifies the channel. The above example would set the card to monitor channel six. When tuned to one channel, this allows Kismet to capture much more data as it doesn't have to divide its time between multiple channels. Consult the documentation if you would like to add more radio cards to completely cover the entire available spectrum.

Cleaning Up

When you are finished using Kismet, hit Q (that's a capital Q) to quit, and then run kismet_unmonitor as root. This takes your wireless card back out of monitor mode, but does not reset its original network parameters. Either eject the card and reinsert it, or configure your SSID and other settings manually to start using wireless as you normally would.

These are just a few of the insanely useful features that Kismet has to offer. On top of everything else, Kismet saves all recorded frames to standard pcap format, so you can use tools like Ethereal or AirSnort to pour over your captured data for later analysis. It can be daunting to get Kismet running at first, but it is worth the effort when serious network analysis is called for.

See Also

- Tons of information on RF Monitoring drivers (*http://airsnort.shmoo.com/*)
- AirSnort on the iBook (*http://www.macunix.net:443/ibook.html*)
- Passive RF Monitoring on the iBook (*http://www.swieskowski.net/code/wifi.php*)

HACK #32 Running Kismet on Mac OS X

Run Kismet natively on OS X using the Viha AirPort driver.

When I wrote the Kismet Hack **[Hack #31]**, the Kismet crew was still looking for someone to work on making the Viha AirPort driver for OS X work with Kismet. Interestingly enough, support for OS X has just been introduced into the CVS tree of Kismet and works quite well. Note that as of this writing, Kismet works with the original AirPort cards, but not with the new AirPort Extreme cards. I'm sure it will support them once an appropriate driver is available. Here is what you need to do to get Kismet running under OS X.

First, you need the Viha AirPort driver from *http://www.dopesquad.net/security/*. Download the 0.0.1a binary, unpack it, and install the driver:

```
root@caligula:~# tar zxf Viha-0.0.1a.tar.gz
root@caligula:~# mv Viha-0.0.1a/WiFi.framework/ /Library/Frameworks/
```

If you have ever run KisMAC **[Hack #24]**, then it has already installed the driver for you, and you can skip this step.

Next, download the Kismet source from *http://www.kismetwireless.net/download.shtml*. You can either use *cvs* to grab a current copy of the source tree, or use the handy patch at *http://www.kismetwireless.net/code/kismet-devel.diff.gz* to bring an existing 2.8.1 tree up to the CVS revision. (This is one way to do it if you don't feel like fiddling with CVS.) Assuming that the *kismet-2.8.1.tar.gz* archive and the *kismet-devel.diff* patch are in your home directory:

```
root@caligula:~# tar zxf kismet-2.8.1.tar.gz
root@caligula:~# cd kismet-2.8.1
root@caligula:~/kismet-2.8.1# patch -p1 < ../kismet-devel.diff
patching file CHANGELOG
patching file CVS/Entries
patching file CVS/Root
patching file FAQ
...
```

Now build the code, explicitly turning on Viha support and turning off pcap support. Kismet will take some time to build, so be patient.

```
root@caligula:~/kismet-2.8.1# ./configure --disable-pcap --enable-viha; make
```

If all goes well, then install Kismet.

```
root@caligula:~/kismet-2.8.1# make install
```

You need to edit both *kismet.conf* and *kismet_ui.conf* (both of which are kept in */usr/local/etc/*). In *kismet.conf*, set suiduser to your normal OS X login name (I use rob, for example). Also define a capture source line for the Air-Port card:

```
source=viha,en1,AirPort
```

Finally, in *kismet_ui.conf*, disable APM support (unless you don't mind a ridiculously inaccurate battery meter at the bottom of your display):

```
apm=false
```

For some reason, Kismet likes a terminal with 26 rows in it when running on OS X, so make sure your terminal is at least that long. If you want color in your terminal (highly recommended), set the TERM to xterm-color:

```
rob@caligula:~$ export TERM=xterm-color
```

or if you are using *tcsh*:

```
[caligula:~] rob% set term=xterm-color
```

Now simply run *kismet* as your normal user (type **Kismet** in the Terminal window), and away you go. Kismet automatically unloads the AirPort driver and fires up the Viha driver (during which time your AirPort menu bar monitor goes away, so don't panic). When you quit Kismet (capital Q), it unloads the Viha driver and starts up the AirPort driver again. I have noticed that it will occasionally fail to reload the AirPort driver. If it does, you can either start and stop Kismet again, or manually kill the Viha driver:

```
root@caligula:~# /Library/Frameworks/WiFi.framework/Resources/driver.sh stop
```

For more details on what you can do with Kismet when it is actually running, see Hack #31. It appears that channel hopping is now controlled by *kismet* itself, so it isn't necessary to run *kismet_hopper* externally. Kismet is under very active development, so I expect that there will be even more features and simpler operation by the time this book goes to press.

HACK #33 Link Monitoring in Linux with Wavemon

Monitor radio parameters in real time using Wavemon, a curses-based tool for Linux.

When using Linux, the standard wireless tools provide a wealth of status information. These tools get their information from the standard kernel interface */proc/net/wireless*. While ideal for providing pinpoint accuracy in measuring signal strength and noise data, these tools are not designed to give an indication of performance over time.

Wavemon (*http://www.wavemage.com/projects.html*) is a terrific little tool that does precisely this. It polls */proc/net/wireless* many times each second to give you a rolling report of how your wireless connection is performing. Its simple curses interface keeps the code quite small, and is ideal for including in embedded distributions (such as Pebble [Hack #53]) to get real-time link data from remote access points.

The main interface provides a nice graphical representation of the current link state (Figure 3-29).

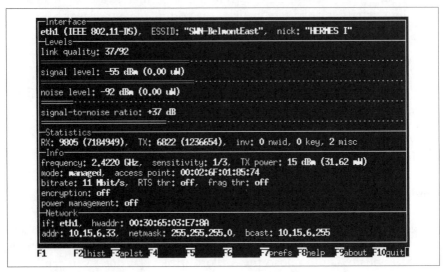

Figure 3-29. Wavemon in action.

All of the statistics are updated in real time, making it ideal for monitoring point-to-point links and fine-tuning antennas on long distance shots. For an even easier to read display, hit F2 to bring up the Level Histogram (Figure 3-30).

This display is easy to read on a laptop even in bright sunshine, making it an ideal tool for outdoor work. The histogram slowly sweeps to the left, giving you a history of the last few moments of wireless connectivity. Since Wavemon runs in a terminal, you can easily run more than one instance to monitor multiple radio links simultaneously.

When you need a high performance signal and noise meter for Linux, Wavemon is hard to beat. The current version is available from Freshmeat at *http://freshmeat.net/projects/wavemon/*.

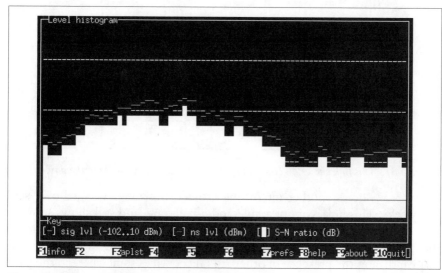

Figure 3-30. Pretty little scrolling waves of data.

HACK #34 Historical Link State Monitoring

Comprehensively track the performance of your wireless links over time.

The monitoring tools mentioned so far give you a good instantaneous reading of received signal and noise levels for a given radio link. While useful for proving a link and installing your gear, remember that radio conditions change over time. Doing the occasional "spot check" doesn't really give you the full picture of what is going on.

For example, take a look at Figure 3-31. This displays radio data for a one-mile link, averaged over several days. You can see that in the middle of each day, the signal drops by as much as 6 dB, while the noise remains steady (remember that these are really negative numbers, so in this graph, a smaller number is better for signal). The repeating pattern we see indicates the effect of *thermal fade*. This particular link is a simple waveguide antenna mounted in the middle of a low sloping roof. As the roof (and the rest of the environment) heats up, the perceived signal is apparently less. At night, when things cool down, the perceived signal increases. The effect of thermal fade in this installation was later mitigated (by about 2 or 3 dB) by relocating the antenna, placing it closer to the edge of the roof. With less hot roof in the path, the effect of the day's heat was reduced. Nothing can completely eliminate the effects of the sun on a long distance path, but without a historical graph, it would be difficult to account for the effect at all.

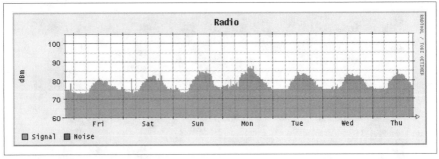

Figure 3-31. This link shows a good deal of thermal fade in the middle of the day.

Figure 3-32 shows another interesting artifact, this time averaged over several weeks. This link is about a mile-and-a-half long, and still shows some of the effects of thermal fade. But look at the noise readings. They are all over the map, reading as high as –89 and jumping to well below –100. This most likely indicates the presence of other 2.4 GHz devices somewhere in the path between the two points. Since the noise remains steady for some time and then changes rapidly to another level, it is probably a device that uses channels rather than a frequency-hopping device. Given the wide variety of perceived noise, I would guess that the most likely culprit is a high-powered 2.4 GHz phone somewhere nearby. It is probably impossible to ever know for sure, but this data might warrant changing the radio to a different channel.

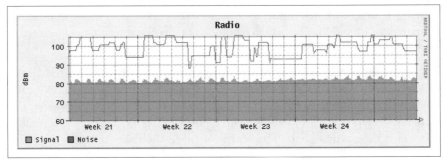

Figure 3-32. A link with a noisy environment.

These graphs were generated using Linux and some freely available tools. A modest Linux server can monitor a large number of radio devices, and the requirements on each of the APs is quite small. I will assume that you are using a DIY AP running Linux **[Hack #51]**, although similar techniques can be used for just about any kind of radio device.

You can monitor signal strength using any available TCP port above 1024 on the APs. Port 10000 is usually a good candidate. On each of the APs to be monitored, as well as on the machine doing the monitoring, add lines like these to *etc/services*:

```
mon0    10000/tcp
mon1    10001/tcp
mon2    10002/tcp
```

Then add a line like this to the */etc/inetd.conf* on the monitored machines:

```
mon0  stream  tcp     nowait  nobody  /usr/local/bin/iwconfig iwconfig eth1
```

Be sure to use the path to *iwconfig* for your system, and specify the device to be monitored at the end. You can add as many *iwconfig* lines as you like, using a different port each time:

```
mon1  stream  tcp     nowait  nobody  /usr/local/bin/iwconfig iwconfig wlan0
```

If you need more ports, add more lines to your */etc/services*. When all of your radio cards are set up, restart *inetd*. You can verify that the changes have taken effect by using telnet:

```
pebble:~# telnet localhost mon0
Trying 127.0.0.1...
Connected to localhost.
Escape character is '^]'.
eth1      IEEE 802.11-DS  ESSID:"NoCat"  Nickname:"pebble"
          Mode:Managed  Frequency:2.457GHz  Access Point: 00:02:2D:1C:BC:CF
          Bit Rate:11Mb/s   Tx-Power=15 dBm   Sensitivity:1/3
          Retry limit:4   RTS thr:off   Fragment thr:off
          Power Management:off
          Link Quality:14/92  Signal level:-83 dBm  Noise level:-96 dBm
          Rx invalid nwid:0  Rx invalid crypt:0  Rx invalid frag:6176330
          Tx excessive retries:7880  Invalid misc:0   Missed beacon:0

Connection closed by foreign host.
pebble:~#
```

To collect the radio data, you need *netcat* installed on the machine that does the collection. *netcat* is a free and insanely useful utility available at *http://www.atstake.com/research/tools/network_utilities/*. Think of it as a scriptable telnet program that will handle just about any kind of network data you want to throw at it. I use *nc* to connect to each of the machines, and scrape the results with a Perl script.

With the *nc* binary installed on your system, use this wrapper to collect the data:

```
#!/usr/bin/perl  -w
use strict;

my $ip = shift;
my $port = shift;
($ip && $port) || die "Usage: $0 ip port\n";
```

```
open(NC, "nc $ip $port |") || die "Couldn't spawn nc: $!\n";

while(<NC>) {
  if(/Signal level:-?(\d+).*Noise level:-?(\d+)/) {
    print "$1 $2\n";
    exit;
  }
}

die "Warning: couldn't find signal and noise!\n";
```

I call it */usr/local/sbin/radio.pl*, and invoke it with the IP address and port number on the command line. It simply returns two unsigned numbers representing the current signal and noise readings:

```
rob@florian:~$ radio.pl 10.15.6.1 mon0
83 96
rob@florian:~$
```

In case you haven't recognized it already, the tool that actually stores the data and draws the pretty graphs is Tobi Oetiker's excellent *rrdtool*. Like many powerful tools, *rrdtool* can be imposing at first (sometimes to the point of frustration). Efficient data collection and accurate visual presentation isn't as simple as you might think. Of course, *rrdtool* will handle just about any data type you track, but getting it working can be tricky the first time.

Personally, I prefer to use a tool like Cacti (*http://www.raxnet.net/products/cacti/*) to manage my *rrdtool* graphs for me. It is simple to install, has an easy to use web interface, and does the dirty work of managing your *rrdtool* databases. With Cacti installed, simply set up *radio.pl* as a data input script, and create a data source for each radio to be monitored. See the Cacti documentation for more details.

When properly configured, Cacti automatically generates Daily, Weekly, Monthly, and Yearly averages for all of your data sources.

If you prefer to roll your own *rrdtool*, then use a command like this to create your database:

```
/usr/local/rrdtool/bin/rrdtool create \
/home/rob/radio/radio.rrd \
--step 300 \
DS:signal:GAUGE:600:0:150 \
DS:noise:GAUGE:600:0:150 \
RRA:AVERAGE:0.5:1:600 \
RRA:AVERAGE:0.5:6:700 \
RRA:AVERAGE:0.5:24:775 \
RRA:AVERAGE:0.5:288:797 \
RRA:MAX:0.5:1:600 \
RRA:MAX:0.5:6:700 \
RRA:MAX:0.5:24:775 \
RRA:MAX:0.5:288:797
```

Be sure that the *rrdtool* binary is in your PATH, and change the print "$1
$2\n"; line in *radio.pl* to something like the following:

```
`rrdtool update /home/rob/radio/radio.rrd --template signal:noise N:$1:$2`;
```

Add a call to *radio.pl* to a cron job that runs every five minutes or so to regu-
larly collect the data:

```
*/5 * * * */usr/local/sbin/radio.pl 10.15.6.1 mon0
```

Finally, once you have collected some data, you can generate a graph like
Figure 3-32 with this command:

```
/usr/local/rrdtool/bin/rrdtool graph - \
 --imgformat=PNG \
 --start="-604800" \
 --title=" Radio" \
 --rigid \
 --base=1000 \
 --height=120 \
 --width=500 \
 --upper-limit=105 \
 --lower-limit=60 \
 --vertical-label="dBm" \
 DEF:a="/home/rob/radio/ radio.rrd":signal:AVERAGE \
 DEF:b="/home/rob/radio/ radio.rrd":noise:AVERAGE \
 AREA:a#74C366:"Signal" \
 LINE1:b#FF0000:"Noise" \
 > graph.png
```

While the other tools mentioned in this chapter will give you a good instantaneous estimate of how well your link is doing, *rrdtool*, *netcat*, and this simple script will give you impressive historical data that can be invaluable for
troubleshooting your network. In addition to signal and noise, *rrdtool* can
also track uptime, network traffic, associated clients, transmission errors,
and any other data you can think of. The reward of having clear historical
graphs is well worth learning to deal with the complexity of *rrdtool*.

HACK #35 EtherPEG and DriftNet

Get a compelling visual representation of what people are looking at on your
network.

While tools like *tcpdump* [Hack #37], Ethereal [Hack #38], and *ngrep* [Hack #41] give
you detailed information about what people are doing on your network, the
information they provide just isn't interesting to most people. They might
understand that their wireless data is vulnerable to eavesdroppers, but some-
how they still have an attitude of "it's hard to do, so it won't happen to me."

For some reason, this attitude is quickly cured when people are shown the
following tools. While they are really simple utilities, I think of them as

revolutionary to network monitoring as the Mosaic browser was to the Internet. Rather than make logs for later analysis, they simply show you what people are looking at online, in real time.

EtherPEG

EtherPEG (*http://www.etherpeg.org/*) is a very clever hack for OS X that combines all of the modern conveniences of a packet sniffer with the good old-fashioned friendliness of a graphics-rendering library. It watches the local network for traffic, reassembles out-of-order TCP streams, and scans the results for data that looks like a GIF or JPEG. It then simply displays that data in a random fashion in a large window. As you can see in Figure 3-33, it's sort of a real-time meta-browser that dynamically builds a view of other people's browsers, built up as other people look around online.

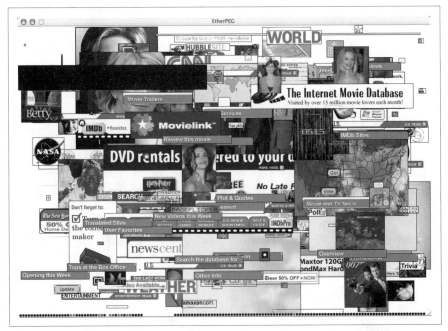

Figure 3-33. EtherPEG in action.

EtherPEG is decidedly not a commercial app designed for extensive eaves-dropping. It is a simple but effective hack that indiscriminately shows all image data that it can assemble. It makes no attempt to display where the images have been downloaded from, or who requested them. It doesn't even save a local copy for later perusal; once you quit the app, all collected data is lost.

The source code is freely available, and compiles easily with a simple make from the Terminal window. If you are looking for a similar (and even more functional) application that will run on an OS other than OS X, read on.

DriftNet

Inspired by EtherPEG, *DriftNet* (*http://www.ex-parrot.com/~chris/driftnet/*) is an image grabber for X11. In addition to decoding image files from sniffed network data, it has a couple of other nifty features. It can save all decoded images for later processing (say, by a screensaver app), and has experimental support for decoding an mpeg audio stream.

As you can see in Figure 3-34, DriftNet's interface is just as simple as Ether-PEG. You can click on individual images to save them to disk, or if you want to save all grabbed images, start up *driftnet* with the –a switch. This starts DriftNet in *adjunct* mode, which doesn't open a window, but simply saves all image data to a temporary directory (which can also be specified with the -d switch). Other applications can then use this ever-growing collection of images as a data source for its own ends.

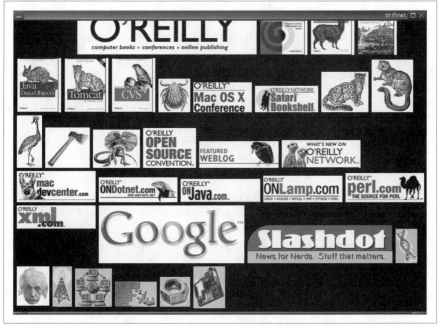

Figure 3-34. DriftNet decoding image data.

DriftNet has received a surprising amount of bad press as being the worst sort of "spyware" utility, and is sometimes billed as usable only for invading other people's privacy. On the contrary, I think that tools like this are tremendously useful. Not only can a systems administrator use such a tool to discourage inappropriate use of a corporate network (by simply leaving it running on a monitor in a public place), it can provide an amazing insight into the mood of a crowd of wireless users. What better way to find out what is going on in the minds of wireless users than to see what they are looking at on their screens? (For the results of one of my experiments in sampling the group subconscious, see my original weblog on the subject at *http://www.oreillynet.com/pub/wlg/1414*.) If nothing else, tools such as DriftNet and EtherPEG help to remind people of the importance of good wireless security practices, and of the use of discretion when using wireless networks in general.

This sort of eavesdropping is only possible because people use insecure protocols and unknowingly broadcast their network traffic in the clear for all to hear. If you are using strong application layer encryption (as described extensively in Chapter 7), this sort of tool is completely useless. If you are concerned about privacy, you should encourage your friends to use freely available encryption tools to protect yourself from wireless voyeurs. I've found that few things encourage them so effectively as running DriftNet or EtherPEG to show them what they themselves are looking at.

HACK #36   Estimating Network Performance

Just how quickly can you squeeze data through your AP?

Many people use online tools like DSL Reports' Speed test (*http://speedtest. dslreports.com/*) to estimate the performance of their Internet connection. When run from a machine directly connected to the Internet, this can give you a fairly good indication of your upload and download capacity.

This tool becomes less useful when trying to estimate the available bandwidth on other networks. For example, on a large wireless network, it is useful to measure the actual capacity of a network link regardless of the speed of the Internet connection. One useful utility for measuring performance is *iperf*. It is a simple, freely available tool that will run on Linux, BSD, OS X, and even Windows. You can download it online at *http://dast.nlanr.net/ Projects/Iperf/*.

In order to measure performance, it needs to be used in pairs (one instance at either end of a link). On one end of the link to be measured, start up *iperf* in server mode:

```
rob@livia:~$ iperf -s
```

Note that it doesn't matter which end is used as the "server," as both upload and download speeds will be tested. On the other end of the link, run *iperf* in client mode, specifying the server to be tested:

```
rob@caligula:~$ iperf -c livia -r
------------------------------------------------------------
Server listening on TCP port 5001
TCP window size: 32.0 KByte (default)
------------------------------------------------------------
------------------------------------------------------------
Client connecting to livia, TCP port 5001
TCP window size: 32.5 KByte (default)
------------------------------------------------------------
[  4] local 10.15.6.33 port 50421 connected with 10.15.6.4 port 5001
[ ID] Interval       Transfer     Bandwidth
[  4]  0.0-10.2 sec  2.95 MBytes  2.43 Mbits/sec
[  4] local 10.15.6.33 port 5001 connected with 10.15.6.4 port 60977
[ ID] Interval       Transfer     Bandwidth
[  4]  0.0-10.0 sec  3.09 MBytes  2.60 Mbits/sec
rob@caligula:~$
```

By default, *iperf* uses port 5001 for its communications. If this port is in use, you can specify a different one with the -p switch on both sides:

```
rob@livia:~$ iperf -s -p 30000
```

You can specify a different port and on the client as well:

```
rob@caligula:~$ iperf -c livia -r -p 30000
------------------------------------------------------------
Server listening on TCP port 5001
TCP window size: 32.0 KByte (default)
...
```

If you don't want just anyone connecting to your *iperf* server, don't forget to kill the server side with a Control-C when you are finished making measurements.

In addition to simple TCP testing, it can also manipulate various TCP parameters, test UDP streams, use multicast or IPv6, and even use a custom defined data stream for testing. Running with the defaults should give you a good basic idea of how much data you can cram through your connection, particularly if it is not being used by any other clients. For more complete details on some of the magic this flexible tool can work, see the online documentation at *http://dast.nlanr.net/Projects/Iperf/iperfdocs_1.7.0.html*.

Watching Traffic with tcpdump

This famous command-line packet capture tool is invaluable for troubleshooting thorny network problems.

Virtually all modern variations of Unix ship with the *tcpdump* utility. Its deceptively simple interface hides a very powerful and complex tool designed to capture data from a network interface, filter it, and print it out so you can get a better grasp of what is really happening on your network. Note that you need to be root to capture packets with tcpdump.

The simplest way to start it is to run it while specifying the network device you would like to listen to:

```
remote:~# tcpdump -i eth0
```

If you are logged into a remote machine while doing this, you will see a flood of traffic fly by, even on an unloaded machine. This is because tcpdump is capturing your *ssh* session traffic and displaying it to your terminal, which generates more traffic, which is again displayed, in an endless loop of wasted bits. This is easily avoided by using a simple filter. For example, you could just ignore all *ssh* traffic:

```
remote:~# tcpdump -i eth0 -n 'port ! 22'
```

Here I also specified the -n switch, which tells tcpdump to skip DNS lookups for every host it encounters. When capturing network data, the name of the game is speed. If your machine is tied up with some other network function (like looking up DNS names), it could miss packets as they fly past, particularly on a busy network. Skipping lookups speeds up capturing, but it means that you will be looking at IP addresses and port numbers instead of names and services.

One common use for tcpdump is to look for ping traffic when troubleshooting connectivity problems. To only see ICMP traffic, specify the protocol in a filter. Don't forget the backslash when specifying protocol names.

```
pebble:~# tcpdump -i wlan0 'proto \icmp'
tcpdump: listening on eth0
16:34:33.842093 10.15.6.33 > www.google.com: icmp: echo request
16:34:33.873784 www.google.com > 10.15.6.33: icmp: echo reply
16:34:34.893981 10.15.6.33 > www.google.com: icmp: echo request
16:34:34.940997 www.google.com > 10.15.6.33: icmp: echo reply
```

Here you can see a user sending echo requests (pings) to *www.google.com*, who then sends echo replies. If you see echo requests with no associated echo reply, this indicates problems somewhere further up the network. If you are sending pings and you don't even see the echo request on your router, you know that the problem is somewhere between your client and your router. Making educated guesses at where the problem might be, combined with judicious tcpdump filters, can quickly find the source of the trouble.

You can also capture all data from a particular host using tcpdump. Use the host directive:

```
pebble:~# tcpdump -i wlan0 'host 10.15.6.88'
tcpdump: listening on eth0
```

```
16:47:16.494447 10.15.6.88.1674 > florian.1900: udp 132 [ttl 1]
16:47:16.494524 florian > 10.15.6.88: icmp: florian udp port 1900
unreachable [tos 0xc0]
16:47:16.495831 10.15.6.88.1674 > florian.1900: udp 133 [ttl 1]
16:47:16.495926 florian > 10.15.6.88: icmp: florian udp port 1900
unreachable [tos 0xc0]
16:47:21.488711 arp who-has 10.15.6.88 tell florian
16:47:21.491861 arp reply 10.15.6.88 is-at 0:40:96:41:80:2c
16:47:28.293719 baym-cs197.msgr.hotmail.com.1863 > 10.15.6.88.1046: . ack 5
win 17128
```

This person is obviously using MSN Messenger, as evidenced by their connection to *baym-cs197.msgr.hotmail.com* port 1863, and by the UDP broadcasts to port 1900 as well. You can also see an ARP response that shows the user's MAC address starting with *0:40:96*, indicating a Cisco card (see "Finding Radio Manufacturers by MAC Address" [Hack #27] for more details). Without even resorting to nmap [Hack #40] or another active scan, we could make a fair guess that this user is using a PC laptop running Windows. This information is revealed in just a few seconds, by observing a mere five or six packets. Had the user been using application layer encryption, this sort of eavesdropping would be impossible. See Chapter 7 for a much more detailed look at wireless security.

Mac OS X is even chattier than MS Windows, revealing the user's name (and occasionally even their photo) in the form of iChat multicast broadcasts. Decoding this data is left as an exercise for the reader, but capturing it is simple enough:

```
pebble:~# tcpdump -i wlan0 -X -s 0 -n -l 'port 5353'
```

This will show you a full dump of packets, both in hex and in ASCII. If you need to analyze large amounts of data, it is usually easier to use a graphical tool like Ethereal [Hack #39] to pour over it. Since your AP probably isn't running Xwindows, you can use tcpdump to capture the actual data. Specifying the -w switch writes all packets to a file in pcap format, which many tools (like Ethereal) will read:

```
pebble:~# tcpdump -i wlan0 -n -w captured.pcap 'port 5353'
```

Now just transfer the *captured.pcap* file to your local machine, and open it up in Ethereal.

For a command-line utility, tcpdump is a surprisingly complete packet capture tool. It has a complex and powerful filter expression language, and can be adapted to capture precisely the data you are after. Be sure to read man tcpdump for many more details on what tcpdump can do for you.

Visual Traffic Analysis with Ethereal

HACK #38 Sift through network data with one of the most advanced protocol analyzers available.

Ethereal is one of the most popular protocol analyzers on the planet. It runs on virtually all major platforms, including Linux, BSD, Mac OS X, and Windows. Like *tcpdump* [Hack #37], it can capture packets directly from a network interface, or analyze data from a previously saved file. While capturing data, Ethereal can give you real-time statistics about which protocols are actively in use (Figure 3-35). Start capturing by selecting *Capture* → *Start...*, select the interface you want to capture from, and click *OK*. Note that you need proper permissions (typically root privileges) to actually capture data.

```
◯ ◯ ◯  ⊠ Ethereal: Capt
┌Captured Frames────────────┐
│ Total     1518   (100.0%) │
│ SCTP         0    (0.0%)  │
│ TCP       1497   (98.6%)  │
│ UDP          2    (0.1%)  │
│ ICMP        18    (1.2%)  │
│ ARP          1    (0.1%)  │
│ OSPF         0    (0.0%)  │
│ GRE          0    (0.0%)  │
│ NetBIOS      0    (0.0%)  │
│ IPX          0    (0.0%)  │
│ VINES        0    (0.0%)  │
│ Other        0    (0.0%)  │
└───────────────────────────┘
  Running   00:01:14

┌───────────────────────────┐
│           Stop            │
└───────────────────────────┘
```

Figure 3-35. Ethereal gives you statistics about the protocols it sees as it captures packets.

If you would like to see these statistics again (with even more detail) after you have finished capturing packets, go to *Tools* → *Protocol Heirarchy Statistics*. You can use this on previously captured dump files as well. If you already have some captured data (say, saved with tcpdump from a remote machine), you can simply click *File* → *Open...* and select the file you'd like to analyze.

Ethereal displays the data it has collected in three ways. The top part of the window shows a summary of the data, with one packet per line. This lists the sequence, time, IP data, protocol, and general description of the packet.

The data can be sorted on any of these fields by clicking the field name at the top. Selecting one packet displays more information in the other two window areas. The middle part of the window shows a hierarchical dissection of the packet, including the Ethernet, IP, TCP, and other layers. This allows you to quickly "drill down" into the particular piece of the packet that you are interested in. The bottom portion of the window shows a hex dump of the actual packet. Bits of the packet are automatically highlighted by selecting parts of the packet in the middle section. For example, selecting the IP source address in the middle section highlights the corresponding 4 bytes in the hex dump at the bottom.

Figure 3-36 shows Ethereal's ability to dissect high-level protocols such as HTTP. Select an HTTP packet at the top, and open the *Hypertext Transfer Protocol* drop-down in the middle section. This shows the contents of the packet in plain ASCII.

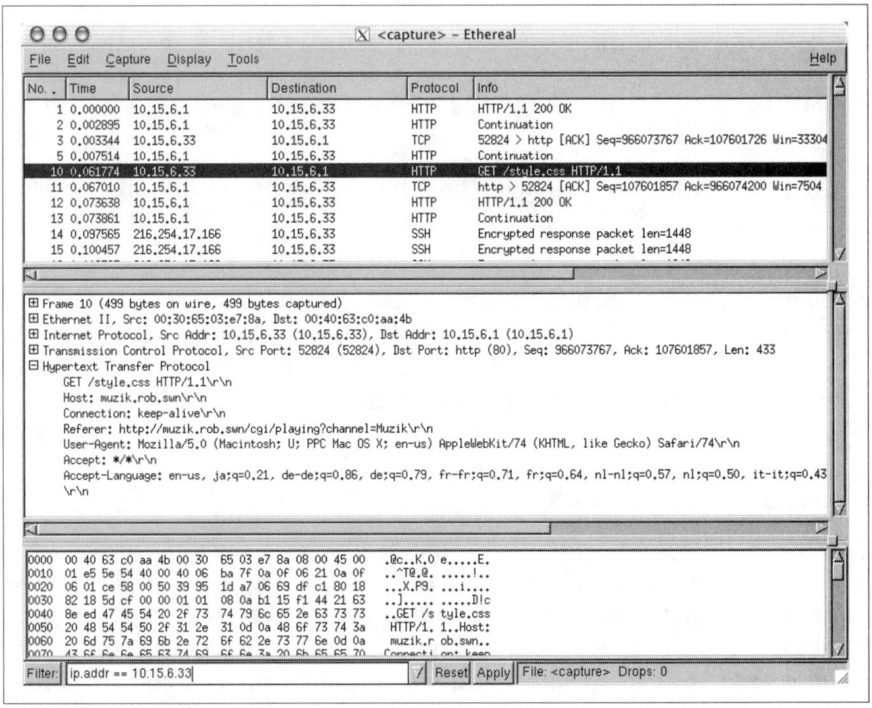

Figure 3-36. Ethereal understands many high level protocols, such as HTTP.

Of course, most TCP conversations are spread across several packets. Ethereal reassembles the entire stream for you by selecting one packet and clicking *Tools → Follow TCP Stream*. Figure 3-37 shows the results of following the above HTTP stream.

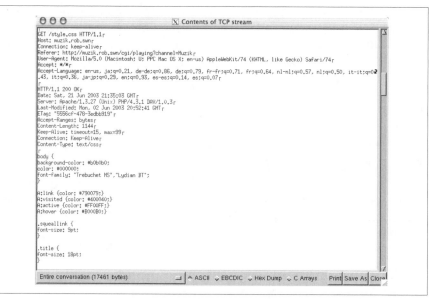

Figure 3-37. Ethereal reassembles a TCP stream to show you a conversation between two hosts.

It is difficult to tell in black and white, but the two conversations are actually displayed in different colors, making it simple to tell at a glance which side is speaking.

Speaking of colors, Ethereal can even display its packet data with color coding, defined by a rich pattern-matching language. This can make any data you are searching for leap out in bold red while showing everything else in pale gray, for example. It uses the same pattern-matching language to specify display filters, which unfortunately isn't the same language used by tcpdump. For an example of how to build a display filter, see "Tracking 802.11 Frames in Ethereal" **[Hack #39].**

This is just a simple example of some of Ethereal's basic features. It can show you as much detail as you care to know about the packets flying around on your wireless network, and is one of the most powerful tools available for tracking down network problems. See the documentation and example capture files at *http://www.ethereal.com/* for some other creative uses for Ethereal.

HACK #39 Tracking 802.11 Frames in Ethereal
Use Ethereal to track wireless frame data it normally can't capture.

In addition to capturing Layer 2 (and greater) traffic on its own, Ethereal can open dump files saved by other tools that incorporate additional data, such as Kismet [Hack #31] or KisMAC [Hack #24]. Recent versions of Ethereal will happily display all 802.11 frame data that these passive monitoring tools can capture (Figure 3-38). This allows you to watch the behavior of devices at the 802.11 protocol layer, which can give you valuable insight into what is actually happening on your wireless network. Keep in mind that Kismet and KisMAC will capture *all* 802.11 they hear, including data for networks you might not be interested in. This is especially true if you capture data while the tools are scanning all available channels.

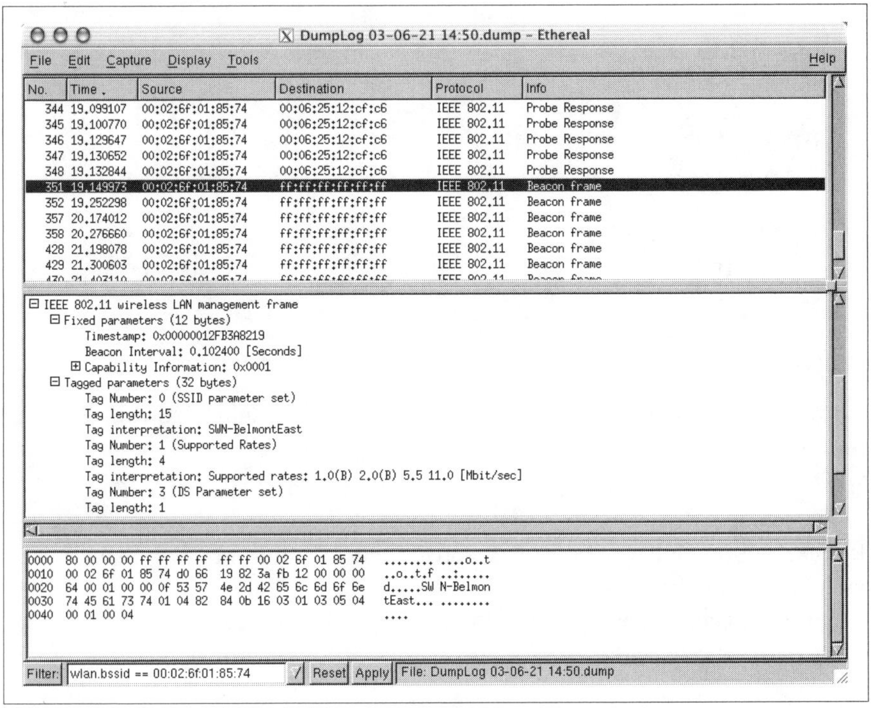

Figure 3-38. Ethereal can display 802.11 frames captured by other programs.

To focus on a particular access point, use a display filter on your data. The simplest way to create a filter from scratch is to build it interactively using the filter editor. At the bottom of the screen, click the *Filter:* button. Next, click *Add Expression*, which opens the filter editor. Select the information in which you are interested in the *Field name* pane. Since we are after the BSS ID of an AP, select *IEEE 802.11 → BSS Id*. Click == as the *Relation*, and enter the MAC address of your AP in the *Value* field. You can see this process in Figure 3-39.

Click *Accept*, then *OK*. Ethereal then filters your data based on the expression you provided. As noted earlier, this language is different than the libpcap filter expression language that tcpdump uses. The resulting expression is

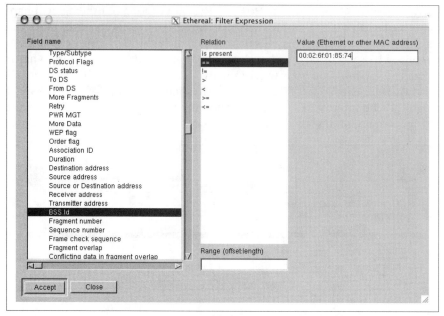

Figure 3-39. Use the IEEE 802.11 BSS Id filter to focus on a particular AP.

shown at the bottom of the main screen, next to the *Filter:* button. You can build more complex expressions by joining filters together with *and* and *or*. Click *Apply* each time you change your filter to see the effect it has on your data.

If you need to analyze a WEP-encrypted packet dump, then you need to provide the WEP key for Ethereal; otherwise, you will only be able to see encrypted packets. Under *Edit → Preferences*, select *Protocols → IEEE 802.11*. Enter your WEP key data here, and Ethereal automatically decrypts it for you (see Figure 3-40).

If you used AirSnort **[Hack #88]** to decrypt a WEP stream, you may need to check the *Ignore the WEP bit* box here. AirSnort decrypts the data, but leaves the WEP bit intact. With this box unchecked, Ethereal will assume that the data is still encrypted, and won't attempt to analyze it further.

Ethereal can filter on virtually every bit in an 802.11 management frame, making it a very useful tool for analyzing a wireless link. Combining Ethereal with Kismet or KisMac makes one of the most flexible and powerful wireless analysis packages available.

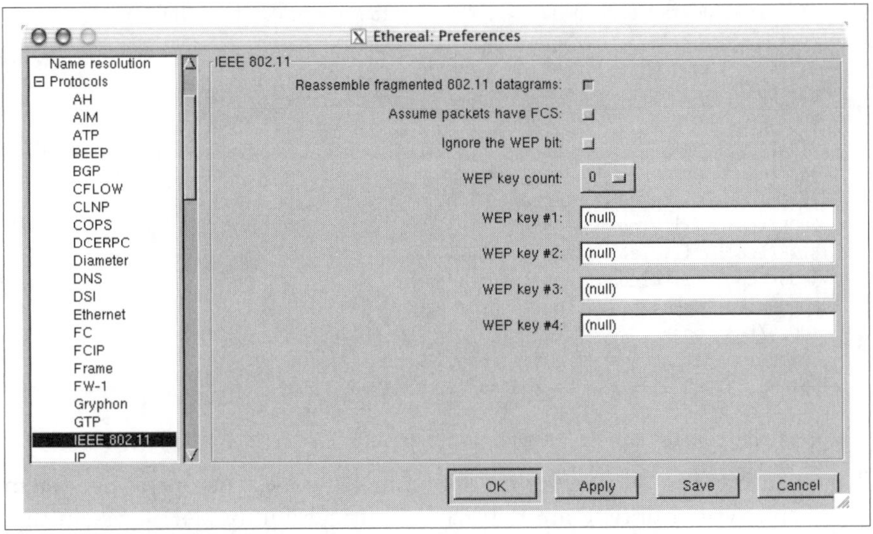

Figure 3-40. Supply your own WEP key under protocol Preferences.

Interrogating the Network with nmap

When you absolutely need to know everything you can about a network or host, nmap can help.

The network monitoring tools discussed so far all achieve their goals by passively listening to traffic on the network. You can often get better results by actually asking machines directly for information rather than waiting for them to divulge it on their own. To find out more information about a particular machine (or an entire network of machines), you need a good active scanning utility. One of the most advanced and widely used network scanners is *nmap*. It is available at *http://www.insecure.org/nmap/*, and is best summarized by the description on the web site:

> Nmap uses raw IP packets in novel ways to determine what hosts are available on the network, what services (ports) they are offering, what operating system (and OS version) they are running, what type of packet filters/firewalls are in use, and dozens of other characteristics.

The most common use for nmap is to scan the TCP ports on a machine to determine which services are available. If run as root, it can also use advanced TCP fingerprinting techniques to make an educated guess about the OS of the target machine.

```
caligula:~# nmap -O 10.15.6.1

Starting nmap V. 3.00 ( www.insecure.org/nmap/ )
Interesting ports on florian.rob.swn (10.15.6.1):
```

```
(The 1590 ports scanned but not shown below are in state: closed)
Port        State       Service
22/tcp      open        ssh
53/tcp      open        domain
80/tcp      open        http
179/tcp     open        bgp
443/tcp     open        https
2601/tcp    filtered    zebra
2605/tcp    filtered    bgpd
3128/tcp    filtered    squid-http
3306/tcp    filtered    mysql
10000/tcp   open        snet-sensor-mgmt
10005/tcp   open        stel
Remote operating system guess: Linux Kernel 2.4.0 - 2.5.20
Uptime 65.988 days (since Thu Apr 17 18:33:00 2003)
```

```
Nmap run completed -- 1 IP address (1 host up) scanned in 33 seconds
```

This scan was run on a server on my home network. The operating system guess and system uptime are both correct (it is a Linux 2.4.19 system that has been up for 65 days, 23 hours, and 43 minutes). Notice how nmap can also detect filtered TCP ports in addition to ports that accept connections. There is no guarantee that these services are actually in use, but since there is a firewall running, it's probably a good guess that at least some of them are active. Ports 10000 and 10005 are actually part of a home-grown monitoring system I'm using, as described in "Historical Link State Monitoring" [Hack #34]. If you are curious about a particular user on your wireless network, nmap can tell you a good deal about the system they are running.

Aside from scanning the ports of a single host, nmap can also scan entire networks. To fingerprint all of the machines on the local network, try something like this:

```
caligula:~# nmap -sS -O 10.15.6.0/24
```

The /24 is *Classless Inter-Domain Routing* (CIDR) notation for the network mask, specifying that all IPs from 10.15.6.0 to 10.15.6.255 should be scanned. If the machine being scanned is running a good intrusion detection system (such as Snort; see *http://www.snort.org/*), it might determine that a scan is in progress and take countermeasures. To try to work around this possibility, nmap provides a number of alternative scanning methods that can be very difficult to detect. The -sS switch tells nmap to use a stealth SYN scan rather than use a standard TCP connect. The scanning tool versus intrusion detection tool arms race has been going on ever since there have been such tools, and will likely continue for quite some time.

You can use nmap to help track down miscreants abusing your network, or simply to take a poll of what your wireless users are running. It is frequently used to probe your own machines to determine whether unexpected services suddenly crop up, or whether your firewall is properly configured. However you use it, nmap will provide valuable insight into the machines present on your wireless network.

HACK #41 Network Monitoring with ngrep

See who's doing what, with a grep for your network interface.

The *ngrep* (*http://www.packetfactory.net/Projects/ngrep*) utility is an interesting packet capture tool, similar to *tcpdump* **[Hack #37]** or Ethereal **[Hack #38]**. It is unique in that it attempts to make it as easy as possible to match which captured packets to print, by using a grep-compatible format (complete with regular expressions and a bunch of GNU grep's switches). It also converts the packets to ASCII (or hex) before printing.

For example, to see the contents of all HTTP GET requests that pass through your router, try this:

```
# ngrep -q GET
```

If you're interested only in a particular host, protocol, or port (or other packet matching criteria), you can specify a *bpf* filter as well as a data pattern. It uses a syntax similar to tcpdump:

```
# ngrep -qi rob@nocat.net port 25
T 10.42.4.7:65174 -> 209.204.146.26:25 [AP]
  RCPT TO:..

T 209.204.146.26:25 -> 10.42.4.7:65174 [AP]
  250 2.1.5 ... Recipient ok..

T 10.42.4.7:65174 -> 209.204.146.26:25 [AP]
  Date: Sun, 8 Sep 2002 23:55:18 -0700..Mime-Version: 1.0 (Apple Message fram
  ework v543)..Content-Type: text/plain; charset=US-ASCII; format=flowed..Sub
  ject: Greetings.....From: John Doe ..To: rob@nocat.net..Content-Transfer-En
  coding: 7bit..Message-Id: ..X-Mailer: Apple Mail v2)....What does t
  hat pgp command you mentioned do again?....Thanks,.....--A Friend....
```

Since *ngrep* prints to STDOUT, you can do post-processing on the output to make a nice printing filter. If you process the output yourself, add the -l switch to make the output line buffered.

The Code

If you're interested in what people on the local wireless network are searching for online, try something like this bit of Perl:

```
#!/usr/bin/perl
use Socket;
$|++;
```

```
open(NG,"ngrep -d en1 -lqi '(GET|POST).*/(search|find)' |");
print "Go ogle online.\n";
my ($go,$i) = 0;
my %host = ( );

while( ) {

  if(/^T (\d+\.\d+.\d+\.\d+):\d+ -> (\d+\.\d+\.\d+\.\d+):80/) {
    $i = inet_aton($1);
    $host{$1} ||= gethostbyaddr($i, AF_INET) || $1;
    $i = inet_aton($2);
    $host{$2} ||= gethostbyaddr($i, AF_INET) || $2;
    print "$host{$1} -> $host{$2} : ";
    $go = 1;
    next;
  }
  if(/(q|p|query|for)=(.*)?(&|HTTP)/) {
    next unless $go;
    my $q = $2;
    $q =~ s/(\+|&.*)/ /g;
    $q =~ s/%(\w+)/chr(hex($1))/ge;
    print "$q\n";
    $go = 0;
  }
  else {
    next unless $go;
    $go = 0;
    print "\n";
  }
}
```

Running the Hack

I call the script go-ogle. This runs an *ngrep* looking for any GET or POST request that includes *search* or *find* somewhere in the URL. Save the code to a file called *go-ogle.pl* and invoke it on the command line. The results look something like this:

```
# perl go-ogle.pl
Go ogle online.
caligula.nocat.net -> www.google.com : o'reilly mac os x conference
caligula.nocat.net -> s1.search.vip.scd.yahoo.com : junk mail $$$
tiberius.nocat.net -> altavista.com : babel fish
caligula.nocat.net -> 166-140.amazon.com : Brazil
livia.nocat.net -> 66.161.12.119 : lart
```

It will very lazily unescape encoded strings in the query (note the ' in the Google query, and the $$$ from Yahoo!). It will also convert IP addresses to hostnames for you (since *ngrep* doesn't seem to have this feature, probably so it can optimize capturing for speed). The last two results are interesting: the "Brazil" query was actually run on *http://www.imdb.com/*, and the last one was to *http://www.dictionary.com/*. Evidently IMDB is now in a partnership with Amazon, and Dictionary.com's search machine doesn't have a PTR record. It's amazing how much you can learn about the world by watching other people's packets.

Note that you must be root to run *ngrep*; for best results it should be run from the router at the edge of your network or from any wireless client associated with a busy AP.

HACK #42 Running ntop for Real-Time Network Stats
See who's doing what on your network over time with ntop.

If you're looking for real-time network statistics, you should check out the terrific *ntop* (*http://www.ntop.org/*) tool. It is a full-featured protocol analyzer with a web frontend, complete with SSL- and GD-graphing support. Unfortunately, ntop isn't exactly lightweight (requiring more resources depending on the size of your network and the volume of Net traffic), but it can give you a very nice picture of who's talking to whom on your network.

ntop needs to run initially as root (to throw your interfaces into promiscuous mode and start capturing packets), but then releases its privileges to a user that you specify. If you decide to run ntop for long periods of time, you'll probably be happiest running it on a dedicated monitoring box (with few other services running on it, for security and performance reasons).

Here's a quick reference on how to get ntop up and running quickly. First, create an ntop user and group:

```
root@gemini:~# groupadd ntop
root@gemini:~# useradd -c "ntop user" -d /usr/local/etc/ntop -s /bin/true ⏎
-g ntop ntop
```

Then unpack and build ntop per the instructions in *docs/BUILD-NTOP.txt*. I assume that you have the source tree unpacked in */usr/local/src/ntop-2.1.3/*.

Create a directory for ntop to keep its capture database in:

```
root@gemini:~# mkdir /usr/local/etc/ntop
```

(Note that it should be owned by root, and *not* by the ntop user.)

If you'd like to use SSL for *https* (instead of standard *http*), then copy the default SSL key to */usr/local/etc/ntop*:

```
root@gemini:# cp /usr/local/src/ntop-2.1.3/ntop/*pem /usr/local/etc/ntop
```

Note that the default SSL key will not be built with the correct hostname for your server. Now we need to initialize the ntop databases and set an administrative password:

```
root@gemini:~# ntop -A -u ntop -P /usr/local/etc/ntop
21/Sep/2002 20:30:23 Initializing GDBM...
```

```
21/Sep/2002 20:30:23 Started thread (1026) for network packet analyser.
21/Sep/2002 20:30:23 Started thread (2051) for idle hosts detection.
21/Sep/2002 20:30:23 Started thread (3076) for DNS address resolution.
21/Sep/2002 20:30:23 Started thread (4101) for address purge.

Please enter the password for the admin user:
Please enter the password again:
21/Sep/2002 20:30:29 Admin user password has been set.
```

Finally, run ntop as a daemon, and start the SSL server on your favorite port (4242, for example):

```
root@gemini:~# ntop -u ntop -P /usr/local/etc/ntop -W4242 -d
```

By default, ntop also runs a standard HTTP server on port 3000. You should strongly consider locking down access to these ports at your firewall, or by using command-line iptables rules.

Let ntop run for a while, then connect to *https://your.server.here:4242/*. You can find out all sorts of details about what traffic has been seen on your network, as shown in Figure 3-41.

Info about host nocat.net

IP Address	208.201.239.5 ▉ [unicast]
First/Last Seen	09/21/02 21:27:16 - 09/21/02 21:35:20 [8:04]
Domain	net
Last MAC Address/Router ▥	00:01:30:B8:23:D0
Host Location	Remote (outside specified/local subnet)
IP TTL (Time to Live)	54:54 [~10 hop(s)]
Total Data Sent	110.8 KB/1,159 Pkts/0 Retran. Pkts [0%]
Broadcast Pkts Sent	0 Pkts
Data Sent Stats	Local (100 %)
IP vs. Non-IP Sent	IP (100 %)
Total Data Rcvd	384.4 KB/1,372 Pkts/0 Retran. Pkts [0%]
Data Rcvd Stats	Local (100 %)
IP vs. Non-IP Rcvd	IP (100 %)
Sent vs. Rcvd Pkts	Sent (45.8 %) Rcvd (54.2 %)
Sent vs. Rcvd Data	Sent (22.4 %) Rcvd (77.6 %)
Further Host Information	[Whois]

Host Traffic Stats

Time	Tot. Traffic Sent	% Traffic Sent	Tot. Traffic Rcvd	% Traffic Rcvd
Midnight - 1AM	0	0.0 %	0	0.0 %
1AM - 2AM	0	0.0 %	0	0.0 %
2AM - 3AM	0	0.0 %	0	0.0 %
3AM - 4AM	0	0.0 %	0	0.0 %
4AM - 5AM	0	0.0 %	0	0.0 %
5AM - 6AM	0	0.0 %	0	0.0 %
6AM - 7AM	0	0.0 %	0	0.0 %

Figure 3-41. ntop provides all sorts of useful real-time information.

While tools like tcpdump and Ethereal give you detailed, interactive analysis of network traffic, ntop delivers a wealth of statistical information in a very slick and easy-to-use web interface. When properly installed and locked down, it will likely become a favorite tool in your network analysis tool chest.

## CHAPTER FOUR

Hardware Hacks
Hacks #43–69

Market forces have brought conventional wireless hardware down to unbelievably low prices in a very short time. The average 802.11b access point costs less than $100 at the time of this writing, and as technologies like 802.11g and 802.11a come to market, prices continue to drop. These inexpensive devices are making it easier than ever for the average person to quickly set up their very own wireless network.

But what can you actually do with an access point once you bring one home? The typical hardware access point is designed to cover a relatively small area, providing local access for a few clients on a private wireless network. The typical consumer grade AP is rated at about 300 ft. range, and generally connects directly to an existing wired network. While the "plug and play" design of these devices is usually adequate to quickly build simple networks, many people find themselves looking for ways to extend their network's range and capabilities. How can you increase your AP's coverage range to a couple of miles? What if you want to force users to look at a particular web page when they first begin to use your network? How can you build a more secure and flexible network than a typical AP allows for? How can end users extend their own range and pick up networks with less than optimal coverage?

This chapter explores a wide variety of methods for answering these questions. I'll present all sorts of information about antennas, feed cables, connectors, and how to use them with your AP or client card. I'll describe methods for extending your AP to run Linux, mounting it in an outdoor case, and increasing its range by several orders of magnitude. When that's just not enough for your application, we give you everything you need to know to build your own access point from scratch.

Add-on Laptop Antennas

HACK #43

Improve the range of your laptop with an add-on antenna.

Possibly the most frequently asked question at any wireless user's group is "how can I make it go farther?" The single most effective means for increasing your range is to add antenna gain. Most people think of adding an external antenna to their access point, or replacing the existing antenna with one of higher gain. While this can help all of your wireless clients, most people ignore the need for a good antenna on the client side. While some laptops (such as the Apple iBook and Sony Vaio, to name two) ship with antennas embedded in the laptop screen, many people are using add-on wireless cards.

These cards leave an annoying little "lump" sticking out of the side of the laptop, parallel with the keyboard, and very close to the table top. This is the laptop's only antenna, and in most cases it can be greatly improved on.

Not all wireless cards accept external antennas. Some (like the Zcomax XI-300 and Proxim RangeLan-DS) have removable antennas, allowing removal of the little plastic "lump," and will accommodate two external antennas using Pigtail adapters [Hack #66]. Others (like some Cisco and Senao/EnGenius cards) have no internal antenna at all, and work only with an external antenna.

Adding an external antenna to your laptop has two important effects. First, most antennas have much higher gain than the tiny dipole antennas contained in many wireless cards. Second, and possibly even more important, an external antenna brings the signal away from the desktop and the body of the computer, giving it more visibility, and making it easier to relocate to find the best possible signal.

While adding a proper external antenna will almost definitely increase your range, not all antennas are especially convenient. Here are three popular antennas that are quite small and unobtrusive.

Poynting (*http://www.poynting.co.za*), a South African antenna manufacturer, produces a number of inexpensive antennas, including a 3.5" square, 8dBi sector. It sells for 176 South African rand, or about $22 U.S. It is small enough to Velcro to the back of a laptop, but offers surprisingly high gain for the size (and price). You can see it online at *http://www.poynting.co.za/antennas/ism_24ghzsinglepatch8dbi.shtml*.

If you use a Lucent/Orinoco/Avaya/Proxim card (or a derivative, such as the AirPort), then you might have luck with the Orinoco Range Extender. It is still a bit overpriced in my opinion, selling for about $65. It looks like a rectangular white popsicle stick with a heavy rubber base and long feed line, and is advertised as a 5dBi omni. If you need more gain, the Deep Dish Cylindrical Reflector design [Hack #70] works quite well with the popsicle stick. The base is nice for sticking the antenna on a nearby table or shelf—but best of all, it is easily detached from the antenna. The stick on its own is very portable, and like the Poynting patch, is well suited for a slab of Velcro on the back of your laptop LCD. Some have even cracked it open, trimmed and re-soldered the feed line, and glued it back together again to make the perfect length of wire (and cut down on unnecessary cable loss.) The Range Extender is available from *http://www.proxim.com/products/all/orinoco/ client/rea/index.html*.

Finally, if cost is an issue, you might consider recycling a discarded "rubber ducky" antenna from a WAP11, WET11, Cisco 350, or other AP. These are small, rugged black omnis or dipoles that offer 3 to 5 dBi gain. Some antennas even sport right-angle elbows. A simple adapter or pigtail will let you use these low-gain antennas with your laptop, which is certainly better than leaving them to collect dust in a drawer. Pick a pigtail with as much flexible feed line as you need, and connect it to your laptop card. As always, be sure to check on the type of connectors you need for both ends of the pigtail (both the laptop card and the antenna will have unusual connectors). When in doubt, see Hack #65, or check the manufacturer's specs online.

HACK #44 Increasing the Range of a Titanium PowerBook

Radio waves just don't penetrate titanium, but that shouldn't keep your TiBook from getting online.

Apple's Titanium PowerBook is arguably one of the most aesthetically pleasing laptops on the market. Its wide-screen display is particularly striking, and like the rest of Apple's entire line, it can accommodate a built-in Air-Port card. Unfortunately, while the choice of titanium for an outer shell might make the TiBook pleasing to the eye and touch, it wreaks havoc with wireless.

The all-metal case acts as an effective Faraday cage, blocking radio signals from anywhere but the tiny plastic antenna ports on either side of the keyboard. To make matters worse, the antenna ports coincide with the exact position that most people rest their hands when not typing. When this happens, it's all too common for connectivity to drop altogether as the client radio desperately tries to find a path to the AP.

Apple is aware of the problem, and is working on improving the situation as new versions of the titanium PowerBook are released. Some users report increased coverage simply by making sure that the antenna connector is firmly seated in the AirPort card, as it can sometimes become dislodged slightly after leaving the factory. But even with a perfectly operating card and antenna, TiBooks routinely see about half of the range of the cheaper plastic iBooks, which have a much more visible internal antenna.

Fortunately, there is hope. Since the TiBooks have a PCMCIA slot, it is perfectly possible to add another wireless card and use it instead of the built-in AirPort. The biggest drawback to this approach is that Apple's nicely integrated wireless tools work only with the internal AirPort card, so you will have to get used to using other means to control your wireless connection. But the two- to four-fold increase in range can be well worth the effort.

The WirelessDriver project lives on SourceForge at *http://wirelessdriver. sourceforge.net/*. As of this writing, it is confirmed to support more than 40 different wireless cards under OS X, and probably supports many more. It works with Prism-based cards as well as Hermes and Aironet cards.

One very popular add-on card is the EnGenius/Senao series, particularly the 2511. It puts out 200mW, and is a particularly sensitive radio. It comes in two versions, with and without an internal antenna. If you use the 2511-CD+EXT2, you need an external antenna like the Poynting patch **[Hack #43]**, as it has no internal antenna of its own. A good choice for a card with an internal antenna and an antenna connector is the Lucent/Orinoco/Proxim Silver or Gold card. Like the internal AirPort card, it puts out only 30mW, but is fairly sensitive, and quite inexpensive (averaging about $40 at this point).

Remember that the best thing you can do to improve the range of any wireless device is to make its antenna as visible as possible to the access point you are trying to communicate with. While an add-on card might not be as convenient as the built-in AirPort card, anything is better than hiding your antenna behind a suit of titanium armor.

HACK #45 WET11 Upgrades

Significantly increase the range, sensitivity, and functionality of your WET11.

The Linksys WET11 (*http://www.linksys.com/products/product.asp?prid=432*) is one of the most inexpensive Ethernet client bridge products on the market. It works with virtually any Ethernet device, and doesn't require any special drivers to configure. Many people use the WET11 to connect devices that otherwise can't accommodate a radio with their wireless network. For example, they are ideal for connecting to networked appliances such as the PlayStation 2 or Xbox to avoid having to run Ethernet cable to your television. They can also be used to get entire networks online when used in conjunction with inexpensive firewalls like the Linksys BEFSR41. Simply connect the WET11 to the WAN port on the firewall, and every device plugged into it can share the WET11's wireless connection. People have had mixed results when using the WET11 directly bridged to a hub or switch, due to the implementation of the tiny device's MAC address handling.

There have been a number of complaints about DHCP not working properly with the WET11, but these issues seem to be resolved by upgrading the firmware to the latest revision, and using the ISC's DHCP server Version 3 or later, available at *http://www.isc.org/products/DHCP/*. As with all embedded hardware devices (particularly those manufactured by Linksys), it is a very good idea to keep up on firmware updates. Updated firmware usually resolves most flaky behavior, and occasionally even gives you a couple of new features.

The WET11 even has a crossover switch for the Ethernet side, making it simple to install regardless of whether you are using a straight-through or crossover cable. Its tiny size and simplicity make it an ideal component for any situation where you need to get an Ethernet device to act as a client to an access point.

But these features aren't nearly enough for wireless hackers. Here are a couple of nifty hacks that are floating around for this fun piece of hardware.

Add an Antenna

The WET11 can easily accommodate an external antenna. Simply unscrew the small "rubber ducky" antenna and replace it with an RP-SMA pigtail [Hack #66]. This alone significantly improves the range of the WET11, and when using a directional antenna, can help reject noise and cause less interference for nearby networks. Save the discarded antenna for use in other projects, such as an add-on antenna for your laptop [Hack #43].

Upgrade the Radio

Possibly the greatest drawback to the WET11 is the cheap radio card installed at the factory. It ships with a low-end, 80mW radio with less-than-average sensitivity. Fortunately, the card is based on the a Prism 2 reference design. If you don't mind voiding your warranty, you can upgrade the card to a much more sensitive, higher power Senao or EnGenius card. The Senao (or EnGenius) 2511 Plus EXT 2 is an ideal card, as it even uses the same internal antenna connector, making the upgrade very easy.

Before you do anything else, upgrade the replacement card with the latest firmware. Unplug the Ethernet and power from the WET11. Remove the rubber feet from the bottom of the WET11 and open the case. Carefully unplug the antenna connector, unscrew the card from the brass stand-offs, and remove the internal card. Unfortunately, you won't be able to reuse the stand-off screws, as the replacement card has a slightly different physical packaging.

Plug in the new card, and reconnect the antenna cable to it. If the PCMCIA card is oriented with the antenna connectors toward the right (and the Senao/EnGenius label is facing you), you want to use the connector on the top. This is the same side that was connected to the original card. Finally, reassemble the case and power it up. You should now be enjoying the benefits of a much more sensitive radio and a full 200mW of power.

Use a Battery Pack

The WET11 is expecting a 5V DC power source. A number of people have reported success using the WET11 with a battery pack in the field. Using four NiMH batteries in a series (at approximately 1.2V each) yields a 4.8V battery, which seems to work fine for several hours with the WET11. The WET11 can accept voltages a bit higher than 5 volts (some say as high as 12V), so you could even theoretically use four Alkaline batteries (4 x 1.5V = 6V). If you make your own battery pack, be sure to observe the proper polarity! Also note that operating time will likely be significantly shorter if you transmit a lot and use the 200mW card as described earlier.

An external battery pack can be handy for generating a signal source when doing a site survey, or for hiding a signal source for a game of wireless hide-and-seek. There is a very detailed discussion with photos online from Belgium at *http://reseaucitoyen.be/?SourcePortable* (be warned, the entire site is in French). With the size and ubiquity of the WET11, it's no wonder that so many people are hacking on it.

HACK #46 AirPort Linux

Turn your Graphite AirPort (or other KarlNet based AP) into a full-fledged Linux router.

Lurking underneath the shiny "War of the Worlds" clam shell of the Graphite Apple AirPort (*http://www.apple.com/airport/*) is a complete computer. Originally designed by KarlNet (*http://karlnet.com/*), the guts of the Apple AirPort essentially are the same as the Proxim RG1000, RG1100, and a few other access points. To network hackers, this presents an enormous opportunity and challenge: if a more capable OS (such as Linux) can be made to run on AirPort hardware, then it should be possible to build a "Super AP" that can perform much more complicated tasks than a standard AP. For example, a Linux AirPort could handle dynamic routing, firewalling, and even manage Internet tunnels, such as IPIP [Hack #54] or GRE [Hack #55].

A number of people have made quite a bit of headway on this project. The single greatest obstacle has been trying to shoehorn a usable system onto the system itself. The AirPort is a very tiny computer with meager hardware resources. It is essentially a 486 CPU (without floating point) with only 4 MB of RAM and 512 KB of flash storage. By today's PC standards, it isn't much more than a pocket calculator.

These severe physical restrictions have led to a number of trade-offs:

- The system needs a lightweight kernel. The kernel of choice at the moment is from the Linux 2.2 series to save on RAM.

- There isn't nearly enough room to store a usable Linux system on the flash, so the root filesystem is kept on an NFS share. This share is mountable over the Ethernet or over wireless.

- With only 4 MB of RAM, application space is very limited. Lightweight applications like *telnetd* are still usable, but running *sshd* is virtually impossible.

- Since the card inside the AirPort is a Hermes-based radio, Host AP [Hack #57] won't work with it. To date, no one (to my knowledge) has gotten Hermes AP [Hack #61] working with AirPort Linux, although it can be done. This means that the wireless must be used in Ad-Hoc mode, and Ethernet bridging isn't possible.

AirPort Linux works by uploading a custom firmware to the AirPort that instructs it to boot from the network. If you decide later that you would like to turn your AirPort back into a traditional AP, you can simply flash the firmware with Apple's original version. To get AirPort Linux running, you need a server capable of providing DHCP, TFTP, and NFS services. Any old Linux or BSD server will do.

Installation

AirPort Linux was pioneered by Till Straumann. His original project is well documented online at *http://www-hft.ee.tu-berlin.de/~strauman/airport/airport.html*; however, the quickest way to get started is to go to *http://www.seattlewireless.net/index.cgi/AirportLinux* and download the *AirportLinux-0.01.tar.gz* package. This is just a collection of all of the software you need to get things going with a bit of documentation.

First, set up the necessary services on your Linux or BSD server. Extract the *AirPortLinux-0.01.tar.gz* archive, and *cd* into it. For simplicity, I will install the software in directories under */remote/*, but you can put them wherever you like:

```
~/AirportLinux-0.01# mvserver/tftpboot /
~/AirportLinux-0.01# mkdir /remote; mvairport /remote
```

The */tftpboot/* directory contains the tiny kernel that the AirPort will boot, and */remote/airport/* contains the root filesystem. Now that the data is in place, configure *tftpd* and NFS. Put a line like this in your */etc/inetd.conf*, and restart *inetd*:

```
tftp      dgram      udp      wait      root      in.tftpd
```

Add the following to */etc/exports* and restart *rpc.nfsd*. Make sure that *portmap* is also running.

```
/remote/airport        airport(ro)
```

We now need to configure *dhcpd* to serve a static IP to the AirPort, and to give it additional boot parameters. To do this, you need the hardware MAC address of your AirPort. The MAC addresses of the Ethernet and wireless cards are listed on the bottom of the unit. If you are booting from the Ethernet (most likely), use the Ethernet ID. If you plan on booting from the AirPort card, use the AirPort ID. Note that wireless booting can be tricky to configure, and is definitely slower than booting from the wire. I recommend using the Ethernet for booting whenever possible.

Now that you have the proper MAC address, create a stanza like the following in */etc/dhcpd.conf*, and restart *dhcpd*:

```
host airport {
          hardware ethernet  00:30:65:FF:AA:BB;
          filename "/tftpboot/vmlinubz.nbi";
          option host-name "airport";
          option option-130 "eth0";
          option root-path "/remote/airport";

     }
```

Naturally, substitute the real MAC address for 00:30:65:FF:AA:BB. Finally, pick an unused IP address on your local network and add an appropriate entry to your */etc/hosts* file:

```
10.15.6.20 airport
```

Now that your server is ready to serve AirPort Linux, you are ready to flash your AirPort hardware.

Flashing the AirPort

The simplest way to flash the AirPort is to use the Java Configurator [Hack #47]. A copy is included in the *AirportLinux-0.01.tar.gz* archive for convenience, in the *etherboot/* directory. Boot the AirPort as you normally would, and make a note of the IP address it is using. Fire up the Configurator, enter the IP address and password for your AirPort, and select *File → Upload new base station firmware....* When prompted for a file, select the *etherboot/etherboot-airport.bin* file from the archive. Wait a few moments, and your AirPort will reboot. After it resets, it is *very* important to hard boot the Air-Port by removing and reapplying the power. It's a good idea to do this any time you flash the firmware on a device, just to be sure you are starting with a fresh boot.

In a few moments, you should be able to ping the AirPort at the IP address you specified; and when it has finished booting, you can *telnet* to it. Log in as root with no password, and you should have a shell on your very own AirPort:

```
$ telnet 10.15.6.20
Trying 10.15.6.20...
Connected to 10.15.6.20.
Escape character is '^]'.

airport login: root


BusyBox v0.60.2 (2002.08.30-19:59+0000) Built-in shell (msh)
Enter 'help' for a list of built-in commands.

#
```

Change the root password with the usual *passwd* command, and your system is ready to use. Configure the interfaces with *ifconfig* and *iwconfig* as you normally would. If you are unable to get to the AirPort after it has rebooted, look closely at the DHCP, TFTP, and NFS logs on your server (many times, they all end up in */var/log/messages*). You should see the AirPort request a DHCP lease, request *vmlinubz.nbi* from *in.tftpd*, and eventually mount */remote/airport* once the kernel has booted.

Putting It Back

If you ever need to turn your AirPort back into a plain vanilla AP, it is as simple as flashing the firmware again. Reboot the AirPort without the Ethernet cable connected. It will create a network called "AirPort xxxxxxxx." Associate your Mac with this network, and run Apple's AirPort configuration utility. It will automatically find the AirPort. Double-click on the Air-Port, and enter the AirPort's hardware password. The AirPort Configuration utility will tell you that there is updated firmware available. Click "Yes" to update the firmware, and when the AirPort reboots, it will be back to its old self.

AirPort Linux isn't for everybody, but it can allow some very tricky things to happen with the AirPort hardware. If this still doesn't provide enough flexibility for your wireless project, you might try building your own AP from scratch **[Hack #51]**.

HACK #47   Java Configurator for AirPort APs

Configure your AirPort or Lucent-based AP from a Java applet.

Jon Sevy has done extensive work with the AirPort, and has released an open source Java client (*http://edge.mcs.drexel.edu/GICL/people/sevy/airport*) that configures the AirPort (including Graphite, Snow, and Extreme) as well as the RG-1000. He has also compiled a tremendous amount of information on the inner workings of the AirPort, and makes extensive resources available online at this site. Since his utility is open source and cross platform, and works very well, I use it in the following examples; see it in action in Figure 4-1.

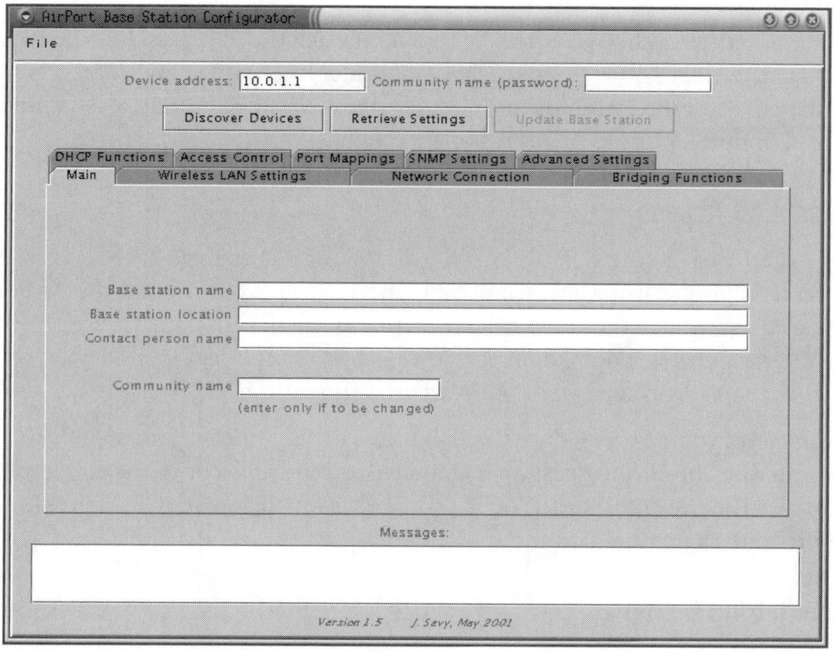

Figure 4-1. The AirPort Java Configurator.

To use the Java Configurator app, you need a copy of the Java Runtime Environment. Download it from *http://java.sun.com/* if you don't already have it. You can start the utility by running the following in Linux:

```
$ java -jar AirportBaseStationConfig.jar &
```

Or simply double-click the AirportBaseStationConfig icon in Windows.

The AirPort can be configured over the Ethernet port or over the wireless. When the application window opens, you can click the *Discover Devices* button to auto-locate all of the APs on your network. When you find the IP address of the AP you want to configure, type it into the *Device address* field, and type the password into the *Community name* field. If you're unsure about the IP address or the password, the AirPort ships with a default password of *public* and an IP address of 10.0.1.1 on the wireless interface (it picks up the wired IP address via DHCP; use *Discover Devices* to find it if you're configuring it over the Ethernet). Once you've entered the correct information, click the *Retrieve Settings* button.

The very first thing you should change is the *Community name*, on the first panel. Otherwise, anyone can reconfigure your AirPort by using the *public* default! While you're there, you can set the name of the AirPort (which shows up in network scans), and also the location and contact information, if you like. These fields are entirely optional, and have no effect on operations.

You should also choose a *network name*, under the *Wireless LAN Settings* tab. This is also known as the ESSID, and identifies your network to clients in range. If you're running a "closed" network, this needs to be known ahead of time by any host attempting to connect.

Local LAN Access

As stated earlier, the default AirPort configuration enables LAN access by default. If you're using DSL or a cable modem, or are installing the AirPort on an existing ethernet network, then this is what you want to use. In the Java Configurator, take a look at the *Network Connection* tab, and check the *Connect to network through Ethernet port* radio button.

From here, you can configure the IP address of the AirPort, either via DHCP, by entering the IP information manually, or by using Point-to-Point Protocol over Ethernet (PPPoE). You'll probably want to use DHCP, unless your ISP requires a manual IP address or PPPoE.

Configuring Dialup

There is also a radio button on the *Network Connection* tab marked *Connect to network through modem*. Use this option if your only network connection is via dialup. Yes, it's very slow, but at least you're wireless. Note that the Dialup and Ethernet choices are exclusive, and can't be used at the same time.

When you check *Connect to network through modem*, the pane presents you with *Phone number*, *Modem init string*, and other dial-up-related fields.

Make sure that *Automatic dialing* is checked, so it will dial the phone when you start using the AirPort. Click on the *Username/Password/Login Script* button to enter your login information. On this screen, you can also define a custom login script if you need to. The default script has worked fine for me with a couple of different ISPs.

Once the AirPort is configured for Dialup, it dials the phone and connects any time it senses Internet traffic on the wireless port. Just start using your wireless card as usual, and after an initial delay (while it's dialing the phone), you're online.

NAT and DHCP

By default, the AirPort acts as both a NAT server and a DHCP server for your wireless clients. DHCP service is controlled by the *DHCP Functions* tab. To turn DHCP on, check the *Provide DHCP address delivery to wireless hosts* box. You can specify the range of IPs to issue; by default, the AirPort hands out leases between 10.0.1.2 and 10.0.1.50. You can also set a lease time here, which specifies the lifetime (in seconds) of an issued IP address. After this timer expires, the client reconnects to the DHCP server and requests another lease. The default of 0 (or unlimited) is probably fine for most installations, but you may want to set it shorter if you have a large number of clients trying to connect to your AirPort.

If you don't have another DHCP server on your network, the AirPort can provide service for your wired hosts as well. Check the *Distribute addresses on Ethernet port, too* box if you want this functionality.

> Only check this box if you don't have another DHCP server on your network! More than one DHCP server on the same subnet is a BAD thing, and will bring the wrath of the sysadmin down upon you. Watching two DHCP servers duke out who gets to serve leases may be fun in your spare time, but can also take down an entire network and leave you wondering where your job went. What were you doing connecting unauthorized gear to the company network, anyway?

If you have more than one AirPort on the same wired network, make sure that you enable only DHCP to the wire on one of them—and again, only if you don't already have a DHCP server.

NAT is very handy if you don't have many IP addresses to spare (and these days, few people do). It also gives your wireless clients some protection from the wired network, as it acts as an effective one-way firewall. In the Configurator, NAT is set up in the *Bridging Functions* tab. To enable NAT, click the

Provide network address translation (NAT) radio button. You can either specify your own private address and netmask, or leave the default (10.0.1.1 / 255.255.255.0).

Bridging

A big disadvantage to running NAT on your wireless hosts is that they become less accessible to your wired hosts. While the wireless users can make connections to any machine on the wire, connecting back through a NAT is difficult (the AirPort provides some basic support for this by allowing for static port mappings, but this is far from convenient). For example, if you are running a Windows client on the wireless, the Network Neighborhood shows only other wireless clients, and not any machines on the wire, since NAT effectively hides broadcast traffic (which the Windows SMB protocol relies on). If you already have a DHCP server on your wired network and are running private addresses, the NAT and DHCP functions of the AirPort are redundant, and can simply get in the way.

Rather than duplicate effort and make life difficult, you can disable NAT and DHCP, and enable Bridging to the wire. Turn off DHCP under *DHCP Functions* (as we just saw), and check the *Act as transparent bridge (no NAT)* under the *Bridging Functions* tab. When the AirPort is operating in this mode, all traffic destined for your wireless clients that happens on the wire gets broadcast over wireless, and vice versa. This includes broadcast traffic (such as DHCP requests and SMB announcement traffic). Apart from wireless authentication, this makes your AirPort seem completely invisible to the rest of your network.

Once bridging is enabled, you may find it difficult to get the unit back into NAT mode. If it seems unresponsive to the Java Configurator (or the Mac AirPort admin utility) while in bridging mode, there are a couple of ways to bring it back.

If you have a Mac, you can do a manual "reset." Push the tiny button on the bottom of the AirPort with a paper clip for about two seconds. The green center light on top will change to amber. Connect the Ethernet port on your AirPort to your Mac, and run the admin utility. The software should let you restore the AirPort to the default settings. You have five minutes to do this, before the amber light turns green and reverts to bridged mode.

WEP, MAC Filtering, and Closed Networks

If you really want to lock down your network at the access point, you have the following choices at your disposal: WEP encryption, filtering on MAC address (the radio card's serial number), and running a "closed" network.

The three services are completely separate, so you don't necessarily have to run MAC filtering *and* a closed network, for example. Combining all of these features may not make your network completely safe from a determined miscreant, but will discourage the vast majority of would-be network hijackers.

To set the WEP keys, click the *Wireless LAN Settings* tab, and enter the keys in the fields provided. Also check *Use encryption* and uncheck *Allow unencrypted data* to require WEP on your network. Give a copy of this key to each of your wireless clients.

With MAC filtering enabled, the AirPort keeps an internal table of MAC addresses that are permitted to use the AirPort. Click the *Access Control* tab, and enter in as many MAC addresses as you like. Only radios using one of the MACs listed here will be allowed to associate with the AirPort. The MAC address of a radio card should be printed on the back of it (a MAC address consists of six hex numbers of the form *12:34:56:ab:cd:ef*).

A "closed" network makes the AirPort refuse connections from radios that don't explicitly set the ESSID, i.e., clients with a blank ESSID, or an ESSID set to ANY. To make your network "closed," check the *Closed network* box under *Wireless LAN Settings*.

Remember that without encryption, all traffic is sent in the clear, so anyone within range could potentially read and reuse sensitive information (such as ESSIDs and valid MAC addresses.) Even with WEP, every other legitimate user can see this traffic. If you need to later restrict access to a user, you must change the WEP key on every wireless client. But for small groups of trusted users, those using these access control methods should discourage all but the most determined black hat without too much hassle.

Roaming

Wireless roaming can be very handy if your network is arranged in a way that you can support it. In order for roaming to be possible, your APs all need to be from the same manufacturer, they all need to reside on the same physical wired subnet (i.e., on the same IP network, with no intervening routers), and they all must have the same network name (ESSID).

In the AirPort, roaming is automatically enabled if this is true. Make sure that all of your AirPorts have the exact same network name under *Wireless LAN Settings*. If, for some reason, you want to disable roaming, just give each AirPort a different ESSID.

Save Your Changes

Once you are satisfied with your settings, click the *Update Base Station* button, and give your AirPort about a minute to reboot. If you changed your network name or WEP settings, be sure to change your local wireless client accordingly before trying to associate with the access point. That's all there is to it.

Apple Software Base Station

#48   Use an OS X machine with an AirPort card as a true access point.

Mac OS 9 had a handy AirPort feature called "Software Base Station." It allowed any Mac with an AirPort card and an Ethernet (or dialup) connection to act like a hardware access point, sharing its Internet connection over the wireless. The early versions of OS X were noticeably lacking this handy feature, but it has been restored in OS X 10.2.

To begin, you need to establish a connection to the Internet over something other than wireless (Ethernet is ideal). You might think that to start a new wireless network, you could simply click on the AirPort icon and select *Create Network*, but this will make an IBSS (peer-to-peer) network. In order to turn your Mac into a true access point, you need to go to *System Preferences → Sharing*, and click on the Internet tab, shown in Figure 4-2.

Check the top box (*Share your Internet connection with AirPort-equipped computers*), but before clicking the *Start* button, you probably want to set up your wireless parameters. Click the *AirPort Options...* button, and you should see a drop-down menu like that shown in Figure 4-3.

Specify a network name and channel, and turn on WEP [Hack #86] if you need it. Click *OK*, then click the *Start* button. Close the control panel, and your AirPort icon should change to include an arrow (Figure 4-4). This means that your AirPort is now operating as a real access point.

To turn off sharing and return to normal AirPort operations, go back to the Sharing control panel (or just click *Open Internet Sharing...* from the AirPort menu bar) and click the *Stop* button. As long as you have Internet sharing enabled, anyone in range of your Mac will see it as a normal access point, and can access the Internet just as if it were a hardware AP. I'm not sure why Apple made this feature a bit obscure to enable, but it can come in handy in a pinch when you need an AP in a hurry.

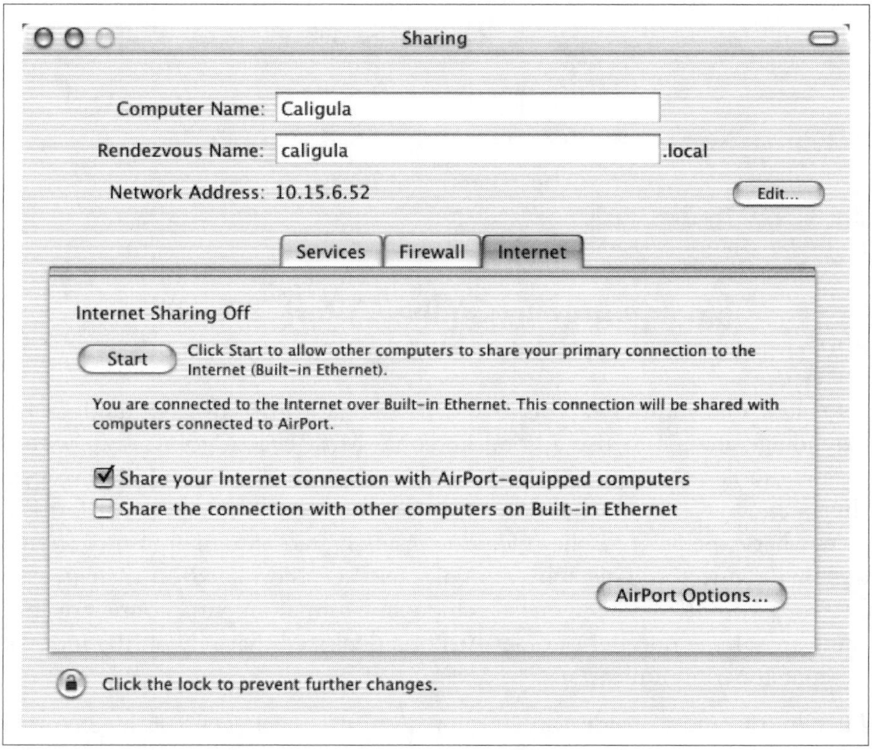

Figure 4-2. Enable Software Base Station in the Sharing Control Panel.

Figure 4-3. Set up your radio parameters under AirPort Options.

Figure 4-4. Software Base Station engaged!

HACK #49   Adding an Antenna to the AirPort
Significantly extend your range when using an AirPort base station.

As stated many times in this book, the single most effective method for extending range is to use a good antenna. Most access points ship with a simple dipole or small omni that doesn't offer much gain, but at least gets the antenna away from the body of the access point. The Apple AirPort is a somewhat expensive AP that includes an integrated antenna but no external antenna connector. This state of affairs has been corrected on their newest AirPort Extreme models, which include an external antenna connector, but there are a huge number of older AirPorts deployed that rely on the internal antenna for communications.

Luckily, the radio inside the Graphite AirPort is a Lucent/Orinoco/Avaya Silver card, which includes an antenna connector of its own. With a little bit of work, it is possible add your own external antenna. All you need is a screwdriver, a dremel tool, a Lucent pigtail [Hack #66], and about half an hour.

As you can see in Figure 4-5, the only ports on the back of a Graphite Air-Port are the modem, power, and Ethernet. The rest of the AirPort is sealed, and there isn't room to squeeze a pigtail in without cutting a hole in the chassis. I found that I used the modem only once since I bought the AirPort, so rather than cut a hole in the side of the AirPort, I could just remove the telephone jack and feed the pigtail through the little square.

There are three Philips head screws on the bottom of the AirPort. Remove them, and carefully remove the bottom half of the shell. There is an internal case that is held to the top by three more screws. Remove them, but don't tilt out the internal case yet. There is a tiny cable connecting the telephone jack to the motherboard, covered with a piece of silver metal tape. Pry up the tape, and carefully disconnect the modem connector. Now you should be able to carefully tilt out the internal case. This is the motherboard and radio card of the AirPort, which attaches to the ports by two short cables (an Ethernet cable and a twisted red and black power cable). Remove them as well.

Figure 4-5. The business end of a Graphite AirPort.

If you have never played with a Lucent/Orinoco/Avaya Silver card before, there is a tiny black plastic cap covering the antenna connector on the edge of the card. Pry out this cap and discard it, as shown in Figure 4-6.

Figure 4-6. The Lucent card with the antenna connector exposed.

Notice how the radio card fits snugly against a black plastic rail on the top half of the outer shell. There isn't enough room to accommodate a pigtail when reassembling the AirPort, so you need to grind away some of this plastic, or possibly use a good pair of cutters to nibble it away. A right-angle pigtail works much better than a straight pigtail, as there isn't much room to maneuver inside the case.

If you would rather just punch a hole in the side of the AirPort case, you can do that now as well. I prefer to feed the pigtail through the modem port, which involves removing the entire port chassis. There are two screws holding a metal plate to the top half of the outer shell. Remove them, and the entire port chassis will pull out of the case. There are two tiny screws holding the telephone jack to this metal plate. You need a tiny Phillips head screwdriver to remove these screws. A jeweler's screwdriver (as you might find in an eyeglass repair kit) works well.

Now reverse the steps, carefully tucking in the cables as you screw everything back together again. Figure 4-7 shows an 8" pigtail fed through the modem port.

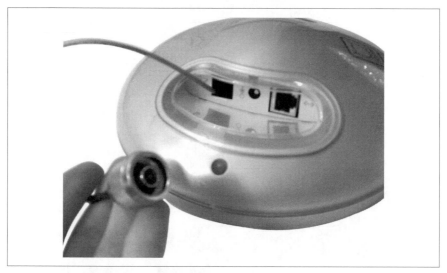

Figure 4-7. AirPort with a standard male N connector.

I didn't have one handy, but a better hack would be to use a chassis mount N or TNC connector to bolt directly to the modem port. That would be more rugged, and would help avoid the possibility of accidentally yanking too hard on the pigtail and damaging the connector or card. Also note that while a pigtail is connected to a Lucent card, the internal antenna is switched off, so you will get very terrible coverage unless you connect the pigtail to an antenna.

This technique can be used for other devices that include an internal card with antenna connectors, such as the Proxim RG1000 or RG1100. Many APs now come standard with external antennas, but if you should encounter one that doesn't, this modification can improve your range significantly.

The NoCat Night Light

#50 Put your AP where everyone can see it—on the ceiling.

Back in March 2003, some friends and I were hanging out at a really good coffee shop in Sebastopol, CA. This particular coffee joint is housed in an old wooden train station building, with very high ceilings, old-style hanging industrial lamps, and even a couple of old trains still on the tracks, serving as small shops.

Unfortunately, there's no wireless available at this shop. (There was, once upon a time, back when O'Reilly was located across the street from it. But that was ages ago, and even then the signal wasn't all that it could have been.) As we sat around drinking our high octane beverages, we got to talking about the best way to provide coverage in such a huge space. The room we were in was a common room, open at all hours (the front entrance is huge, and doesn't even have a door.) While you could put an access point in one of the enclosed shops in the building, coverage in the open area would likely be spotty at best. You would want the AP to be located high up off the ground, where everyone could see it.

Almost simultaneously, we all looked up and noticed the lamps hanging from the wooden rafters. What if you could house an AP in a package the size of a large light bulb, and install it in an existing light socket? This seemed like a good idea, but how would you get network access to it without running CAT5 to the socket? Easy: Powerline Ethernet.

With the recent release of the Siemens' SpeedStream series, such an insane, caffeine-induced idea as an AP in a light bulb might be a possibility. These devices are quite small, about the size of a standard wall wart (Figure 4-8). They sport a CF wireless adapter that acts as the AP (actually, it's the same card as the popular Linksys WCF11 but with a different sticker.) The brilliant bit is that the wireless network bridges directly to the AC power, so a standard Powerline Ethernet adapter anywhere on the same power circuit can provide Internet access to as many APs as you care to plug in. At a mere $85 retail, we couldn't resist picking one up and seeing what we could do with it.

One of our first concerns was practical rather than technical. Obviously, if you're going to replace a light bulb with an access point, the room will likely get darker. That is, unless the AP can also provide light as well. After fooling with a couple of lighting ideas, we finally soldered some copper romex onto a fluorescent bulb as a prototype. The romex is rigid enough to hold the lamp steady, and easy to solder to. The fluorescent bulb would obviously be dimmer than a 300-Watt spot lamp, but it would be better than

Figure 4-8. The tiny SpeedStream Powerline AP.

nothing. And as a flourescent runs much cooler, it probably wouldn't turn the guts of the access point to liquid. This solved the light issue well enough for the moment, but how could we connect the whole thing to a standard light bulb socket?

One trip to the hardware store later, we had a variety of Edison plugs, sockets, and adapters. We settled on a simple extender type of device, with a female socket on one side and a male plug on the other. Again, the contacts were copper, making it easy to solder on more romex (Figure 4-9). We had the basic design together, but what could we possibly use for housing?

Tupperware, of course. Adam painted the inside of a Tupperware bowl white, and the entire device just managed to squeeze inside. We first attempted to take the SpeedStream unit apart to save space, but it's already tightly packed inside (much of the unit is occupied by a large transformer). Besides, keeping the original enclosure made us all feel a bit more relaxed about plugging the thing in. The Edison plug poked through the bottom of the bowl, where we simply screwed on another connector to keep it tightly attached.

So with all of the technical considerations accounted for, all that was left was the all-important marketing phase of the project. Some electrical tape and one vinyl sticker later, the NoCat Night Light was born! See it in all of its glory in Figure 4-10.

But how well would it actually work? Wouldn't the fluorescent throw off all sorts of noise that would interfere with the AP? We certainly thought so.

Figure 4-9. The AP, Edison connector, and bulb connected with romex.

Figure 4-10. The completed "light bulb."

Unfortunately, we didn't have a machine handy with which to do real throughput testing, but DSL reports showed a very respectable 2 Mbps or so. This was well above the rated capacity of the cable modem network we were using, so we were definitely satisfied with the results.

One big improvement to the design would be to replace the fluorescent bulb with a bright LED array, or even a simple socket so you could use whatever (low temperature) light source you like. This design makes much more sense than Siemen's original, as it gets the AP up off of the ground and above your head, where presumably many more people can see it. Adding more APs is as simple as screwing in a light bulb, as they bridge directly to the same AC Powerline segment, and terminate at the same Ethernet.

Keep in mind that this design is a prototype, and while it works in casual testing, it hasn't been tested for hours of continuous use. At the very least, it would be a good idea to insulate the bare contacts and find a better way of ventilating the fluorescent bulb (or replacing it altogether with an LED array). Build it at your own risk, but by all means have fun while doing it.

HACK #51   Do-It-Yourself Access Point Hardware

Use one of these popular embedded PC boxes as a building block for your access point project.

There is a huge variety of PC-compatible hardware available that is perfectly capable of serving as an access point. If budget is a concern, you can certainly dust off that old PC that is collecting dust in the closet (provided that it is roughly of 486/50 vintage or so; 386 machines, while nostalgic, are probably too painfully slow to deal with by today's standards). Some people choose to use a full-blown tower case with an old 486 or Pentium processor as a combination access point and file server. One node on the NoCat network is an old Apple G3 running Yellow Dog Linux, as that was what we had lying around!

But if you are planning on building out a large network project, it is advisable to standardize your hardware platform. This is a good idea from an aesthetic point of view, as well as for reliability and ease of troubleshooting. While your dusty old 486 might be just taking up space, brand new embedded machines are coming down in price. These are tiny, fanless machines that are designed to run off of DC power, which boot from cheap compact flash RAM. This means no moving parts, simple ventilation requirements, and potentially very long uptimes.

Not all embedded solutions are necessarily cost effective. One notorious example is the PC/104 hardware used in industrial applications. Although it offers relatively low performance, this hardware has a reputation for robustness and ease of programming, as well as the standard PC/104 "stackable" bus. But even its extreme popularity in the industrial world hasn't done much to bring down its price, relative to what is available in the general purpose computing world.

Whatever hardware platform you choose, be sure that it meets your needs. When choosing a piece of hardware, you should remember to consider the number and type of radio and network interfaces, cooling and power requirements, size, RAM and CPU available, and of course, cost. Here are a number of solutions that DIY networks have found to bring a high performance-to-price ratio.

Soekris (http://www.soekris.com/)
> Affectionately known as the "little green box," the Soekris solution is a popular choice among do-it-yourself networkers. There are a number of Soekris models that work well as access points, with and without PCMCIA. All Soekris boards will boot from Compact Flash and come standard with multiple Ethernet interfaces, a mini-PCI slot, hardware watchdog, serial console, and an AMD 133 MHz processor. They are all fanless boards and use a DC power supply (see Figure 4-11).

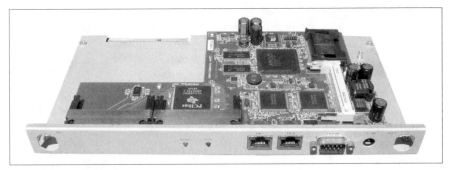

Figure 4-11. The Soekris net4521.

> At the time of this writing, the Soekris net4521 (with two PCMCIA slots, two Ethernet ports, a mini-PCI slot, and 64 MB RAM) sells for about $250.

OpenBrick (http://www.openbrick.org/)
> Another popular embedded solution is the OpenBrick. The typical OpenBrick has a 300 MHz (fanless) Geode processor, an on-board NIC, a PCMCIA slot, and boots from Compact Flash. It runs on DC power, and unlike the Soekris, also has USB ports (although it does not have a mini-PCI slot.) It comes standard with 128 MB RAM, and also has room for a 2.5" hard drive.

The OpenBrick (Figure 4-12) is designed to serve as a tiny server or client workstation, and as such, has virtually all standard PC functionality (VGA and NTSC video out, PS/2, parallel and serial ports, audio, etc.). Its additional features also make for a higher price tag, with the going rate about $360 as of this writing.

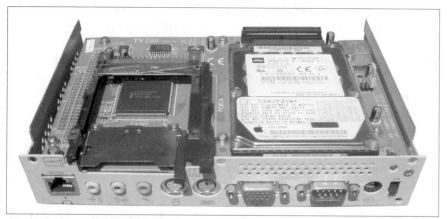

Figure 4-12. The OpenBrick.

Via-based computers (http://www.via.com.tw/)

There are a number of Via-based computers on the market. They are generally marked as desktop PCs, although small, fanless cases that take a DC power supply are becoming commonplace. As they are intended to be used as general purpose PCs, they typically have 500 MHz or better Via processors, on-board NICs, an IDE interface, USB, and a PCI slot. Using an inexpensive CF-to-IDE adapter [Hack #52], these boards (or, indeed, any PC) can be made to boot from Compact Flash for a hardware solution with no moving parts.

If you are looking for a fanless solution, be sure to get the 500 MHz version, as the 800 MHz and faster Via boards require a processor fan. Via motherboards (Figure 4-13) are around $100 at the time of this writing, without case, RAM, or storage.

The Fujitsu Stylistic series

This collection simply wouldn't be complete without mentioning the Fujitsu Stylistic 1000 series (Figure 4-14). This is a very popular surplus market tablet PC that has "hack me" written all over it. It has three PCMCIA slots, one of which is the boot device. It can boot from Card Flash using a CF to PCMCIA adapter, and is unique in that it has an integrated LCD display and battery. The 1000 series has a 486 DX4/100 processor, is expandable to 40 MB RAM, can use a cordless pen for

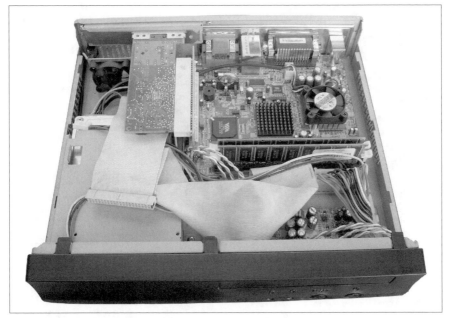

Figure 4-13. A Via EPIA 800MHz PC.

input, and has served just fine as a hardware gateway (I use one myself for my node on SeattleWireless). Fujitsu still makes the Stylistic series, although new machines are quite expensive (on par with modern laptops). The older 1000s or 1200s can frequently be found on the surplus market for less than $100.

Running your own custom access point can be considerably more challenging than the plug-and-play devices you can buy in consumer electronic stores, but building such devices can be much more rewarding as well. Bringing the power and flexibility of Linux or BSD to the access point itself can lead to all sorts of interesting possibilities that just can't be accomplished with a $75 over-the-counter access point.

HACK #52 Compact Flash Hard Drive

Make your own tiny hard drive with no moving parts and very low power consumption.

One challenge when building your own embedded device is finding enough storage for the operating system and any data you need to keep track of. While 2.5" laptop hard drives probably have the highest ratio of storage space to physical space, they introduce a couple of challenges for an embedded system. A hard drive is a mechanical device, with fairly strict environmental operating conditions (for both temperature and humidity). They

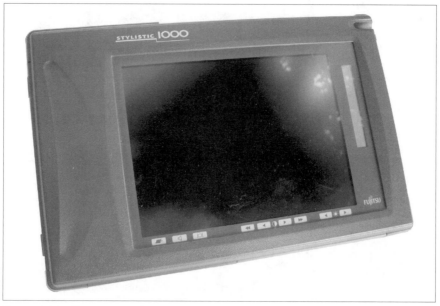

Figure 4-14. The Fujitsu Stylistic 1000.

generate noise, draw a fair amount of power, and above all, are quite fragile. In other words, you probably wouldn't want to consider leaving one in a relatively unprotected plastic box on your roof through the winter or summer.

A very popular alternative to traditional hard drives is to use flash RAM instead. Flash memory uses only a tiny fraction of the power that a hard drive uses, and can operate over a much wider range of environmental conditions. It is very tiny, lightweight, and noiseless. It can be rewritten many thousands of times, and can even be dropped on the floor without fear of loss of data. While it isn't nearly as cost effective in terms of price per bit, the popularity of digital cameras has driven flash memory prices down remarkably. If your application can fit in 32 to 512 MB of space, then flash storage is a viable alternative to 2.5" hard drives.

Many types of flash media can be used as a standard IDE device by using a simple converter, shown in Figure 4-15. One device I particularly like to use is the CFADPT1 from Mesa Electronics. Their memory devices are available online at *http://www.mesanet.com/diskcardinfo.html*. It can be used on a standard IDE chain or on the SFF IDE found in laptops. As the SFF IDE bus provides power on the data cable (standard IDE doesn't), you need to connect a spare floppy power connector to the adapter when using it with standard IDE.

Figure 4-15. CompactFlash to IDE adapter.

Once a CompactFlash card is inserted into the IDE adapter and attached to your computer, no further configuration is necessary. CF drives require no special drivers, and appear to be standard IDE devices to the host computer. Partition and format them as you would any other IDE device. Once an OS is installed, you can even boot from them.

Mesa also carries hard-to-find SFF IDE ribbon cable with connectors installed for a reasonable price—just ask. A number of suppliers carry CF-to-IDE adapters, and the going rate is about $20. While SmartMedia and Memory Stick adapters are also available, CF-to-IDE tends to be the cheapest way to go.

At the time of this writing, 512 MB compact flash cards are available for under $100, 256 MB cards are available for around $50, and 128 MB cards are going for an unbelievable $20. These are ideal for running a micro Linux distribution, such as Pebble **[Hack #53]**. Note that while you won't need one of these for use with the Soekris **[Hack #51]** as it boots from CF directly, these adapters will allow any computer with an IDE interface to eliminate its most unreliable component: the hard drive.

Pebble

#53

Use this tiny Debian-based distribution for your own custom wireless access point.

Terry Schmidt of NYCwireless has done terrific work in getting together a stripped down Linux distribution specifically tailored for wireless access points in general, and for the Soekris [Hack #51] platform in particular. This distribution is called Pebble, and is freely available at *http://www.nycwireless. net/pebble/*. It aims to balance functionality with size, weighing in at about 47 MB. As it is based on Debian, customizing the installed software is very straightforward. Unlike some *very* tiny distributions, it uses standard libraries and binaries. This significantly simplifies upgrades, and it means that custom packages don't have to be built from source and linked to custom, stripped-down libraries.

- Based on Debian GNU/Linux 3.0r1 (Woody)
- Linux Kernel 2.4.20 with IPv6 modules
- HostAP 0.0.2 and utils
- bridge-tools
- djbdns caching dns server
- NoCatAuth running as nonroot user, post 0.81 nightly
- openSSH server 3.4p1
- openSSL 0.9.6c patched
- pcmcia-cs
- ppp and pppoe
- Zebra 0.92a-5

There are also a number of shell niceties, including wget, elvis, tcpdump, perl, and even lynx. It runs well on every Soekris model, and will spawn a serial console on those machines (or any machine that has a serial port available). It runs on virtually any 486 class machine (or better) with at least 32 MB RAM. If you don't need all of the functionality provided in the standard distribution, you can easily strip out the components you don't need, to fit it into an even smaller space. For example, eliminating Perl, NoCatAuth, djbdns, and a couple of nonessential shell utilities will easily let Pebble fit on a 32 MB flash card (although since 128 MB flash cards are now selling for $20, perhaps this is something of a waste of effort).

If you are running from flash memory, one of the most useful features in Pebble is that it mounts the bootable medium read only, and creates a temporary RAM disk for its temporary files. This means that once it is configured, the flash is never written to, which considerably extends the lifetime of your flash.

Since it is based on Debian, you can easily install and remove packages using the standard *apt-get* utility. Pebble is under active development, with contributions from many interested embedded networkers. If you can spare the tiny amount of space required for Pebble, I highly recommend trying it for your own access point application.

HACK #54 Tunneling: IPIP Encapsulation
IP tunneling with the Linux IPIP driver.

If you have never worked with IP tunneling before, you might want to take a look at the Advanced Router HOWTO (*http://www.tldp.org/HOWTO/Adv-Routing-HOWTO/*) before continuing. Essentially, an IP tunnel is much like a VPN, except that not every IP tunnel involves encryption. A machine that is "tunneled" into another network has a virtual interface configured with an IP address that isn't local, but exists on a remote network. Usually, all (or most) network traffic is routed down this tunnel, so remote clients appear to exist on the network as if they were local. This can be used to allow clients from the Internet to access private network services, or more generally, to connect to any two private networks together using the Internet to carry the tunnel traffic.

If you want to perform simple IP-within-IP tunneling between two machines, you might try IPIP. It is probably the simplest tunnel protocol available, and also works with *BSD, Solaris, and even Windows. Note that IPIP is simply a tunneling protocol, and does not involve any sort of encryption. It is also only capable of tunneling unicast packets; if you need to tunnel multicast traffic, take a look at GRE tunneling [Hack #55].

Before we rush right into our first tunnel, you need a copy of the advanced routing tools (specifically the *ip* utility.) You can get the latest authoritative copy from *ftp://ftp.inr.ac.ru/ip-routing/*. Be warned, the advanced routing tools aren't especially friendly, but they allow you to manipulate nearly any facet of the Linux networking engine.

In this example, I assume that you have two private networks (10.42.1.0/24 and 10.42.2.0/24) and that these networks both have direct Internet connectivity via a Linux router at each network. The "real" IP address of the first network router is 240.101.83.2, and the "real" IP of the second router is 251.4.92.217. This isn't very difficult, so let's jump right in.

First, load the kernel module on both routers by typing as the root user:

```
# modprobe ipip
```

Next, on the first network's router (on the 10.42.1.0/24 network), do the following:

```
# ip tunnel add mytun mode ipip remote 251.4.92.217 local 240.101.83.2↵
ttl 255
# ifconfig mytun 10.42.1.1
# route add -net 10.42.2.0/24 dev mytun
```

And on the second network's router (on the 10.42.2.0/24), reciprocate:

```
# ip tunnel add mytun mode ipip remote 240.101.83.2 local 251.4.92.217↵
ttl 255
# ifconfig mytun 10.42.2.1
# route add -net 10.42.1.0/24 dev mytun
```

Naturally, you can give the interface a more meaningful name than mytun if you like. From the first network's router, you should now be able to ping 10.42.2.1, and from the second network's router, you should be able to ping 10.42.1.1. Likewise, every machine on the 10.42.1.0/24 network should be able to route to every machine on the 10.42.2.0/24 network, just as if the Internet weren't even there.

If you're running a Linux 2.2.x kernel, you're in luck: here's a shortcut that you can use to avoid having to use the Advanced Router tools package at all. After loading the module, try these commands instead:

```
# ifconfig tunl0 10.42.1.1 pointopoint 251.4.92.217
# route add -net 10.42.2.0/24 dev tunl0
```

And on the second network's router (on the 10.42.2.0/24 network):

```
# ifconfig tunl0 10.42.2.1 pointopoint 240.101.83.2
# route add -net 10.42.1.0/24 dev tunl0
```

That's all there is to it.

If you can ping the opposite router, but other machines on the network don't seem to be able to pass traffic beyond the router, make sure that both routers are configured to forward packets between interfaces:

```
# echo "1" > /proc/sys/net/ipv4/ip_forward
```

If you need to reach networks beyond 10.42.1.0 and 10.42.2.0, simply add additional route add -net lines. There is no configuration needed on any of your network hosts, as long as they have a default route to their respective router (which they definitely should, since it *is* their router, after all).

To bring the tunnel down, bring down the interface on both routers and delete it, if you like:

```
# ifconfig mytun down
# ip tunnel del mytun
```

(or, in Linux 2.2):

```
# ifconfig tunl0 down
```

The kernel will very politely clean up your routing table for you when the interface goes away.

See Also

- Advanced Routing HOWTO, *http://www.tldp.org/HOWTO/Adv-Routing-HOWTO/*
- Advanced Routing Tools (iproute2), *ftp://ftp.inr.ac.ru/ip-routing/*

HACK
#55
Tunneling: GRE Encapsulation

IP tunnels with GRE for supporting multicast and Cisco devices.

GRE stands for *Generic Routing Encapsulation*. Like IPIP tunneling [Hack #54], GRE is an unencrypted encapsulation protocol. The main advantages of using GRE instead of IPIP are that it supports multicast packets, and that it also interoperates with Cisco routers.

Just as with the IPIP tunneling hack, I assume that you have two private networks (10.42.1.0/24 and 10.42.2.0/24), and that these networks both have direct Internet connectivity via a Linux router at each network. The "real" IP address of the first network router is 240.101.83.2, and the "real" IP of the second router is 251.4.92.217.

Again, as with IPIP tunneling, you also need a copy of the advanced routing tools package (there is no shortcut for GRE tunnels in Linux 2.2 that I've been able to find). Once you have the *iproute2* package installed, begin by loading the GRE kernel module on both routers:

```
# modprobe ip_gre
```

On the first network's router, set up a new tunnel device:

```
# ip tunnel add gre0 mode gre remote 251.4.92.217 local 240.101.83.2 ⏎
  ttl 255
# ip addr add 10.42.1.254 dev gre0
# ip link set gre0 up
```

Note that you can call the device anything you like; *gre0* is just an example. Also, that 10.42.1.254 address can be any available address on the first network, but shouldn't be 10.42.1.1 (the IP already bound to its internal interface.) Now, add your network routes via the new tunnel interface:

```
# ip route add 10.42.2.0/24 dev gre0
```

The first network is finished. Now for the second:

```
# ip tunnel add gre0 mode gre remote 240.101.83.2 local 251.4.92.217 ⏎
  ttl 255
# ip addr add 10.42.2.254 dev gre0
# ip link set gre0 up
# ip route add 10.42.1.0/24 dev gre0
```

Again, the 10.42.2.254 address can be any available address on the second network. Feel free to add as many ip route add ... dev gre0 commands as you need.

That's it! You should now be able to pass packets between the two networks as if the Internet didn't exist. A traceroute from the first network should show just a couple of hops to any host in the second network (although you'll probably notice a fair bit of latency when crossing the 10. 42.2.254 hop, unless you're *really* well connected). If you're having trouble, check the notes in the IPIP example and don't panic. Your best friend when debugging new network configurations is probably a packet sniffer like *tcpdump* [Hack #37] or Ethereal [Hack #38].

To bring the tunnel down, run this on both routers:

```
# ip link set gre0 down
# ip tunnel del gre0
```

See Also

- Advanced Routing HOWTO, *http://www.tldp.org/HOWTO/Adv-Routing-HOWTO/*

- Advanced Routing Tools (iproute2), *ftp://ftp.inr.ac.ru/ip-routing/*

HACK #56   Running Your Own Top-Level Domain
Set up your own TLD in BIND for ease of navigation.

If you administer a network that uses private addressing, you've almost certainly encountered the disassociated schizophrenia of trying to maintain zone files that properly reflect internal and external IP addresses. With the introduction of Views in Bind 9, supporting multiple address ranges in a single domain has been significantly streamlined.

While using views is one way to attack the problem, consider the ease of setting up your own top-level domain. Normally, zone entries in *named.conf* look something like this:

```
zone "oreillynet.com" {
        type master;
        file "data/oreillynet.com";
};
```

This is an entry appropriate for an authoritative DNS server for the *oreillynet.com* subdomain. The actual top-level domains (i.e., *.com*, *.net*, *.org*, *.int*, etc.) are only delegated to the mysterious 13 known as the root DNS servers. Even though your servers won't be consulted by the rest of the Internet, it can be handy to set up your very own TLD that works only on your local network.

For example, suppose you have a group of machines that use the private 192.168.1.0/24 network. These machines aren't directly reachable from the Internet, and you don't really want to advertise their DNS information to would-be network crackers. Try a non-standard TLD:

```
zone "bp" {
        type master;
        file "data/bp";
        allow-transfer { 192.168.1/24; };
        allow-query { 192.168.1/24; };
};
```

The bp is short for BackPlane—and, more to the point, the bp is just plain short. With the preceding code added to your zone file, set up a master record for bp just as you would any other domain:

```
$TTL 86400
@    IN SOA  ns.bp. root.homer.bp. (
                2002090100      ; Serial
                10800           ; Refresh after 3 hours
                3600            ; Retry after 1 hour
                604800          ; Expire (1 week)
                60              ; Negative expiry time
                )

        IN NS           ns.bp.

ns      IN A 192.168.1.1

homer IN A 192.168.1.10
bart  IN A 192.168.1.11
lisa  IN A 192.168.1.12
```

Reload named, and you should be able to simply ping homer.bp. If you'd like other name servers to maintain slave copies of your TLD, just add them as usual:

```
zone "bp" {
        type slave;
        file "db.bp";
        masters { 192.168.1.1; };
};
```

In this way, you can extend your new TLD across your entire private network architecture. If you're running tunnels over the Internet **[Hack #54]** to connect remote offices or friends, support for your TLD could theoretically grow to be as large as you like. This is exactly what some wireless community networks (like NoCatNet and SeattleWireless) are doing. For example, users on SeattleWireless can browse to *http://www.rob.swn/* to hit a web server that I host on the wireless network. This shortcut of using a custom TLD saves a lot of typing, doesn't require Internet access to work, and is much easier than remembering IP addresses.

Getting Started with Host AP

#57   Use a Prism II radio card with Linux as if it were a hardware access point.

The Host AP driver will allow a Prism-based radio card to operate as a BSS Master or Slave, and can also do IBSS mode. PCMCIA, PCI, and mini-PCI radios are all supported. It is highly recommended that you use a 2.4 Linux or later kernel if you use Host AP. To get started with Host AP, first download the driver at *http://hostap.epitest.fi/*. If you need to run a Hermes-based card (such as the Lucent/Orinoco/Avaya/Proxim), take a look at Hack #61.

Once the driver is unpacked, you simply run a *make* with the name of the driver you want to build: *make pccard* builds the PCMCIA driver, *make plx* builds the non-PCMCIA (plx-based) PCI PC Card driver, and *make pci* builds the standard PCI driver. The hardware-independent driver code is automatically built regardless of the driver you choose. It doesn't hurt to build all of the drivers, unless space is a critical consideration on your system. To install the drivers, run *make install_pccard*, *make install_plx*, or *make install_pci* respectively.

PCMCIA

If you are installing the PCMCIA driver, the make process automatically copies *hostap_cs.conf* to your */etc/pcmcia/* directory, so that your cards will be properly detected when they are inserted. It doesn't hurt to stop and start PCMCIA services once you have installed the Host AP driver. Once installed, the wireless device will be called *wlan0* (and the second is called *wlan1*, etc.).

Setting up radio parameters is very straightforward. If you are using the PCMCIA driver, all of the wireless parameters are set in */etc/pcmcia/wireless.opts*.

Here's an example *wireless.opts* for BSS Master (i.e., Host AP) mode:

```
#
# wireless.opts
#

case "$ADDRESS" in

*,*,*,*)
  INFO="A card in Host AP Master mode"
  ESSID="NoCat"
  MODE="Master"
    CHANNEL="6"
  RATE="auto"
  ;;

esac
```

You may be thinking, "My God, it's full of stars...." But if you have ever worked with *network.opts*, the syntax is exactly the same. If you haven't, those asterisks allow for tremendous flexibility.

The script is passed a string in $ADDRESS that gives details about the card that was inserted, so you can have different entries for different cards. The address matching syntax is:

```
scheme, socket, instance, MAC address)
```

The scheme allows for setting up as many arbitrary profiles as you like. The most common use for schemes is on a client laptop, where you may have different network settings for your office wireless network than for your home network. You can display the current scheme by issuing the cardctl scheme command as root, and change it by using a command like cardctl scheme home or cardctl scheme office. Both *wireless.opts* and *network.opts* are scheme-aware, allowing you to change your network and wireless settings quickly with a single command.

The second parameter, socket, is the socket number that the PCMCIA card was inserted into. Usually, they start with 0 and go up to the number of PCMCIA slots you have available. To find out which is which, insert a card in one slot and issue the cardctl status command.

The third parameter, instance, is used for exotic network cards that have more than one interface. I haven't come across one of these, but if you have a network card that has more than one network device in it, use this to set different parameters for each device, starting with 0.

I find the last parameter very useful, as you can match the setting to a specific MAC address. You can even include wildcards, to match a partial MAC address, like this:

```
*,*,*,00:02:6F:*)
```

This would match a Senao/EnGenius card inserted in any slot, in any scheme. Keep in mind that the *wireless.opts* is only called to set radio parameters. Network settings (such as IP address, default gateway, and whether to use DHCP) are set in *network.opts*, just like any other PCMCIA network device.

One further caveat when using the PCMCIA Host AP driver: some machines (notably the Stylistic 1000) have a problem loading the Host AP driver with some Prism II cards. The symptom is that the card is detected on insert, but mysteriously fails to initialize, reporting an obscure error to the effect of "GetNextTuple: No more items". If you are having trouble with the driver, try adding this line to your *hostap_cs.conf* (replacing any existing module "hostap_cs" line):

```
module "hostap_cs" opts "ignore_cis_vcc=1"
```

Normally, the driver attempts to verify that one entry on the card's acceptable voltage table matches the voltage reported by your PCMCIA slot. In some cases, this voltage can be incorrectly reported, causing the driver to fail to initialize. This option causes the driver to ignore the reported voltage and load anyway. It works like a charm on my Stylistic 1000 with a Senao 200mW card.

PCI

Configuration of a PCI or mini-PCI Prism II card is much the same as any other network device. At some stage, you need to configure the radio parameters manually with calls to *iwconfig*. This is best done in the boot-up process after the kernel modules are all loaded, but before your device configures its IP stack. Simply create an initialization script with a line like this:

```
iwconfig wlan0 essid "NoCat" mode "Master" channel 6 rate "Auto"
```

Copy this script to */etc/init.d/*, and symlink it to an appropriate place in */etc/rc2.d/*, or wherever the appropriate place is for your default run level. Unfortunately, every Linux distribution has a slightly different mechanism for processing the boot up *rc* scripts, so if in doubt, consult your distribution's documentation.

Once your radio parameters are configured, treat the *wlan0* device as if it were any other Ethernet interface. Give it an IP address, set up your routing, and bind processes to its IP as you normally would. The Host AP driver takes care of all of the details of managing your wireless clients for you. If you ever need to change the radio parameters of the card (whether using PCMCIA or PCI), you can always change parameters and view the current status with *iwconfig*:

```
root@pebble:~# iwconfig wlan0
wlan0     IEEE 802.11b  ESSID:"NoCat"
          Mode:Master  Frequency:2.437GHz  Access Point: 00:02:6F:01:85:74
          Bit Rate:11Mb/s   Tx-Power=24 dBm   Sensitivity=1/3
          Retry min limit:8   RTS thr:off   Fragment thr:off
          Encryption key:off
          Power Management:off
          Link Quality:0  Signal level:0  Noise level:0
          Rx invalid nwid:0  Rx invalid crypt:0  Rx invalid frag:0
          Tx excessive retries:0  Invalid misc:0   Missed beacon:0
```

That is all you need to do to bring up a simple Host AP configuration. If you are curious about how to tweak your Host AP to perform more elaborate functions, or about how to monitor its status and that of all of your connected clients, see the other hacks in this section.

Make Host AP a Layer 2 Bridge

Make a simple Ethernet bridge with Host AP and one other network interface.

So far, we have seen how to set up your Host AP machine as a routed or NAT'd network appliance. But what if you want to bridge directly to your Ethernet network or another wireless card?

Bridging is very straightforward to implement. You need a copy of the bridge utilities from *http://bridge.sourceforge.net/*, as well as a kernel with 802.1d Ethernet bridging enabled. The basic procedure for configuring a bridge is to remove any existing IP configuration on the devices you want to bridge, then create a logical bridge device with the interfaces you want to bridge together. Finally, you configure an IP address and routes for the logical bridge device, so you can still use the network from the bridge device itself (as well as access any services provided by the bridge device from the rest of the network).

Suppose we want to bridge a Prism card running Host AP (*wlan0*) with the first Ethernet device (*eth0*). Try this, preferably from the console:

```
pebble:~# ifconfig eth0 0.0.0.0
pebble:~# ifconfig wlan0 0.0.0.0
pebble:~# brctl addbr br0
pebble:~# brctl addif br0 eth0
pebble:~# brctl addif br0 wlan0
pebble:~# ifconfig br0 10.15.6.2
pebble:~# route add default gw 10.15.6.1
```

When you first create the bridge device, it takes a moment or two for the bridge to "learn" the layout of your network. It can take several seconds for traffic to begin to pass through the bridge when first brought up, so don't panic if you don't immediately see traffic.

If you have one bridge only on your network, you can also safely turn off Spanning Tree:

```
pebble:~# brctl stp br0 off
```

This prevents the bridging code from needlessly sending 802.1d negotiation traffic to nonexistent bridges. You can see the configuration of your bridge at any time by using brctl show:

```
pebble:~# brctl show
bridge name     bridge id            STP enabled     interfaces
br0             8000.00026f018574    no              eth0
                                                     wlan0
```

If you are interested in which MACs have been found on the bridge inter-faces, use `brctl showmacs <interface>`:

```
pebble:~# brctl showmacs br0
port no mac addr                is local?      ageing timer
   2    00:02:6f:01:aa:ff       yes               0.00
   1    00:03:93:6c:11:99       no              135.69
   2    00:30:65:03:00:aa       no                0.08
   1    00:40:63:c0:aa:bb       no                0.16
   1    00:a0:24:ab:cd:ef       yes               0.00
```

Generally, bridges are "set and forget" devices. Once configured, your bridge maintains itself, barring a huge amount of traffic or untoward miscreants fiddling with it. Be sure to read the documentation available at *http://bridge.sourceforge.net/,* as well as the documents listed at the end of this hack.

Caveats

Not all network devices allow bridging. Specifically, some radio cards (notably the Lucent/Orinoco/Avaya/Proxim Gold and Silver cards) prohibit Ethernet bridging in the radio firmware. If you need to bridge, I highly recommend upgrading these cards to a Prism card, such as the very popular Senao/EnGenius models. These cards not only allow bridging, but are more powerful and sensitive as well.

Also keep in mind that, as easy as a simple bridge is to configure, it isn't the most secure device on the planet. If you have any interest in controlling the packets that flow across your bridge (and you should), then you will want to implement some firewalling on your bridge. But unfortunately, standard netfilter commands don't work with bridges under Linux 2.4. Be sure to read "Bridging with a Firewall" **[Hack #59]** if you need more control over your bridge.

See Also

- The Linux Bridge STP HOWTO (*http://www.linux.org/docs/ldp/howto/BRIDGE-STP-HOWTO/*)
- The Linux Bridge and Firewall mini HOWTO (*http://www.tldp.org/HOWTO/mini/Bridge+Firewall.html*)

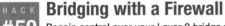

Bridging with a Firewall

#59   Regain control over your Layer 2 bridge with iptables and ebtables.

As we saw in the previous hack **[Hack #58]**, creating an Ethernet-to-wireless bridge is very straightforward. While this allows for very easy integration with your existing network, it isn't always the best decision from a security point of view. Rather than simply connect two networks together at Layer 2, wouldn't it be nice to be able to tightly control the flow of packets between the two networks?

You might think that you could simply use *iptables* to control network access, as you normally would with any other network device. In the experimental Linux 2.5 kernels, this is the case. But when 802.1d bridging is in effect in Linux 2.4, the netfilter code never sees bridged packets. In order to make traffic visible to standard firewall tools, you'll have to patch your kernel.

There are two Linux 2.4 patches available that allow you to manipulate your bridge as a firewall: *ebtables* and *bridge-nf*. The first patch implements *ebtables*, a new packet filter specifically designed for Ethernet bridges. The second provides netfilter functionality for your bridge, so you can manipulate it using *iptables*. Both patches are available at *http://ebtables.sourceforge.net/*. While you're there, be sure to grab a copy of the *ebtables* utilities as well.

If you're running Linux 2.5 or later, you're in luck. Both *ebtables* and *bridge-nf* are now built into the kernel, so you don't have to patch your kernel.

Patching the Linux 2.4 Kernel

Extract a clean copy of Linux 2.4.20, and patch your kernel source by doing the following:

```
rob@florian:/usr/local/src$ tar jvxf ~/linux-2.4.20.tar.bz2
rob@florian:/usr/local/src$ patch -p0 < ~/ebtables-v2.0.003_vs_2.4.20.diff
patching file linux-2.4.20/net/bridge/br_private.h
patching file linux-2.4.20/include/linux/if_bridge.h
patching file linux-2.4.20/net/core/dev.c
...
rob@florian:/usr/local/src$ patch -p0 < ~/bridge-nf-0.0.10-against⏎
-2.4.20.diff
patching file linux-2.4.20/include/linux/netfilter.h
patching file linux-2.4.20/include/linux/netfilter_ipv4.h
patching file linux-2.4.20/include/linux/netfilter_bridge.h
...
rob@florian:/usr/local/src$
```

This assumes that you put your kernel sources in */usr/local/src/*, and that the patches are in your home directory, but feel free to keep your code wherever you like. Now that your kernel source is patched, configure and build your kernel as you normally would. Be sure to include 802.1d Ethernet Bridging (CONFIG_BRIDGE) when you configure it.

Setting Up a Firewall

With your new kernel installed, you can now manipulate the firewall exactly as you would expect using *iptables*. You can also use *ebtables* to do all sorts of interesting things at the MAC layer. For example, to ignore all traffic from a given IP that doesn't match a known MAC address, you could try this:

```
# ebtables -A FORWARD -p IPv4 --ip-src 10.15.6.10 -s ! 00:30:65:FF:AA:BB ↵
-j DROP
```

This prevents other users from "camping" on known IP addresses. While it won't help much with MAC spoofing attacks, this will help keep average users from stepping on other people's IP addresses. You can also use it in reverse to lock a MAC address into a particular IP:

```
# ebtables -A FORWARD -p IPv4 --ip-src ! 10.15.6.10 -s 00:30:65:FF:AA:BB ↵
-j DROP
```

This will prohibit the machine with the specified MAC address from using any IP but 10.15.6.10.

These are just a couple of examples of the power and flexibility of *ebtables*. You can also do all sorts of neat things like MAC redirection and NAT, or filter on protocol types (need to drop all IPv6 traffic? No problem!). For more information, check out the *ebtables* web site as well as man ebtables.

MAC Filtering with Host AP
#60   Filter MAC addresses before they associate with your Host AP.

While you can certainly perform MAC filtering at the link layer using *iptables* or *ebtables* [Hack #59], it is far safer to let Host AP do it for you. This not only blocks traffic that is destined for your network, but also prevents miscreants from even associating with your station. This helps to preclude the possibility that someone could still cause trouble for your other associated wireless clients, even if they don't have further network access.

When using MAC filtering, most people make a list of wireless devices that they wish to allow, and then deny all others. This is done using the iwpriv command.

```
# iwpriv wlan0 addmac 00:30:65:23:17:05
# iwpriv wlan0 addmac 00:40:96:aa:99:fd
  ...
# iwpriv wlan0 maccmd 1
# iwpriv wlan0 maccmd 4
```

The addmac directive adds a MAC address to the internal table. You can add as many MAC addresses as you like to the table by issuing more addmac commands. You then need to tell Host AP what to do with the table you've built. The maccmd 1 command tells Host AP to use the table as an "allowed" list, and to deny all other MAC addresses from associating. Finally, the `maccmd 4` command boots off all associated clients, forcing them to reassociate. This happens automatically for clients listed in the table, but everyone else attempting to associate will be denied.

Sometimes, you only need to ban a troublemaker or two, rather than set an explicit policy of permitted devices. If you need to ban a couple of specific MAC address but allow all others, try this:

```
# iwpriv wlan0 addmac 00:30:65:fa:ca:de
# iwpriv wlan0 maccmd 2
# iwpriv wlan0 kickmac 00:30:65:fa:ca:de
```

As before, you can use `addmac` as many times as you like. The `maccmd 2` command sets the policy to "deny," and `kickmac` boots the specified MAC immediately, if it happens to be associated. This is probably nicer than booting everybody and making them reassociate just to ban one troublemaker. Incidentally, if you'd like to remove MAC filtering altogether, try `maccmd 0`.

If you make a mistake typing in a MAC address, you can use the `delmac` command just as you would `addmac`, and it (predictably) deletes the given MAC address from the table. Should you ever need to flush the current MAC table entirely but keep the current policy, use this command:

```
# iwpriv wlan0 maccmd 3
```

Finally, you can view the running MAC table by using */proc*:

```
# cat /proc/net/hostap/wlan0/ap_control
```

The *iwpriv* program manipulates the running Host AP driver, but doesn't preserve settings across reboots. Once you're happy with your MAC filtering table, be sure to put the relevant commands in an *rc* script to run at boot time.

Note that even unassociated clients can still listen to network traffic, so MAC filtering does very little to prevent eavesdropping. To combat passive listening techniques (like we do with Kismet in Hack #31), you will need to encrypt your data.

HACK #61 Hermes AP

Enable BSS master mode on Hermes-based radios.

Hermes-based radio cards (like the tremendously popular but confusingly named Lucent/Orinoco/Avaya/Proxim silver and gold cards) are notoriously difficult to operate in BSS [Hack #12] master mode. By design, the cards themselves are actually not able to provide BSS master services on their own. You might find this surprising, since they are the radio card embedded in the original AirPort AP, as well as the RG1000, RG1100, AP1000, and many others. Before these cards can operate as a BSS master, they need additional firmware uploaded to the card. This *tertiary firmware* is uploaded to the card's RAM, and is lost if the card loses power. To make matters even more difficult, the firmware in question is licensed software, and can't legally be distributed by anyone but the manufacturer.

The ingenious Hermes AP project (*http://hunz.org/hermesap.html*) addresses both of these tricky issues. It consists of a set of modified drivers, a utility for uploading the tertiary firmware, and a simple script that downloads the firmware from Proxim's public FTP server. Hermes AP isn't trivial to get running, but can be the perfect piece of software if you absolutely need a host-based Orinoco AP.

To get Hermes AP running, you need a kernel with Dev FS enabled. This allows the kernel to manage the */dev* directory, dynamically creating device files for every physical device that the kernel supports. Run a make menuconfig, and select *Code maturity level options → Prompt for development and/or incomplete code/drivers.* Now go back to the main menu, and under *File systems* enable */dev file system support*, as well as *Automatically mount at boot.* When running Dev FS, it's also a good idea to disable */dev/pts file system support,* as Dev FS will automatically manage your ptys for you.

Before you recompile your kernel, copy all of the source code under the *drivers/* directory from Hermes AP over top of the existing drivers in the kernel (right over top of the files in *linux/drivers/net/wireless/*). Now build your kernel and modules as you normally would, and reboot.

Your Orinoco card should come up as usual with the new driver, but won't support BSS Master mode yet. First, cd to the Hermes AP source directory. To download a copy of the tertiary firmware from Proxim's site, run the *hfwget.sh* script in the *firmware/* directory. Next, build the *hfwload* utility by running make in the *hfw/* directory. This utility uploads the tertiary firmware to your card. Copy the utility and the card firmware somewhere handy (I keep mine in */usr/local/hermesap*) and run a command like this at boot time, before the interface comes up:

```
# cd /usr/local/hermesap; ./hfwload eth1 T1085800.hfw
```

Note that the card must not be configured as up when you load the firmware; if it is already up, an ifconfig eth1 down will bring it down for you. If all goes well, an *iwconfig* should show that *eth1* is in Master mode! You can now configure the radio with an ESSID, WEP keys, and any other features as you normally would.

Hermes AP is still beta software, but it seems to run quite well. Personally, I still prefer Host AP and a good Senao/EnGenius card to Hermes AP (as the radio cards are more powerful and sensitive, and Host AP is under active development and sports more fun features) but for some situations, Hermes AP can be ideal.

HACK #62 Microwave Cabling Guide

There are myriad antenna feed cables available. Which is the right one for the job?

Not all coaxial cable is appropriate for 2.4 GHz use. The same piece of cable that delivers high quality video and audio to your TV is nearly useless for connecting microwave antennas. Choosing the proper type and length of cable is just as important as choosing the right antenna for the job. A 12 db sector antenna is useless if you lose 18 db in the cable that connects it to the radio. While all cable introduces some loss as signal travels through it, some types of cable do better than others at 2.4 GHz.

LMR is a kind of coax cable made by Times Microwave, and is possibly the most popular type of cable used for extending 802.11b networks. LMR uses a braided outer shield and solid center conductor, and comes in various sizes.

Heliax is another kind of microwave cabling made by Andrew. It is made of a semi-rigid corrugated outer shell (a sort of flexible copper tubing), rather than the braided strands found in coax. The center conductor can either be solid or a corrugated tube inner conductor. It is designed to handle loads MUCH greater than (legal) 802.11b installations, is very expensive, and can be difficult to work with. It is also extremely low loss. The foam dielectric type part numbers start with LDF.

Don't mess with air dielectric unless you enjoy the challenge of keeping your feed lines pressurized with nitrogen. Air dielectric cable at 802.11b power levels is like the proverbial elephant gun to kill the mosquito.

In addition to Times Microwave and Andrew's offerings, Belden also makes a very common piece of cable that works okay in the 2.4 GHz range. You'll frequently see references to "9913"; this is Belden 9913.

The properties of some common cables are provided in Table 4-1. Generally speaking, the thicker and better built the cable, the lower the loss (and the higher the cost). Cable in excess of half an inch or so in thickness is difficult to work with, and it can be hard to find connectors for it. Whenever possible, order the specific length you need, with the proper connectors preinstalled, rather than try to cut and crimp it yourself. A commercial outlet will usually have the tools and experience needed to make a well-built cable. The best cable in the world won't help you if your connector isn't properly installed.

Table 4-1. Attenuation, size, and approximate cost of microwave coax

Cable type	Diameter	Loss in db/100' at 2,500 MHz	Approximate price per foot
LMR-200	0.195"	16.9	$0.37
LMR-400	0.405"	6.8	$0.64
LMR-600	0.509"	4.4	$1.30
LMR-900	0.870"	3.0	$3.70
LMR-1200	1.200"	2.3	$5.50
Belden 9913	0.405"	8.2	$0.97
LDF1-50	0.250"	6.1	$1.66
LDF4-50A	0.500"	3.9	$3.91
LDF5-50A	0.875"	2.3	$2.27
LDF6-50	1.250"	1.7	$10.94
LDF7-50A	1.625"	1.4	$15.76

To sum up: use the best quality cable you can afford, at the shortest length possible. A couple of dB here and there really adds up when dealing with the very low power levels of 802.11b. If you want to put an antenna on the roof, you might look into weatherproof enclosures for your AP, and mount it as close to the antenna as possible. Then run your Ethernet cable as long as you need (up to 100 meters!)

HACK #63 Microwave Connector Reference

Be able to tell one microwave connector from another with this field reference.

So you have the radio, an antenna, and a length of cable. How do you connect them together? You need to use connectors that work well in the 2.4 GHz range, fit the kind of cabling you're using, and mate with each other. Practically all common connectors have two halves, a male and a female (or a pin and a socket). A few of the more exotic types (such as the APC-7; see later in this section) are sexless, so any connector will match up with any other. Here are the most common connectors you are likely to encounter in the microwave bestiary.

The BNC (Figure 4-16) is a small, cheap connector using a quick-connect half turn (the same connector found on 10base2 Ethernet). The BNC isn't well suited for 2.4 GHz use, but is mentioned here because, with the death of 10base2, the connectors are frequently sold for pennies per pound. Don't be tempted.

Figure 4-16. BNC is the "Bayonet Neill Concelman" connector.

The TNC (Figure 4-17) is a threaded version of the BNC. The fine threads help eliminate leakage at microwave frequencies. TNCs work well all the way through 12 GHz, and are usually used with smaller (and higher-loss) cable.

Figure 4-17. TNC is a threaded BNC.

An N connector (Figure 4-18) is a larger, threaded connector found on many commercial 2.4 GHz antennas. It is much larger than the TNC. It works very well on thicker cable (such as LMR-400) and operates well up to 10 GHz. The N is probably the most commonly encountered connector when dealing with 802.11b-compatible gear.

The connector commonly referred to as a "UHF" connector looks like a coarse-thread version of the N (Figure 4-19). It's not usable for 2.4 GHz, but is sometimes confused with the N. According to the ARRL Microwave manual, it's a PL-259 (which mates with the SO-239 socket). It's not designed to work at microwave frequencies. Avoid.

Figure 4-18. N is Neill's connector.

Figure 4-19. The so-called "UHF" connector.

SMA connectors (Figure 4-20) are very popular, small, threaded connectors that work great through 18 GHz. Their small size precludes using them with large, low-loss cable without using a pigtail.

The SMB (Figure 4-21) is a quick-connect version of the SMC.

The SMC (Figure 4-22) is a very small version of the SMA. It is designed to work well through 10 GHz, but accepts only very small cables.

The APC-7 (as seen in Figure 4-23) is a 7mm-sexless connector, usable through 18 GHz. It is a high grade connector manufactured by Amphenol, and is expensive, fairly rare, and very low loss.

Remember that each connector in the system introduces some loss. Avoid adapters and unnecessary connectors whenever possible. Also, commercially built cables tend to be of higher quality than cables you terminate yourself (unless you're really good and have the right tools.) Whenever possible, try to buy a pre-made cable with the proper connectors already

Figure 4-20. SMA is the Sub-Miniature connector, variation A.

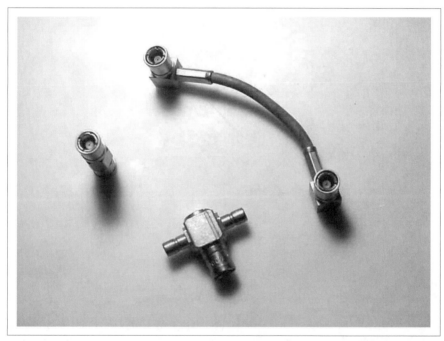

Figure 4-21. SMB is the Sub-Miniature connector, variation B.

attached, at the shortest length you can stand. 802.11b gear doesn't put out much power, and every little bit helps extend your range and reliability. It's very easy to make a bad cable, and bad cables can cause no end of trouble.

When matching cables to your equipment, you may encounter connectors of reverse gender (sometimes called "reverse polarity," or male and female

Figure 4-22. SMC is the Sub-Miniature connector, variation C (tiny!).

Figure 4-23. APC-7, or Amphenol Precision Connector, 7mm.

ends swapped with the same threads), reverse threading (lefthand instead of righthand thread), or even reverse gender reverse threading (both). For example, the popular WAP11 uses an RP-TNC. Make sure you know what you're getting before you order parts online!

Antenna Guide

How do you know which antenna is the best for the job? This guide will explain.

The single most effective way to extend the range of your access point or client radio is to add an external antenna. Contrary to popular belief, antennas do *not* give you more signal than you started with (that's what amplifiers are for). They focus the available signal in a particular direction, much like what happens when you turn the focus head of a flashlight. It doesn't make the bulb any brighter, it just focuses what you have into a tighter space. Focusing a flashlight gives you a brighter beam that covers a smaller total area, and likewise, more directional antennas give you a stronger perceived signal in a smaller area. All antennas are somewhat directional, and the measure of their directionality is referred to as *gain*. Typically, the higher the gain, the better the range (in the direction that the antenna radiates best in).

Another important characteristic of antennas is the phenomenon of polarization [Hack #84].

There are a few general types of antennas suitable for use at microwave frequencies. Each works well for its own application, and no single antenna works best for every application. When actually shopping for antennas, be sure to look at the actual radiation pattern of your antenna to be sure that it fits your needs.

Plan your goals ahead of time, and configure your network to meet those goals. The following sections describe the most common types of antennas, listed in rough order of increasing gain.

Omni

Omnidirectional antennas (or *omnis*) radiate outward in horizontal directions in roughly an equal manner. Imagine putting an enormous donut around the center pole of an omni: that's what the radiation pattern looks like. Omnis are good for covering a large area when you don't know which direction your clients might come from. The downside is that they also receive noise from every direction, and so typically aren't as efficient as more directional antennas.

As you can see in Figure 4-24, they look like tall, thin poles (anywhere from a few inches to several feet long), and tend to be expensive. The longer they are, the more elements they have (and usually the more gain and the higher the price.) Small "rubber ducky" antennas ship standard with many access points, such as the Linksys WAP11 or the Cisco 350. Omni antennas are mounted vertically, like a popsicle stick reaching skyward. They gain in the

HACK
#64   **Antenna Guide**

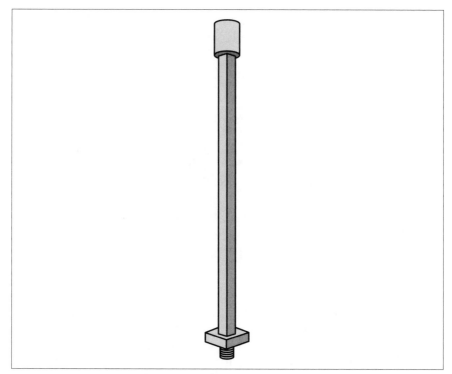

Figure 4-24. Omnis range from tiny extenders to tall, building-mounted poles.

horizontal, at the expense of the vertical. This means that the worst place to be in relation to an omni is directly beneath (or above) it. The vertical response improves dramatically as you move away from the antenna.

Sector (or Sectoral)

Sectors antennas come in a variety of packages, from flattened omnis (tall, thin, and rectangular) to small flat squares or circles (Figure 4-25). A close cousin of the sector is the *patch* antenna, which shares most of the same properties. Some are only a few inches across, and mount flat against a vertical wall or on a swivel mount. They can also be ceiling mounted to provide access to a single room, such as a meeting room, classroom, or tradeshow floor. As with omnis, cost is usually proportional to gain.

Picture an omni with a mirror behind it, and you'll have the radiation pattern of a sector antenna. Sectors radiate best in one direction, with a beam as wide as 180 degrees or as narrow as you like. They excel in point-to-multipoint applications, where several clients will be accessing the wireless network, all coming from the same general direction.

Figure 4-25. Sector antennas tend to be flat and thin.

Yagi

As you can see in Figure 4-26, a *yagi* looks something like an old television aerial. Some yagis are simply bare, like a flat Christmas tree, and are pointed vaguely in the direction of communications. Others are mounted in long horizontal PVC cans. They can work well in point-to-point or point-to-multipoint applications, and can usually achieve higher gain than sectors.

The typical beam width can vary from 15 degrees to as much as 60, depending on the type of antenna. As with omnis, adding more elements means more gain, a longer antenna, and higher cost.

Waveguides and "Cantennas"

An increasingly popular antenna design is the waveguide. The so-called "cantennas" are simple antennas for home-brew designers to build, which offer very high gain for relatively little effort. Waveguides most closely

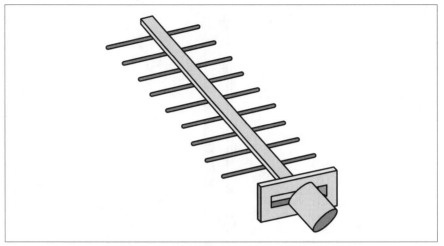

Figure 4-26. Yagis come in various shapes, but all have multiple elements.

resemble plumbing, in that they are boxes or cans with nothing in them but
a tiny radiator. Figure 4-27 shows an ambitious design, made from extruded
and milled aluminum.

Figure 4-27. A 16dBi, horizontally polarized waveguide that acts like an omni.

The Pringles can and coffee can antennas are examples of simple (but effective) home-brew cylindrical waveguide antennas. A rectangular waveguide

can behave like a sector or an omni, depending on how it is constructed. We will look at these antennas in detail in Chapter 5.

Parabolic Dish

In some ways, a dish is the opposite of an omni. Rather than try to cover a wide area, a dish focuses on a very tight space. Dishes typically have the highest gain and most directionality of any antenna. They are ideal for a point-to-point link, and nearly useless for anything else.

Figure 4-28 shows a mesh antenna, although solid variations exist. Dishes come as small as 18" across or as big as you like (a 30-foot dish is possible, but probably not very convenient). A dish that can send an 802.11b signal more than 20 miles can be as small as a few feet across. In terms of gain for the buck, dishes are probably the cheapest type of antenna. Some people have been successful in converting old satellite and DSS dishes into 2.4 GHz dishes; see Chapter 5 for two of these designs. Generally speaking, the difference between a mesh reflector and a solid reflector has little to do with gain, but is a consideration when mounting your dish, as solid dishes tend to pick up more load from the wind.

Figure 4-28. A 24 dBi parabolic dish.

Putting It All Together

When trying to estimate what antennas will be required for a particular installation, I find it helpful to draw an overhead picture of the project site. Sketch out where you intend to install your equipment and where you expect your network clients to come from. Also include any obstacles (such as walls containing metal, or intervening buildings and trees on a long distance shot.) This should help to determine your desired coverage area, as well as help suggest optimal placement of your access points and antennas.

For example, if you are trying to cover a large office with obstacles in the center (such as an elevator shaft or bathrooms), access points at opposite ends of the room with sector antennas pointed inward might make more sense than a single AP in the center with an omni. On a long distance shot, it might make more sense to go around an intervening tree or building by adding an extra hop, rather than trying to shoot through it with high gain dishes. Knowing the approximate radiation pattern and gain of your antennas ahead of time will help to focus your energy in the direction that you intend to use it, so you can design the most efficient network possible.

HACK #65   Client Capability Reference Chart

A quick guide to what's what in the world of consumer wireless gear.

Wi-Fi has decidedly shifted from a niche market to a mass market in just a little over a year. As a result, there is a bewildering assortment of wireless equipment available on the market. While the various descriptions will dazzle you with the latest bells, whistles, and didgeridoos, most wireless hackery requires only the answer to a few key questions: How much does it cost? How much power does it put out? How sensitive is the radio? What other equipment will it communicate with?

Unfortunately, the answer to the first question ("How much does it cost?") is changing so rapidly that by the time this book makes it to press, anything I included here would be irrelevant. While new hardware is being introduced all the time, the specifications of existing hardware remain relatively unchanged. Table 4-2 shows the vital statistics of many popular radio cards.

For brevity, the table's Receive Sensitivity column uses the following convention: the numbers are the power levels required (in dBm) to receive data at 11 Mbps, 5.5 Mbps, 2 Mbps, and 1 Mbps respectively. Remember that these are negative numbers, so, for example, a rating of –94 is much more sensitive than a rating of –87 (by a whopping 7 dB!) A "*" means that the rating for that speed is unavailable.

Table 4-2. Common wireless client capabilities matrix

Name	Interface	Tx power	Rx sensitivity	Antenna connector	Chipset
3Com AirConnect	PCMCIA	30mW	-81 / -84 / -85 / -87	Dual MMCX	Prism 2.5
Addtron AWP-100	PCMCIA	20mW	-76 / * / * / -80	None	Prism
Cisco 340 (AIR-LMC340)	PCMCIA	30mW	-83/-87/-88/-90	Dual MMCX	Aironet
Cisco 350 (AIR-LMC350)	PCMCIA	100mW	-85/-89/-91/-94	Dual MMCX	Aironet
D-Link DWL-520	PCI	30mW	-80/-83/-86/-89	Reverse SMA	Prism
D-Link DWL-650	PCMCIA	30mW	-84/-87/*/-90	None	Prism 2
D-Link DWL-650+ (proprietary 22Mb)	CardBus	30mW	unpublished?	None	TI
EnGenius/ Senao/NetGate (2511 Plus EXT2)	PCMCIA	200mW	-89/-91/-93/-95	Dual MMCX	Prism 2.5
EnGenius/ Senao/NetGate (2011CD)	PCMCIA	100mW	-87/-89/-91/-93	Dual MMCX	Prism 2.5
Linksys WPC11	PCMCIA	25mW	-76/*/*/-80	None	Prism 2
Linksys WMP11	PCI	30mW	-82/*/*/*	Reverse SMA	Prism 2
NetGear MA101	USB	20mW	-84/-87/-89/-91	None	n/a
NetGear MA401	PCMCIA	30mW	*/*/*/*	None	Prism 2
Orinoco (Silver or Gold)	PCMCIA	30mW	-82/-87/-91/-94	Lucent	Hermes
ZcomMax (XI-325H)	PCMCIA	100mW	-92/*/*/-85	MMCX	Prism 2.5

Note that some client cards use minor variations under the same trade name. For example, the Cisco Aironet series can come with or without external antenna connectors. Units with AIR-PCM model numbers have permanent molded antenna connectors, while AIR-LMC models have external connectors with no internal antenna. Likewise, some manufacturers offer cards with different transmit power under similar names, but that have different model numbers. Be sure to check your model numbers before purchasing!

There is an interactive hardware capability chart available from Seattle-Wireless (*http://seattlewireless.net/index.cgi/HardwareComparison*). This chart is generally kept up to date as new equipment appears on the market, and can be particularly handy, since some manufacturers bury the technical details of their products in the back of the manual (if they publish them at all). If you have a piece of hardware that isn't listed, you can add it to the list yourself, and save other people the effort of digging around for the real specs.

Pigtails

#66   Use a short length of feed line to connect your wireless device to an antenna.

While some wireless equipment has no external antenna connector available at all, many devices ship with a tiny, non-standard port to accommodate an external antenna. Most antennas use a standard microwave connector [Hack #63]. Typically, to connect one to the other, you need a short length of cable with one of each sort of connector. This connector is commonly referred to as a *pigtail* adapter. A pigtail in all its glory is depicted in Figure 4-29.

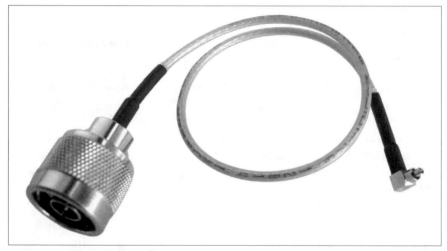

Figure 4-29. A Lucent pigtail with an N male end.

Pigtails are available from a number of sources. They typically sell for $10 to $20, depending on the length and type of cable, and what connectors you need on each end. Be sure that you know what sort of connector [Hack #65] you need on the card side as well as on the antenna side. Most 802.11 manufacturers will also sell you a pigtail adapter for a phenomenally inflated price ($80 to $100 or more, for virtually the same piece of cable).

Pigtails have extremely high loss compared to a larger cable (such as LMR400), and usually use a cable such as LMR100 or LMR195. It is generally a good idea to keep your pigtail lengths as short as possible, and run larger, lower-loss cable for the bulk of your antenna run. Be sure to observe the type of connector, as well as the gender (male or female) that you need for either end. Adapters and gender changers can help in a pinch, but remember that excessive adapters will add unnecessary loss to your overall system.

The client card end of a pigtail is typically available in straight or right-angle versions. Both connectors have identical loss, but the best choice depends on the physical layout of your equipment. Most times, a right-angle connector is preferred, but depending on how your cable needs to run, a straight connector may work better. Also remember that the small end of the pigtail is very fragile, and will snap easily if pulled or forced into the connector. Use care when installing or removing pigtails, and whenever possible, tie off the cable to help eliminate cable stress on the connector. It is common to use a nylon zip tie to fasten the cable to the card itself, the chassis, or another stationary part.

When you are sure of the sort of pigtail you need for your application, consult the list of hardware vendors [Hack #67].

802.11 Hardware Suppliers
#67
Where to get hard-to-find parts and supplies.

Generally speaking, the typical consumer channels are great for obtaining radios, access points, and routers. But external antennas, adapters, pigtails, and cable can be harder to come by. On their quest for long-distance networking, many people find themselves dealing with general-purpose radio suppliers who have a great deal of knowledge about microwave gear, but very little experience with 802.11 devices.

Here is a list of popular suppliers for 802.11-related equipment. Among these vendors, you will find virtually everything you need for long-distance networking, from antennas and feed line to outdoor enclosures and weatherproofing supplies. Many of them will build cables to custom lengths with whatever connectors you require, for a reasonable fee. They offer a nice selection of various 802.11-specific equipment, as well as general-purpose radio gear. These vendors are listed for reference only, and shouldn't be interpreted as an endorsement by either myself or O'Reilly.

- Aeralix, Peabody, MA (*http://www.aerialix.com*)
- Antenna Systems and Supplies, Schaumburg, IL (*http://www. antennasystems.com*)

- Down East Microwave, Frenchtown, NJ (*http://www.downeastmicrowave. com*)
- ElectroComm, Denver, CO (*http://www.ecommwireless.com*)
- FAB Corp, Tampa Bay, FL (*http://www.fab-corp.com*)
- HD Communications, Ronkonkoma, NY (*http://www.hdcom.com*)
- Hyperlink Tech, Boca Raton, FL (*http://www.hyperlinktech.com*)
- NetGate, Spokane, WA (*http://www.netgate.com*)
- NetNimble, Sacramento, CA (*http://www.netnimble.net*)
- Pasadena Networks, Pasadena, CA (*http://www.pasadena.net*)
- Superpass, Waterloo, Ontario, Canada (*http://www.superpass.com*)
- The RF Connection, Gaithersburg, MD (*http://www.therfc.com*)

With competition in the 802.11 market heating up, combined with the often confusing intricacies of wireless networking specifications, many vendors are realizing the importance of customer service. A good vendor should provide a great deal of information about their products online, and be willing to answer questions about your particular application.

Home-Brew Power over Ethernet

H A C K #68

Power your access point without running a separate power cable by using free pairs on the CAT5.

A number of access point manufacturers (Lucent, Symbol, and D-Link, to name three) are now offering Power over Ethernet (PoE) add-ons for their access points. A PoE module inserts DC voltage into the unused wires in a standard Ethernet cable (pairs 7–8 and 4–5). The idea is to supply the AP's power and UTP Ethernet connectivity requirements via a single Ethernet cable. This works great in areas where you may not have power easily accessible, such as a roof. This also allows you to more easily place the AP closer to the antenna, thus reducing signal loss over antenna cabling. Ethernet signal travels well over CAT5 cable; a 2.4 GHz signal doesn't do as well over antenna cabling. Also, Ethernet cabling is much cheaper than antenna cable such as LMR400. The following hack demonstrates how to build a simple PoE module pair.

> Don't try this unless you have some knowledge of electricity. 12v isn't going to kill you, but you may cause serious damage to your access point and other equipment. Don't blame me if something goes wrong. I'm not an electrical engineering major, I'm just a networking guy who wanted cheap PoE modules, and decided to write about how I did it.

Step by Step

1. Solder wires to the DC Male Power Plug. Solder one pair (two wires twisted together) to the inner-contact connection. These will be the positive power wires. Solder another pair to the outer-contact connection. Notice that on this DC Male Power Plug, there are three connectors. One is for the center pin, one is for the outer surface, and one goes to the plug-housing. You do not need to solder anything to the plug-housing connector. Figure 4-30 shows what it should look like when finished.

Figure 4-30. The completed power plug.

2. Drill a hole in your two-port mount housing. Mount the Male DC plug in the housing, as shown in Figure 4-31.

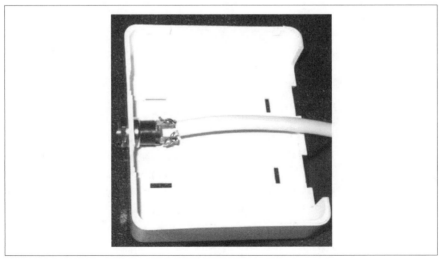

Figure 4-31. The DC plug is mounted in the housing.

3. Connect the wires in your two-port jack as follows (note that this is the Intel Symbol, Orinoco Standard, *not* the Cisco standard for wiring):

Input jack		Output jack		DC plug
Pin 1	<->	Pin 1		
Pin 2	<->	Pin 2		
Pin 3	<->	Pin 3		
		Pin 4	<->	DC Positive Wire 1 → Center Connector
		Pin 5	<->	DC Positive Wire 2 → Center Connector
Pin 6	<->	Pin 6		
		Pin 7	<->	DC Negative Wire 1 → Outer Connector
		Pin 8	<->	DC Negative Wire 2 → Outer Connector

4. Wire the one port wall mount jack as follows:

Output plug		Inputjack		DC plug
Pin 1	<->	Pin 1		
Pin 2	<->	Pin 2		
Pin 3	<->	Pin 3		
		Pin 4	<->	DC Positive Wire 1 → Center Connector
		Pin 5	<->	DC Positive Wire 2 → Center Connector
Pin 6	<->	Pin 6		
		Pin 7	<->	DC Negative Wire 1 → Outer Connector
		Pin 8	<->	DC Negative Wire 2 → Outer Connector

5. Plug in and test. The completed modules are shown in Figure 4-32.

The DC resistance of Cat5 is about 3 ohms per 100 feet per conductor, so a 250-foot cable has at least 7 ohms resistance. Most of the time, the APs draw much less than 0.8A, so you would still be above 6V at the AP. In fact, the access points typically use linear regulators to drop the voltage down to 5V on their insides, so as long as you're giving them something better than 6V at the terminals, they're likely to work.

There is a good calculator online at *http://www.gweep.net/~sfoskett/tech/poecalc.html* that calculates the voltage drop for a given length of CAT5. Use it to estimate how much power you need to provide at one end of your cable run in order to power your access point.

—*Terry Schmidt*

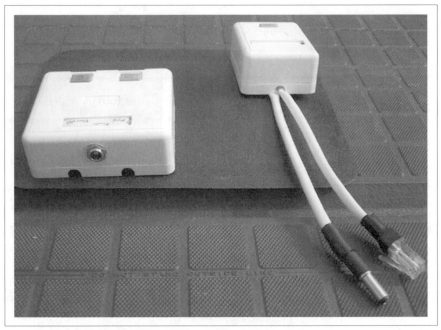

Figure 4-32. The completed PoE modules.

Cheap but Effective Roof Mounts

Install wireless gear on your flat roof without piercing it with mounting hardware.

If you intend to make a long distance wireless link, you will likely need to get your antennas up as high as they can comfortably go. For many people, adding a dedicated tower is out of the question (for aesthetic and local ordinance reasons), so the next logical place for gear is the rooftop.

Ideally, the equipment should be installed in such a way that it doesn't pierce the roof of the building, lest the rainy season come and bring expensive roof repair bills with it. If you are working with a flat roof, you may find it useful to build a small "sled" on which to mount your gear. Figure 4-33 shows a typical plywood sled with a 24 dBi dish mounted on it.

It consists of a piece of plywood that is a few feet square around with sections of 2×4 screwed to it from above. This gets the wood slightly up and off of the roof's surface to allow rainwater to flow past as it normally would. The sled is weighed down with cinder blocks, and has a cheap aluminum tripod mount (found at Radio Shack) bolted to it. Figure 4-34 shows a detail of the "experimental" equipment housing.

Figure 4-33. A simple piece of plywood, raised with a couple of 2x4s and held down with cinder blocks.

In this installation, cost was one of the primary concerns. The owner had a Stylistic 1000 that needed housing, and the cheapest deal we could find at the time was a rubberized mailbox (just a couple of dollars at the hardware store). When closed, the mailbox is practically water tight, but unfortunately, it has a matte black finish, which would likely soak up the sun and overheat the electronics inside. This was mitigated by wrapping the box in a cheap mylar windshield reflector, which keeps the inside of the box surprisingly cool, even on hot summer days. Note that the Stylistic has no ventilation requirements, so an airtight box was an ideal choice. The cables were

Figure 4-34. This rubber mailbox has a 1-year uptime, and is still going strong!

run through a hole cut in the side of the mailbox that was then filled in with Silicone compound.

This choice of mounting hardware may sound ridiculous, but you can't argue with this node's uptime: one year and counting! Granted, this is in Northern California, where the winters are quite mild, and the summers aren't usually too hot. But then again, this node isn't even running on a Compact Flash card, but instead uses an 8-year-old PCMCIA hard drive (found installed in the Stylistic when purchased from the local surplus electronics store). We originally installed it just to see how long such a setup would last, and were pleasantly surprised at the results. The only downtime this node has suffered has been to upgrade the radio card.

The other end of the link isn't on a flat roof, so we couldn't use a sled. Fortunately, there was plenty of signal available at the pitched edge of the roof, allowing us to use a recycled DSS dish mount. You can see it in action in Figure 4-35.

By adding a short piece of pipe, the DSS dish mount was extended enough to accommodate another 24 dBi dish. The metal box beneath the eaves is a $10 metal sprinkler box with an Orinoco RG-1100 installed in it. By bolting directly to wooden studs, we avoided piercing the tar paper on the roof. The

Figure 4-35. A recycled DSS mount and a short length of pipe made an ideal dish mount.

two white lines running to the box are Ethernet and power for the RG-1100. The owner had a considerable amount of Ethernet cable on hand, and decided to run the data separate from power, rather than bother with full-blown PoE **[Hack #68]**. These cables were later tacked back and run under the eaves, and were virtually invisible from the ground.

Another approach is to avoid the use of plywood altogether, and simply make a base out of wide wooden planks (as in Figure 4-36). These can be weighed down with sandbags, and the pole steadied with guy wires if necessary. These materials can be easier to get up on a roof than a sheet of plywood, and won't have as much potential wind load. If you're curious about the white antenna feed line in the photo, yes, it is in fact Heliax. The omni and yagi terminate in a metal sprinkler box (screwed to one of the boards), which contains a Soekris net4511 **[Hack #51]**. The Soekris is fed Ethernet and power over a piece of outdoor CAT5, which enters the building through a skylight. The 12-dBi yagi feeds a link to another part of town a couple of miles away, and the 9-dBi omni provides local service.

Roof mounts don't necessarily need to be elaborate. Antennas for 2.4-GHz gear tend to be small and have little wind load, allowing you to get away with surprisingly little for structural support. Whenever working on roofs,

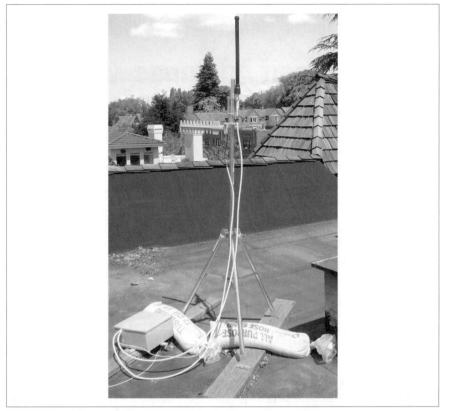

Figure 4-36. A simpler sled design, using two boards and another aluminum tripod.

remember to take your time, bring a friend, and work only in good weather when you have plenty of daylight. Building your own rooftop node can be very exciting, but remember that roofs can be dangerous places, no matter how many times you have been up on them.

## CHAPTER FIVE

Do-It-Yourself Antennas
Hacks #70–79

The price of wireless networking hardware has fallen dramatically in a very short time. Wireless adapters now come standard with many computers, and access points are commonplace. Even the price of antennas and related components has fallen sharply as high demand and extreme competition have driven the industry to an increasingly high-volume, low-margin business.

But this hasn't stopped people from experimenting with finding out just how little it takes to build a working network. There is something almost magical about radio networking. Tales of war driving (and even war walking) aside, just imagine that today in many cities around the world, dozens of invisible networks exist on any given street corner. As you sit at a cafe eating your lunch, you may be completely unaware of the dozens of people simultaneously using the environment around you to communicate with people around the world. I believe that it is largely this mysterious, intangible aspect of unseen global communications that draws people to embark on their own antenna projects. The deeply rewarding feeling of making something useful out of virtually nothing is worth much more than saving a few dollars on a network component.

When comparing antenna designs, there are a number of important factors to keep in mind. The first antenna property that people usually refer to is *gain*. The gain of an antenna is a measurement of how well it radiates in the direction you intend it to, measured in decibels. This measurement is actually the antenna's performance as compared to an imaginary invention called an *isotropic radiator* (this is the *i* in dBi). Imagine an infinitely small light suspended in the vacuum of space. It radiates light equally in all directions, and by definition has no gain in any direction. Now take this light and place it in the head of a flashlight. Without increasing the brightness of the bulb, you can turn the head of the flashlight to focus its beam in a particular direction. This is gain. By directing the energy in a particular direction, you both make the light cover a smaller area, and appear to be brighter in the area it does cover. The higher the gain, the tighter and brighter the beam appears to be. Also note that antenna gain is *reciprocal*, meaning that it works for both transmit and receive. Adding an antenna to either end of a radio link will help performance for both ends of the link.

Another important property to keep in mind when designing or purchasing an antenna is that it must be tuned to the frequency for which you are using it. An antenna that is well matched to the radio it is connected to is said to have a low *Standing Wave Ratio*, or SWR. The SWR of an antenna is measured using an SWR meter or reflectometer. It is a measurement of how much energy actually leaves the antenna versus how much energy is reflected back at the radio from the antenna itself. At (legal) 802.11-power levels, a badly mismatched antenna with a high SWR simply results in poor performance. At higher power levels, a mismatched SWR can actually damage your radio or amplifier. As we will see in the antenna designs in this chapter, the antenna is tuned by manipulating a number of factors, including the size of various active components, and their relative distance away from reflective components.

One property of antennas that is frequently overlooked by beginners is their *front-to-back ratio*. This is a measurement of how much energy radiates in the expected direction (at the center of the strongest beam) versus the average amount of energy radiated in the opposite direction. A high front-to-back (or F/B) ratio means that most of the energy goes in the direction that the antenna is pointed. A low F/B ratio means that more energy is lost in the reverse direction, potentially causing unwanted interference with nearby devices. This is particularly important if you are using two or more antennas adjacent to each other, pointed in different directions. A higher F/B means that it is less likely that adjacent antennas will interfere with each other.

Finally, one last important property of antennas to keep in mind is their *polarization*. Briefly, this refers to the orientation of the electrical and magnetic parts of the radio wave as they leave the antenna. Polarization is discussed in greater detail in "Taking Advantage of Antenna Polarization" [Hack #84]. There is also a comparison of the various general types of antennas and their typical uses in "Antenna Guide" [Hack #64].

The following hacks describe a number of inexpensive, highly effective antenna designs that you might find useful for your own wireless networking project.

HACK #70 Deep Dish Cylindrical Parabolic Reflector

This simple design provides high gain without pigtails or modifying your AP.

I needed a parabolic reflector to eliminate off-property coverage. This design can reduce signal from some areas while enhancing signal in other areas. I designed this reflector to be installed in outdoor enclosures with WAP-11 access points, but it is becoming quite popular with people building indoor LANs, as well as with people building very short point-to-point links. This design offers very high performance and easy availability (scissors, tape, cardboard, tin foil, and 20 minutes, and you are in business). See it in action in Figure 5-1.

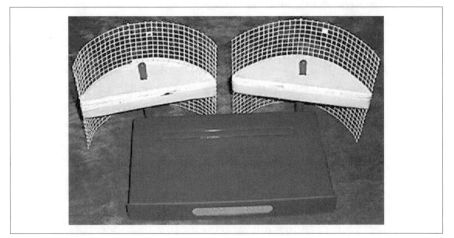

Figure 5-1. Add a reflector without modifying the AP.

This antenna is so easy to make, tune, and install, and it performs so well, that it is foolish not to try one before electing to purchase a commercial antenna, if for no other reason than you can check to see whether you are purchasing enough commercial antenna gain to make the link you want to make.

Advantages over other antennas:

- No pigtail [Hack #66] required
- No modification to AP (no voiding of warranty)
- No matching (SWR) problems
- No purchased parts
- Trivially easy construction
- Very low probability of error
- As good as or better performance than the Pringles can antenna [Hack #72]

- Superior front-to-back/front-to-rear ratio
- Improves wireless LAN privacy
- Reduces interference

This design can easily complete links up to one kilometer by sitting two WAP-11s in windows at each end of a link with clean line of sight. The 6-inch version of the antenna gives you about 10 to 12 dB of gain over the stock antenna. With a WAP11, this equates to approximately 27 to 33 dB of *Effective Isotropically Radiated Power* (EIRP). This means you wind up with an apparent power in the favored direction between 500 mw and 2 Watts.

Of course, that gain has to come from somewhere. It comes from the back side of the reflector, so power that is normally transmitted in that direction is "bounced" forward. That feature of this antenna can be used to enhance the privacy of your wireless network, which was my reason for designing it in the first place. The rest is just gravy (but it is very real and rather tasty gravy). The approximate radiation pattern of a 9-inch reflector is shown in Figure 5-2.

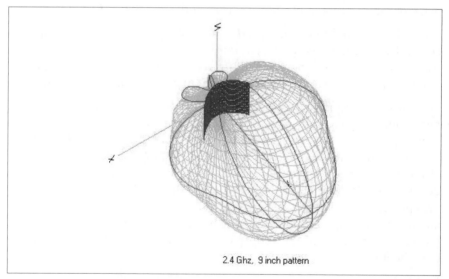

2.4 Ghz, 9 inch pattern

Figure 5-2. Approximate radiation patter for a 9" reflector.

To build this reflector, you can use the sample template in the Appendix, or download the original reflector template from *http://www.freeantennas.com/projects/template/parabolic.pdf*. The drawing can be scaled using a copy machine to make a dish of any reasonable size. The gain computations for various sizes of the dish are also provided on the web site, as well as rough graphs showing beam width and gain/frequency. This reflector is frequency independent, meaning it works with any wireless gear, on any band.

There is a square drawn upon the diagram. It will help you to ensure that your scaling does not corrupt the aspect ratio of the template. In other words, if the square is still square after you enlarge or reduce the template, you still have a good template.

Focal length varies proportionally with the size of the dish, so the focal point is also shown in the drawings. Positioning of the feed point (focal point) is the most critical aspect of a deep dish parabolic. Errors of 1/4" or more are unacceptable at these frequencies. It may help to "fiddle" with the positioning as small irregularities (~1/4" or greater) will move the focal point slightly. If the dipole is not in the focal point, you will lose gain. Parabolic reflectors also lose gain if your finished reflector varies much from the correct curve.

The reflector is designed to be fed by a dipole, which is why it is not circular. A dipole is long and cylindrical, while the focal point on a circular dish is circular. The focal point on this design is a cylinder. Many access points (such as the WAP-11) use one or more dipoles as their antenna. This reflector is the optimal shape for such an antenna. Some units, such as the WET-11, do *not* use dipoles as their antenna. You can download a modified template for the WET-11 at the address listed at the end of this hack.

The reflector should be made from a piece of square material to shape the curve. If you need to reduce height for packaging reasons, a shorter antenna will work but will lose roughly 3 dB for each halving of reflector height. It is also important to try to get the dipole lined up in the center of the reflector.

Front-to-back ratio is a measurement of how well a directional antenna rejects interference from directions other than the desired direction. The front-to-back ratio with this antenna depends upon the size of the wire mesh you use to make the antenna. Finer mesh yields only slightly better gain but yields much better front-to-back ratio. Modeling shows the F/B ratio to be better than ~25 dB if you use 1/4" or smaller mesh. My calculated gain figures presume the reflector is 55 percent efficient. If you use a solid sheet of aluminum or copper as your reflector, your gain figures may be a little bit higher than these. The radiation pattern is narrower in the vertical plane than the horizontal plane.

People have made good reflectors from Pringles cans, large tin cans, wire screen, aluminum sheet, and tin roofing material. Any flat metal surface or screen, such as tinfoil taped to cardboard, will work. You can build one of these in less than a half an hour using an old shoe box and a roll of tin foil.

The original article that this Hack is based on is available online at *http://www.freeantennas.com/projects/template/index.html*.

—*Michael Erskine*

HACK #71 "Spider" Omni

Possibly the smallest and simplest omnidirectional antenna there is.

This is one of the simplest and smallest antenna designs I've seen for 2.4 GHz. It isn't much larger than a standard N connector—because that is exactly what it is made of. It has been dubbed the *spider omni*, since it looks a bit like a crazed spider crawling up your antenna feed (Figure 5-3). Technically, it is a ground plane antenna, but practically speaking, it acts like a vertically polarized 3 dB omni.

Figure 5-3. A spider omni.

The spider is very simple to construct if you have a good soldering iron and some basic tools. You need a standard N connector and about a foot or so of solid copper 12-2 romex (common 12-gauge electrical wiring). You also want a good vice to hold onto the pieces as you solder them, as well as a pair of needle nose pliers, some good solder, and a bottle of flux.

First, cut five pieces of bare copper romex, each about 3 cm long. Straighten out each piece as best as you can. Using needle nose pliers, make a small 180-degree bend on one end of four of the pieces. Now, tin the bent tip of each piece, as well as one end of the remaining straight piece. This will make your soldering job much easier later.

If you don't know what tinning is, you may want to get the help of a friend who has experience with soldering. To *tin* means to cover the end of a piece of wire with solder before actually soldering it to your project. This helps the solder to flow better, and ultimately makes a better bond between the metal surfaces.

Now solder the straight piece to the gold cup on your N connector [Hack #63]. Don't use too much solder; there should be just enough to fill the cup without overflowing. Prepare to solder the four legs directly onto the N connector's chassis. You need to use a lot of heat, and liquid flux will help the solder to flow better and bond to the body of the connector. I found it easiest to clamp the straight piece of wire, rather than the threaded bottom of the N connector. This helps to keep the heat from dissipating into your vice while you solder to the chassis.

Take your time, and don't use too much solder on the legs. When you are finished, let the whole thing cool for several minutes, as the chassis will be quite hot.

Now, trim all of the leads to about 20 mm past the edge of the housing. Trim the center lead to about 20 mm past the end of the gold cup. Bend the four radials connected to the housing down at a slight angle. Physically mounting the omni is straightforward if you use heavy feed line, such as LMR 400. Mount the antenna with the center lead pointing up.

The spider omni doesn't provide a tremendous amount of gain (about 3 dB or so, as far as I can tell from informal tests) but it does work quite well for what it is. Higher gain antennas are certainly possible (as we see will see later in "Cut Cable Omni Antenna" [Hack #76]), but tend to be more complicated and much larger. For many applications, you just can't beat the size and cost of this tiny little antenna.

Pringles Can Waveguide
#72   How to make the infamous Pringles cantenna.

At the Portland Summit in June 2001, Andrew Clapp presented a novel yagi antenna design (*http://www.aeonic.com/~clapp/wireless/*). It used a bolt, metal tubing, washers, and PVC tubing to make an inexpensive "shotgun" yagi, either 18" or 36" long. While his antenna shows between 12 and 15 dBi gain (which is impressive for such a simple design), it's also quite large. When we returned from Portland, some members of our local group and I realized that, if we were careful, we could fit a full wavelength inside of a Pringles can (see Figure 5-4). This would show a reduced total gain, but would also make the entire antenna much more compact.

Figure 5-4. The complete Pringles can antenna.

This now infamous hack takes about an hour to construct. Table 5-1 shows a list of the parts you need to get started.

Table 5-1. Part list for a Pringles can waveguide

Part	Approximate cost
All-thread, 5 5/8" long, 1/8" OD	$1.00
Two nylon lock nuts	$0.10
Five 1" washers, 1/8" ID	$0.10
6" aluminum tubing, 1/4" ID	$0.75
A connector to match your radio pigtail (we used a female N connector)	$3.00
One 1/2" piece of 12 gauge solid copper wire (we used ground wire from house electrical wiring)	Negligible
A tall Pringles can (any flavor, Ridges are optional)	$1.50
Scrap plastic disc, 3" across (for example, another Pringles can lid)	Negligible
Total:	$6.45

Of course, buying in bulk helps a lot. You probably won't be able to find a 6" piece of all-thread; buy the standard size (usually 1 or 2 feet) and a 10-pack of washers and nuts while you're at it. Then you'll have more than enough parts to make 2 antennas, all for about $10.

You also need the following tools.

- Ruler
- Scissors
- Pipe cutter (or hacksaw or dremel tool, in a pinch)
- Heavy-duty cutters (or dremel again, to cut the all-thread)
- Something sharp to pierce the plastic (such as an awl or a drill bit)
- Hot glue gun (unless you have a screw-down type connector)
- Soldering iron

Front Collector Construction

Mark and cut four pieces of tubing, about 1.2" (1 15/64"). Where did I get this number? First figure out the wavelength at the bottom of the frequency range we're using (2.412 GHz, or Channel One). This will be the longest that the pipe should be:

```
W = 3.0 * 10^8 * (1 / 2.412) * 10^-9
W = (3.0 / 2.412) * 10^-1
W = 0.124 meters
W = 4.88 inches
```

We'll be cutting the pipe to quarter wavelength, so:

```
1/4 W = 4.88 / 4
1/4 W = 1.22"
```

Now figure out what the shortest range we'll ever use is (2.462 GHz, or channel 11 in the United States):

```
W = 3.0 * 10^8 * (1 / 2.462) * 10^-9
W = (3.0 / 2.462) * 10^-1
W = 0.122 meters
W = 4.80 inches
1/4 W = 1.20"
```

Practically speaking, what's the difference between the shortest pipe and the longest pipe length? The answer is about 0.02", or less than 1/32". That's probably about the size of the pipe cutter blade you're using. So, just shoot for 1.2", and you'll get it close enough.

Cut the all-thread to exactly 5 5/8". The washers we used are about 1/16" thick, so that should leave just enough room for the pipe, washers, and nuts.

Pierce a hole in the center of the Pringles can lid big enough for the all-thread to pass through. Now is probably a good time to start eating Pringles. (We found it better for all concerned to just toss the things; "Salt & Vinegar" Pringles are almost caustic after the first 15 or so. Heed the recommended serving size!)

Cut a 3" plastic disc, just big enough to fit snugly inside the can. We found that another Pringles lid, with the outer ridge trimmed off, works just fine. Poke a hole in the center of it, and slip it over one of the lengths of pipe.

Now, assemble the pipe. You might have to use a file or dremel tool to shave the tips of the thread, if you have trouble getting the nuts on. The pipe is a sandwich that goes on the all-thread like this:

```
Nut Lid Washer Pipe Washer Pipe Washer Pipe-with-Plastic Washer Pipe Washer
Nut
```

You can see the collector assembly clearly in Figure 5-4. Tighten down the nuts to be snug, but don't overtighten (I bent the tubing on our first try; aluminum bends *very* easily). Just get it snug. Congratulations, you now you have the front collector.

Preparing the Can

By now you should have eaten (or tossed) the actual chips. Wipe out the can, and measure 3 3/8" up from the bottom of the can. Cut a hole just big enough for the connector to pass through. We found through trial and error that this seems to be the "sweet spot" of the can. On our Pringles "Salt & Vinegar" can, the N connector sat directly between "Sodium" and "Protein."

Element Construction

Straighten the heavy copper wire and solder it to the connector. When inside the can, the wire should be just below its midpoint (ours turned out to be about 1 1/16"). You lose a few db by going longer, so cut it just shy of the middle of the can.

We were in a hurry, so we used hot glue to hold the connector in place on our first antenna. If you have a connector that uses a nut and washer, and you're really careful about cutting the hole, these work very well (and aren't nearly as messy as hot glue). Just remember that you're screwing into cardboard when you connect your pigtail. It's very easy to forget and accidentally tear the wall of the can.

Now, insert the collector assembly into the can and close the lid. The inside end of the pipe should *not* touch the copper element; it should be just forward of it. If it touches, your all-thread is probably too long.

How can one estimate gain without access to high end radio analysis gear? Using the Link Test software that comes with the Orinoco silver cards, you can see the signal and noise readings (in dB) of a received signal, as well as your test partner's reception of your signal. As I happen to live 0.6 mile (with clean line of sight) from O'Reilly headquarters, we had a fairly controlled test bed to experiment with. We shot at the omni on the roof, and used the access point at O'Reilly as our link test partner.

To estimate antenna performance, we started by connecting commercial antennas of known gain and taking readings. Then we connected our test antennas and compared the results. We had the following at our disposal:

- Two 10 dBi, 180-degree sector panel antennas
- One 11 dBi, 120-degree sector panel antenna
- One 24 dBi parabolic dish
- The Pringles can antenna

Table 5-2 shows the average received signal and noise readings from each, in approximately the same physical position.

Table 5-2. Average received signal and noise readings

Antenna	Signal	Noise
10dBi A	-83db	-92db
10dBi B	-83db	-92db
11dBi	-82db	-95db
24dBi	-67db	-102db
Pringles can	-81db	-98db

The test partner (AP side) signal results were virtually the same. Interestingly, even at only 0.6 mile, we saw some thermal fade effect; as the evening turned into night, we saw about a 3 db gain across the board. (It had been a particularly hot day: almost 100 degrees. I don't know what the relative humidity was, but it felt fairly dry.)

Yagis and dishes are much more directional than sectors and omnis. This bore out in the numbers, as the perceived noise level was consistently lower with the more directional antennas. This can help a lot on long-distance shots, as not only will your perceived signal be greater, but the competing noise will also seem to be less. More directional antennas also help keep noise down for your neighbors trying to share the spectrum as well. Be a good neighbor and use the most directional antennas that will work for your application (yes, noise is everybody's problem).

The Pringles can seemed to have large side lobes that extend about 45 degrees from the center of the can. Don't point the can directly at where you're trying to go; instead, aim slightly to the left or the right. We also found that elevating the antenna helped a bit as well. When aiming the antenna, hold it behind the connector, and *slowly* sweep from left to right, with the Link Test program running. When you get the maximum signal, slowly raise the end of the can to see whether it makes a difference. Go slowly, changing only one variable at a time.

Remember that the can is polarized, so match the phase of the antenna you're talking to (for example, if shooting at an omni, be sure the element is on the bottom or the top of the can, or you won't be able to see it). See the earlier discussion on antenna polarization for how you can use this effect to your advantage.

We were fortunate enough to have a member of our community group bring a return loss meter to one of our meetings, and were able to get some actual measurements of how much signal was returning to the radio. The results weren't as good as I had hoped, but they showed that the antenna was usable, particularly at lower frequencies. Most likely, failing to take into account the thickness of the washers made the entire front element a little too long. There isn't nearly enough power leaving the radio to cause damage due to high return loss, but it does point out that the antenna isn't as well-tuned as it could be.

For a simpler, higher-gain waveguide antenna, read the next Hack. The original article that this Hack is based on is available online at *http://www.oreillynet.com/cs/weblog/view/wlg/448*.

HACK #73 Pirouette Can Waveguide

Build a simpler, higher-gain antenna-in-a-can.

Since the Pringles can story was published, I have received a phenomenal amount of email from people who have tried it for themselves. While some people simply enjoyed making a recycled antenna out of a piece of trash, many people told me "you know, that's not a bad design, but some friends and I found a better way to do it...". One such person was Gregory Rehm. He took my Pringles can design, and another coffee can design that I was working on, and pitted them against his own designs (including a 40 oz stew can) in a Wireless Shoot-Out Battle Royale. His experimentation and excellent analysis is documented on his web site at *http://www.turnpoint.net/wireless/has.html*. It is very entertaining to read (and in case you're too filled with suspense to wait until you can check his site, his stew can won by a mile).

As it turns out, it is much simpler to make a tin can waveguide antenna than to bother with cutting pipe and spacing washers apart on all-thread. He has an excellent how-to posted online at *http://www.turnpoint.net/wireless/cantennahowto.html*, complete with photos, diagrams, and formulae.

Another common can that approaches the ideal diameter for 2.4 GHz is the Pepperidge Farm Pirouette can (see Figure 5-5). It makes a much simpler, sturdier, and more efficient antenna than a Pringles antenna, and the best part is, you get to eat the cookies!

Figure 5-5. The Pirouette "cantenna."

Essentially, you are looking for a can that is about 3 1/2" in diameter. Make an N connector with a 1.2" intentional radiator (just as used in the Pringles Can Waveguide [Hack #72]), and attach it to the Pirouette can about 1.9" from its back surface.

Presto, you have an instant waveguide without cutting a single piece of pipe!

See Also

- The ARRL Antenna Book (*http://www.amazon.com/exec/obidos/tg/detail/ -/0872598047/*)
- The ARRL Microwave Experimenter's Guide (*http://www.amazon.com/ exec/obidos/tg/detail/-/0872593126/*)

HACK
#74   Primestar Dish with Waveguide Feed

Use a cantenna waveguide in conjunction with a recycled satellite dish.

Primestar was recently purchased by Direct TV, who is now phasing out all the Primestar equipment. This means that the dishes are being trashed, and are available for other uses such as the one I describe here. It is easy to turn a surplus Primestar dish into a highly directional antenna for the very popular IEEE 802.11 wireless networking. The resulting antenna has about 22 dB of gain, and is fed with 50 ohm coaxial cable. Usually LMR400 or 9913 low-loss cable is used if the source is more than a few feet from the antenna. (See "Microwave Cabling Guide" [Hack #62] for more details on cabling options.)

Figure 5-6 shows the Primestar dish in action.

Figure 5-6. Primestar dish on the roof.

To build your own, you'll need the following parts and a couple of hours:

- A Primestar dish (you may use any old dish, but if it is bigger than the Primestar, the gain will be higher)
- A juice can (about 4 inches in diameter and at least 8 inches long)
- A chassis mount N connector

After deciding on a place to mount your antenna, remove the apparatus at the feed position of the dish. Be sure to save the mounting hardware. Using a can opener, cut one end of the juice can out, drink the juice, and wash the can out. Solder a quarter wavelength (1.15") of wire onto the center conductor of the chassis mount N connector.

Using a punch or whatever other tools you deem necessary, mount the N connector so that it is about 1.2" from the closed end of the juice can. It is also a good idea to put a drip hole at the lowest point of the can to ensure that water doesn't build up inside. After having one of these on my roof for a few months, I learned it would be a good idea to put a plastic lid on the open end of the can so that the inside doesn't rust. During the time mine has been up, it has rusted and I have lost a couple of dB of signal strength. These two details may be correlated.

Mount the juice can so that the opening is just at the focus of the dish. In my installation (see Figure 5-7), I didn't quite achieve this, but I only lost a dB or two by taking the easy route. I still have about 25 dB signal-to-noise ratio, so the loss wasn't important to me. The easy route is to mount the can as far back as you can along the mount, by punching two holes through the can and bolting it in. The perfectionist's method would be to find the best feed place (which I found to be just a little farther back) and use some PVC tubing to extend the mount so the feed is in the perfect position. In some installations, every decibel will count, which should be taken into consideration.

Figure 5-7. The inside of the feed can.

Other Considerations

This antenna is very directional. You must have it aligned very carefully or you will lose a lot of signal. It also needs to be mounted securely, so the wind won't be able to rotate it even a few degrees.

This antenna is an offset fed dish, which means that the feed horn (our juice can) is not positioned as much in the way of an incoming signal, so it doesn't shadow the dish. This makes the aiming a bit tricky, because it actually looks like it is aimed down when it is aimed for the horizon (as you can see in Figure 5-6). You can use the scale on the dish mount to determine the elevation it is aimed at. The dish isn't as directional in the up/down directions as it is side to side. This is fortunate, because without turning the mounting upside down a standard mount will only get it a few degrees above the horizon. I sacrificed a dB of gain here by not turning it over, mostly because I mounted it on a vent pipe, and didn't want to put that kind of wind load on it. As already mentioned, I don't really need the extra signal either.

IEEE 802.11a

As if this hack weren't already hackish enough, this antenna is easily adapted for use with 802.11a gear at 5.8 GHz. Simply scale the dimensions on the feed can and the excitation antenna to 2.4 / 5 = 48% of the dimensions just mentioned. Remember that wavelength goes down as frequency increases, so antennas of equivalent gain at higher frequencies are actually smaller.

The original article that this Hack is based on is available online at *http://www.wwc.edu/~frohro/Airport/Primestar/Primestar.html*.

—Rob Frohne

HACK #75 BiQuad Feed for Primestar Dish
Make an even higher gain antenna out of a recycled Primestar dish.

The Primestar dishes are high-gain, low-cost, parabolic reflectors with an offset feed. They have superior sidelobe performance when compared with a wire grid antenna, reducing the chance that somebody off of the axis of your link will be able to interfere with it.

Additionally, the spacing between the feed slot and the feed mounting bar is small. It is about 55 mm, which is less than a half wavelength at 2.4 GHz. Failure to couple efficiently to the dish's wide aperture or to minimize radiation into the mounting bar results in poor gain and/or significant sidelobes.

The feed is oriented for vertical polarization in Figure 5-8. To make it horizontal, merely rotate the feed by 90 degrees. You will lose about 3 dB of gain when using the horizontal mode, as the biquad's radiation pattern is a better match for the dish's oblong shape when vertical polarization is used.

Figure 5-8. The biquad feed mounted on the dish.

Construction of the Biquad

I used Printed Circuit board scraps for the 110×110 mm reflector, but it will be just as effective if made out of sheet brass or copper. Aluminum can be used if soldering of the rigid coax is not required at the feed point.

The reflector's "lips" are 30 mm high, and serve to reduce coupling into the mounting bar. Note that they are only required along the main edge axis of the reflector. The lips cut down radiation from the rear lobes of the biquad by about 6 dB. The best SWR is obtained when the biquad loop is about 15 mm above the ground plane, and the SWR may be adjusted by varying this distance.

A piece of 3/4-inch copper piping makes a tight fit with the mount supplied on the Primestar dish. The rigid 0.141-diameter coax is soldered to the ground plane to provide physical support for the structure. If the biquad element is constructed carefully, there will be no component of radiation along the axis of the coax, there will be no current induced into the coax outer conductor, and a balun is not needed.

To make the element, take a piece of 1.2-mm bare or enamelled copper wire exactly 244 mm long. Bend it in half, and then make the bends at the half-way point on each leg (where the solder joints will be). Next, bend the 4 remaining right angles so that the element sides are rectangular and there is about a 1.5 mm gap for soldering to the feed. The widths of the 2 quad elements will be approximately 30.5 mm from wire center to wire center. Figure 5-9 shows the completed feed.

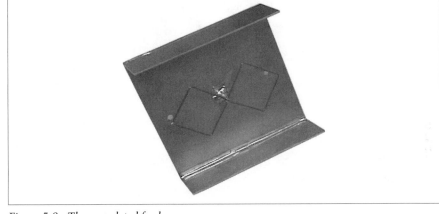

Figure 5-9. The completed feed.

You may use a standard coax cable to connect at this point if you do not have rigid cable available, but you will have to figure out how to support the loop physically. The best SWR is obtained when the loop is about 15 mm above the ground plane, and when the reflector is mounted about 10 mm in front of the Primestar's feed bracket.

That's all there is to it, folks—you now have a dish with 27–31 dBi of gain and negligible sidelobe radiation (<40 dB). The beam width is about 4 degrees. Figure 5-10 shows a model of the BiQuad's radiation pattern.

BiQuad Antenna for PCS Cellular Radio

Need a little bit more range for your cell phone? You can make a BiQuad for 1,900 MHz exactly the same as the preceding one, but you must start with a 304-mm long pice of wire, and fold it into 8 arms that are approximately 39.5 and 38.5 mm long. The ground plane needs to be a little larger—use one about 160 mm (6.2 inches) square. If you don't have a coaxial RF input jack on your cell phone, you can couple the signal into its existing antenna using a single quad as a matching stub. It's not perfect, but in practice it works well. Solder an alligator clip to either of the high voltage apex (39 mm from the

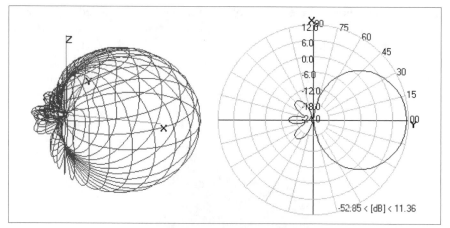

Figure 5-10. Approximate radiation pattern for the BiQuad.

feed) of a single 152 mm loop, and clip that to the antenna stub you are currently using. Now you can put 100 feet of coax between your phone and the antenna on your roof to operate even in fringe areas.

The original article upon which this Hack is based is available online at *http://www.trevormarshall.com/biquad.htm.*

—*Trevor Marshall*

H A C K **Cut Cable Omni Antenna**
#76   Make a high-gain omni out of bits of feed cable.

Most of the designs on the Web for a 2.4 GHz omni antenna seem to involve brass tubing and LMR-400 cable, none of which are readily available to me. I then found a coax-only design for 444 MHz that was based on the same idea. The only reasonable cable I could get my hands on was RG-213 from Maplin (*http://www.maplin.co.uk/*). I thought I'd give it a try by scaling the 444 MHz design up to 2.4 GHz and using RG-213. In order to get about a 6 db gain from the antenna, it needs 8 sectors, with a 1/4-wave section at the top and a fly lead with an N-connector at the bottom.

It should take about two to three hours to build an antenna using this design, but don't worry if it takes longer. You will get quicker, especially as you need to make the jig only once. Figure 5-11 shows the completed antenna.

Each sector of the antenna needs to be 1/2 a wavelength long, multiplied by the velocity factor of the cable. The velocity factor of RG-213 is 0.66. If you decide to use a different cable (such as LMR-400), then you need to get the

Figure 5-11. The completed omni antenna.

velocity factor of that cable (which will be different), and recalculate all the dimensions.

```
                   V * C     0.66 * 299792458
1/2 wavelength = ------  = ----------------  = 0.0405m  = 40.5mm
                 2 * F      2 * 2441000000

V = Velocity  Factor of RG213 = 0.66
C = Speed of light = 299792458
F = Frequency  of Signal = 2441000000 (mid  point of 2.4Ghz range)
```

The 1/4 wave element is not adjusted by the Velocity factor, as it is in the open, so it works out at just 31 mm long, giving a total antenna length of 355 mm + fly lead.

All of the parts needed to make this antenna are available cheaply from either Maplin or any DIY shop. You need the following:

- 1 meter RG-213U cable (available by the meter from Maplin). This is enough for two antennas. Buy more for whatever fly lead length you want.
- 1 N connector. Depending on what you want to connect the antenna to, use either male or female connectors, and inline or bulkhead. Remember that inline connectors need to fit 10 mm diameter RG-213 cable.
- 20 mm PVC conduit (available from any DIY store) It should have a 20 mm inside diameter, and 22 mm outside.
- 22 mm pipe clips (depending on how you want to mount the antenna). Pipe clips make mounting the antenna easy.

You also need the following standard tools.

- Millimeter ruler for measuring
- Junior hacksaw
- Stanley blade knife
- Pliers
- Standard soldering iron (you don't need a heavy duty one) and solder
- Scraps of wood to make a jig to aid soldering
- Bench or vice to hold the cable while you cut it

Cutting the Pieces

After much trial and error, I found that the neatest way to cut the cable is actually with a junior hacksaw. It gives a much cleaner finish than wire cutters. Each sector consists of a short length of RG-213 cable, with the central core sticking out each end.

When building the antenna, the exact length of each piece of RG-213 is not that important; it is the overall length of each sector that counts. I found that cutting the cable to 37 mm with 6 mm of core sticking out each end gets enough overlap to easily solder the segments together. If you allow 1 mm for the width of the hacksaw when cutting the sectors apart, it means you need 37 + 6 + 6 + 1 = 50 mm of cable for each sector. Making 8 sectors + 1/4 wave section comes to 420 mm of cable for the antenna + cable for the fly lead.

The best way to cut each sector is to make the cuts where each end of the sheathed section of the sector will be, before making the cut between each sector. Figure 5-12 displays the top three sections of the antenna, and the 1/4-wave section, showing the order that the cuts should be made.

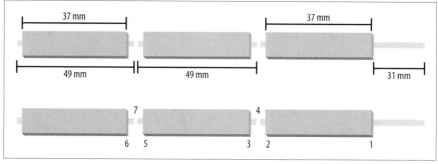

Figure 5-12. Segment lengths.

The best way to make the cuts is to mark them out on the cable first. When sawing the cable, you'll find it has a tendency to deform and bend, so lightly sawing round the outside sheath first—but not cutting through—helps guide the actual cut. I use the junior hacksaw to gently saw round the cable sheath to make the mark for each section.

The first mark will be at 31 mm from the end of the cable, which is for the 1/4-wave section at the top. Once you make the mark, it is time to cut around the cable. You want to cut through the sheath and shielding, and just into the central insulation, but not into the central copper wires. You may need to practice a bit first, but you should be able to feel it as you cut through the shielding into the central insulation. By leaving plenty of sheathed section either side of the cuts, the shielding stays in place when being cut.

Now with pliers, gently twist off 31 mm of sheath and shielding at the end of the cable. This should leave the central insulator exposed. Using the Stanley knife, score round through the central insulator (not too hard, or you will cut the central cable). Now twist off the insulation (Figure 5-13). You should be able to see the twist in the central cable through the insulation, which will show you which way to twist off the insulation, resulting in the central core twisting more tightly.

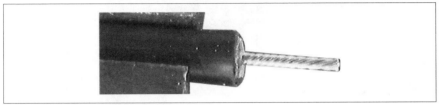

Figure 5-13. The center conductor is exposed.

The next mark is 37 mm down (68 mm from end of the cable), and is the cut for the other end of the sheathed section of the top sector. The next mark is 13 mm down (this section consists of 6 mm core from each sector and 1 mm for the cut between sectors; 81mm from the end) and is the top of the sheathed section of the second sector. The next mark is again 37 mm down, then 13 mm, then 37 mm, and so on, until you have each of the sheathed sections marked out.

You can now start making the cuts, remembering to cut only through the sheath and shielding, and just into the central insulation. First make the cut at 37 mm down, then make the next cut another 13 mm down. You may find that some of the shielding pulls out when you make this cut, as the 13 mm length of sheath cannot hold the shielding tight enough. Don't worry, it doesn't matter.

Now you are ready to cut off the top sector from the cable. Cut through the whole cable at the midpoint of the two cuts you just made; that is, about 43.5 mm from the end of the sheath, or 74.5 mm from the end of the cable. See position 4 in Figure 5-12. Just carefully saw the whole way through the cable. Now you can pull off the sheath and shielding from the each end.

Now score round the insulation as you did before, being careful not to cut the central cable. Carry on, making cuts 37 mm down from the end of the sheath, and then 13 mm further down (50 mm from the end of the sheath). Then cut through the cable in the middle of the two cuts. Another sector made. You need 8 sectors total. Make the same cuts as usual for the eighth sector as it will make top of the fly lead as well. Now that you have all 8 sectors, you need to check round the end of each sector to make sure that none of the shielding is touching the central cable, as odd strands can get left.

Next, you need to make a gentle V-shaped cut with the Stanley knife at each end of the sectors to expose the shielding, which is where the central core of the next sector will be soldered. See Figure 5-14 for an example V cut.

Figure 5-14. A gentle V cut.

Make sure that the V cuts at each end of the sector line up; otherwise, when you come to solder the antenna together, the whole thing will be twisted all around. Once you have all eight sectors finished, it is time to put them together.

Build a Jig

If you do not have a handy helper to hold the sectors together, then you will find it easier to make a small jig from scraps of wood to hold the sectors together as you solder them. The clamps on the righthand side of Figure 5-15 need to be no more than 30 mm long. The baseboard of the jig must extend to the right far enough to take the whole length of the completed antenna, as the baseboard will need to support the antenna during the soldering since the antenna is not rigid enough to support itself. Don't make the clamps too tight, as you need to be able to easily lift the cable out after it has been soldered.

When you are ready to solder the sectors together, take care that each sector is correctly spaced. The overall length of each sector needs to be 40.5 mm. Measure from one end of the shielding of the sector that you are adding to the same end on the next sector, and slide the sectors together/apart until the distance between them is 40.5 mm. Try to get it as accurate as you can, as it affects the direction the antenna transmits in if you get it wrong. There should be a small 3 mm gap between the sheaths of each sector. Figure 5-16 shows the details of a soldered sector.

Figure 5-15. A jig to hold your cable while soldering.

Figure 5-16. A soldered section of cable.

Once you have soldered each sector together, lift the sector up, turn it over, and move it down the clamp to get ready for the next sector. This results in a nice straight antenna. When soldering, remember to heat both the shielding and core so that the solder runs smoothly and fixes them together.

Once complete, test the cable with either a bulb and battery or a multimeter. The center of the fly lead should form a circuit to the 1/4-wave section, and to the shield of the fly lead to the shield of the top section. Now test that there are no crossed connections by ensuring there is no circuit between the center of the fly lead and the shielding of the top sector, and there is no circuit between the 1/4-wave section and the shielding of the fly lead.

Now fix the N connector of your choice onto the end of the fly lead. The type of connector you use depends on what you want to connect to. I use inline connectors, but you could use any connector you like. Slide the antenna into a length of conduit. It should be a snug fit, so you may need to gently ease it in. Now find an old soft drink bottle top, and pop it on the top end of the antenna.

Voila, one complete antenna! Securing the antenna in the conduit is best left until you are ready to mount it somewhere. You can cut 5 cm slots in the bottom of the conduit and use a jubilee clamp to grip the fly lead, drill a hole through the conduit and use a cable tie to hold the fly lead, use a bulk-head mount connector on a bottle cap and glue it to the bottom of the conduit, or glue the fly lead in place. It's up to you.

Disclaimer

I should point out now that I don't claim that the design just described is fit for any purpose, and don't accept any liability for use of the design, or any antenna based on this design. If you want to build an antenna using this design, then you are responsible for ensuring that it doesn't breach any laws where you are, and is compatible with any hardware you connect it to. If in doubt, buy a commercial antenna.

The original article on which this Hack is based is available online at *http://wireless.gumph.org/articles/homemadeomni.html*.

Slotted Waveguides

Make a high-gain, horizontally polarized omni or unidirectional antenna. And it looks cool too!

Unlike wideband antennas like the BiQuad [Hack #75], slotted waveguides are resonant antennas, and have a relatively narrow operating frequency range. The designs described in this Hack have an adequate bandwidth for any WLAN, but they have been carefully designed and must be equally carefully constructed.

The major attraction of a slotted waveguide design is its simplicity. Once you have built the first one, it is very simple to build many more. The gain varies little across the 802.11b spectrum, dropping a little bit at the extreme ends. A finished 8-element directional is shown in Figure 5-17.

How a Waveguide Antenna Works

A waveguide is a very low-loss transmission line. It allows us to propagate signals to a number of smaller antennas (slots). The signal is coupled into the waveguide with a simple coaxial probe; as it travels along the guide it traverses the slots. Each of these slots allows a little of the energy to radiate. The slots are in a linear array pattern, and the total of all the radiated signals adds up to a very significant power gain over a small range of angles close to the horizon. In other words, the waveguide antenna transmits almost all of its energy at the horizon, usually exactly where we want it to go. Its exceptional directivity in the elevation plane gives it quite a high-power gain. Additionally, unlike vertical colinear antennas, the slotted waveguide transmits its energy using *horizontal* polarization, which is the best type for distance transmission.

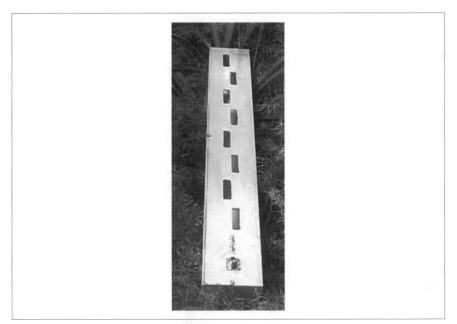

Figure 5-17. An 8-element slotted waveguide.

Unidirectional Waveguide Antennas

I am going to describe 2 unidirectional designs. The first has 8 slots and is about 30 inches long. The second has 16 slots and is about 5 feet long. Simple to construct, the 8-slot has been provided as a good starting point for an antenna novice. I built my 8-slot prototype using only hand tools.

The 16-slot design has been made to radiate over a wider beamwidth by the addition of "wings" to each side of the guide, flush with the front (slotted) surface. It is, of necessity, higher Q, and the higher gain is obtained over a narrower bandwidth. They can be expanded aluminum or sheet, and should extend 9.6 inches beyond the sides of the guide. They act as a ground plane for the slots. Do not change this dimension; it is two electrical wavelengths.

Omnidirectional Slotted Waveguide Antennas

The slotted waveguide has achieved most of its success when used in an omnidirectional role. It is the simplest way to get a real 15-dBi gain over 360 degrees of beamwidth.

Horizontal polarization **[Hack #84]** in a wide area network can often double the number of users that can interconnect without interference. When using horizontally polarized BiQuads or Patch antennas (provided that they have been tested for good cross-polarization performance) at the client site, these omnis will be 20 dB stronger than the signal from a similar vertical collinear. Conversely, vertically polarized receiver antennas will prefer the vertically polarized colinear over the slotted waveguide by a similar amount. Transmission on an immediately adjacent channel (say, channels 5 or 7), normally not permissible because of interference, is now possible. So a judicious intermingling of horizontally polarized clients can talk with a horizontal central station on the same or adjacent channels that other clients are using with vertical polarization.

To make the unidrectional antenna radiate over the entire 360 degrees of azimuth, a second set of slots is cut in the back face of the waveguide. When looking straight at the face of the waveguide, you will be able to see clearly through both slots.

Unfortunately, unless a lot of slots are used, the antenna becomes more like a bidirectional radiator, rather than an omnidirectional. This antenna was invented in the 1940s, and as our simulation and measurement technologies have become more accurate, it is apparent that the slotted waveguide designs we used in the past are far from optimum. The most common defect is a "tilt" in the radiation pattern at the extreme ends of the frequency range. This occurs when the wavelength of the signal travelling down the guide differs from the slot spacing.

My current favorite uses 32 slots to get 15 dBi of gain, radiated in a uniformly omnidirectional manner. The large number of slots makes it easier to dissipate the energy from the waveguide. As with the 16-slot unidirectional, two sets of "wings" (one set at each slot surface) are required to get equal radiation of energy over a full 360 degrees. Note that a higher Q is necessary to get all the slots illuminated evenly.

Note that the gain versus frequency curve peaks at 2,440, and it radiates well over all 14 channels.

Highly Directional Slotted Waveguide Antennas

Sometimes it is useful to have a highly directional antenna. For example, when installing a point-to-point link between two buildings, it is not desirable to have a wide angle of coverage. Any interference from other 802.11b devices (or microwave ovens) that are in the radiation zone will affect your link integrity.

The ideal antenna for such a situation is a dish, such as Primestar's. When using my BiQuad feed, it is possible to reject interference outside the dish's primary 5-degree cone by 30 dB or more.

But if a 16-slot waveguide antenna is turned to a horizontal position, parallel with the ground, it radiates vertical polarization. Its directivity in this plane is extremely good. So, if you don't have a dish handy, consider the possibility of using a pair of these slotted waveguides, parallel to the ground. They will work very well.

Construction Details for the 8-Slot Unidirectional Antenna

The base extrusion for all of my slotted waveguides is 4"×2" O.D. rectangular aluminum tubing with approximately 1/8-inch thick walls. Inside dimensions are 3.756×1.756 inches (95.4 mm×44.6 mm). These inside dimensions are critical, and must be within +/- 0.040 inches or +/-1mm if the antenna center frequency is to be +/- 1 channel. I cut the end inserts from a 5/16"×1 3/4" flat aluminum bar extrusion.

Waveguide antennas are fairly critical in their constructional dimensions, and are easiest to make with a CNC milling machine. I have computed these designs so that they would be easy to replicate; if you are plus or minus 1 mm, the design will work fine—but you must be careful. I used a jig, a hand operated DeWalt heavy duty cut-out tool, a 1/4-inch router bit, and lots of water to machine the slots. This worked fine (even if it was a little tedious). Really, folks—plus or minus 1 mm will not kill your antenna!

Coupling the Signal into the Waveguide

As I said previously, we are propagating the WLAN signal down a waveguide and then using it to excite a number of elemental radiators, or slots. The first task is to get the signal into the waveguide with a feed probe. First, obtain a suitable N connector. Take a piece of 20 mm×40 mm copper or brass shim, and form it into the shape of a cone. Use Figure 5-18 as a template.

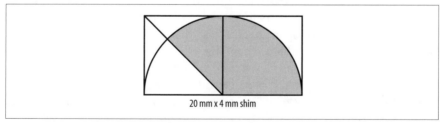

20 mm x 4 mm shim

Figure 5-18. A template for the feed cone.

Solder it to the inner conductor of your Type N connector. Its length should be 20 mm, and its largest diameter should be about 15 mm. When soldered to the N connector, it should protrude exactly into the center of the waveguide and no further. The finished feed cone is illustrated in Figure 5-19.

Figure 5-19. The completed feed cone.

Both ends of the waveguide need to be terminated for RF. The easiest way I found to do this was to cut 3.75-inch pieces of 5/16" × 1.75" aluminum bar stock. I do not recommend that you make the end plugs sloppily, but good electrical contact is not required.

Remember not to have any screws protruding into the waveguide for more than 1/8 inch, especially the screws holding down the N connector. They will affect performance.

8+8 Slot Omnidirectional Antenna

The total length of air inside the 8+8 slot omnidirectional waveguide, from end to end, is 765 mm. Mount the N connector in the center of the widest side: 27.5 mm from one end (the "base") of the airspace in the waveguide, and offset 10 mm from the centre line of the face, in the direction as the offset of the first slot. The wavelength of the radiation passing down the waveguide is longer than a wavelength in free air (it is 161 mm in this design).

The first slot is centered 1.0 wavelength from the base, at a maximum of the H field in the waveguide. This length is 161 mm from the base of the airspace. It is the H component of the field that induces the energy into the slots and makes them radiate. Each slot is 59 mm long, and extends outwards from the centerline for a width of 17 mm. The waveguide excites each edge of the slot, depending on its position across the wide surface of the guide. If it straddled the exact center, each edge of the slot would be excited in antiphase (the waves cancel each other out), and there would be no radiation. So as we offset the edges of the slots, the more the offset, the greater the energy that is dissipated into each slot. The electrical length of each slot should be 59 mm. Do not allow too much kerf at the ends (it should be 2 mm radius max). I recommend finishing the cut with a 1/8-inch router bit (or a file). Or you might use the 1/8 bit in a CNC machine to cut the entire rectangular outline. Remember, even though these slots are arranged *verti-cally*, they radiate *horizontal* polarization.

For the 8+8 slot omnidirectional, slots 2–8 are centered at distances of 241, 322, 403, 483, 564, 644, and 724 mm from the base of the airspace, staggered across the centerline. It doesn't matter which direction the first one is cut, but they must alternate. The end plate should create a 765-mm airspace. Looking straight on at the front of the guide, you can see right through both the front and back slots.

8-Slot Unidirectional Antenna

The total length of air inside the 8-slot unidirectional, from end to end, is 760 mm. Mount the N connector in the center of the widest side, 25 mm from the base of the airspace in the waveguide. The wavelength of the radiation passing down the waveguide is 160 mm in this design. The first slot is centered 1.0 wavelength from the base, at a maximum of the H field in the waveguide. This length is 160 mm from the base of the airspace. Each slot is 58 mm long, and extends outwards from the centerline for a width of 20 mm. The waveguide excites each edge of the slot depending on its position across the wide surface of the guide. If it straddled the exact center, each edge of the slot would be excited in antiphase and there would be no radiation. So, as we offset the edges of the slots, the more the offset, the greater the energy that is dissipated into each slot. The electrical length of each slot should be 59 mm. Do not allow too much kerf at the ends. Remember, even though these slots are arranged vertically, they radiate horizontal polarization.

Slots 2–8 are centered at distances of 240, 320, 400, 480, 560, 640, and 720 mm from the base of the airspace, staggered across the centerline. It doesn't matter which direction the first one is cut, but they must alternate. The end plate should be to create a 760 mm airspace.

Constructional Details for 16- and 16+16-Slot Design

The correct wavelength for these designs is 161 mm. The gain for the 16-slot unidirectional is 15 dBi–17 dBi, verified on my test range, across the whole band. On the range, the 16 slotter gives slightly higher gain than my Hyperlink Technologies model 2419G Mesh Parabolic, which is "rated" at 19.1 dBi gain.

The slot width for the 16 slotter is 15 mm, and it is 12 mm for the 32 slotter; otherwise, the key dimensions are the same.

The original article upon which this Hack is based is available online at *http://www.trevormarshall.com/waveguides.htm*.

—*Trevor Marshall*

H A C K
#78
The Passive Repeater

Use a passive device that requires no power to shoot around obstacles.

Everyone you know is getting signals 5, 10, 15, or even more miles per hop. You need only to go four miles, but there's a hill in the middle—it's not distance, it's the obstacle that's killing you. You know you could put a repeater station on the hill, but there's no power, and you can't afford the cost of a solar power system big enough to ride out a few cloudy days. What you need is a *passive repeater*.

Suppose the hill is right at the half-way point. Just to make sure you get a big enough signal, you buy two 24 dBi parabolic dishes, mount them on a 20-foot pole, and have lots of clearance in the now line-of-sight paths to the end stations. Both ends are also provided with 24 dBi dishes. You anticipate the joy of getting high speed down to your house for the first time, but when you turn your gear on, there's no signal to be seen. Argh! What went wrong?

Let's think about how our system is supposed to work. If we didn't have the obstacle in the middle of the path, our endpoint antennas would ensure that we had a strong signal over our four-mile path. Our signal from the originating end had to go only half the distance, so we know the signal at the two-mile point is four times bigger than it would be at four miles (due to the *inverse square law*; see "Calculating the Link Budget" [Hack #81]). Our thinking is that this signal in the cable is supposed to get launched from the second antenna and beam strongly to your house, since it has to go only a relatively easy two-mile hop.

Well, actually the system is working just the way you thought. The reason you can't see a signal is that it's just too weak. First, let's predict how much signal we'd see if we had a clear four-mile path.

At 2.4 GHz, the free space path attenuation (loss) can be calculated like this:

    Loss (in dB) = 104.2 + 20 log *d*

where *d* is in miles (if you'd rather use kilometers, use 92.4 as the constant instead of 104.2, or substitute 32.4 if you prefer your distance in meters). With an algebraic (scientific) calculator, get the path loss for four miles by keying in:

    104.2 [plus key (+)] 20 [times key (x)] [log key] 4 [equals key (=)]

you'll see 116.24 in the display. For the terminally lazy (or those without a calculator), consult the precomputed lookup table [Hack #81] to find a rough estimate of loss for a given distance.

How much signal is available over our nonobstructed four-mile path? Let's assume that we have 24 dBi antennas on each end and that our radios are in a box near each antenna. Let's allow a 3 dB loss for pigtails, connector attenuation, and transmission line (coax).

We use dBs for our ratios since it makes it easy to calculate total path gains and losses. Just add the dB for each element in the path, and the sum is the effective path.

```
Coax  +  Antenna  +  Free Space Loss  +  Antenna  +  Coax
 -3   +    24     +      -116          +    24     +   -3  =  -74
```

It looks like we'll get 74 dB less out of the connector at our receiver than we put in at the transmitter. That's about 25 million times smaller, so it's a good thing that our receivers can detect weak signals!

Now let's put the hill back in place and put the passive repeater on top, coupling the antenna leads directly into each other with an appropriate "barrel" connector. To calculate our signal, we note that the distance is half, so we'll see 6 dB more signal over a 2-mile path, which is −68 dB. (Do the calculation and you'll see for yourself.)

The calculation is very simple since we have the same antennas everywhere. When we connect our two antennas together on the hill, we just add the connector-to-connector loss for the two 2-mile paths, and we get −136 dB less at the receiver than we put in at the transmitter when our passive repeater is in place.

If we have a 200 mW transmitter (23dBm) when we have the 4-mile unobstructed path, we get −51 dBm for our receiver. A great signal, as we expected. But with the passive repeater in the middle of the obstructed path, we get only −113dB and, sorry to say, we won't get any bandwidth. Even the thermal noise of the antenna would exceed the tiny signal provided by our passive repeater. In fact, if the hill is about 500 feet high, diffraction over the top is likely to give us a path loss 35 or 45 dB worse than free space loss. So the signal from the passive repeater is about 200 times smaller than what just falls over the hill.

So have we proven that passive repeaters don't work? While it looks pretty bad, let's look at another example. Let's keep the 4-mile distance, but say that we live just 500 feet from the ridge. We are still obstructed and can't get a direct signal, but let's do the calculation for a passive repeater on this ridge.

We don't have to recalculate the 4-mile minus 500 feet path, since it's virtually the same as the full 4-mile path, or −74 dB. Our second hop is now about 1/10 mile, so this hop gives us −84 dB. Adding up our components in this hop, we get −3 + 24 + −74 + 24 + −3 = −42 dB. Coupling our antennas together at the passive repeater, we add the two paths and get −74 + −42 =

116 dB. Our 23 dBm transmitter now gets us –93 dBm at the receiver end. Not a great signal, but we should be able to get 1 Mb/s connections through the passive repeater. Of course, you could argue that you should just put your radio on the peak and run 500 feet of cable, and that might be a reasonable alternative. The passive repeater is just barely working for us here.

However, there are situations where you can't just run a cable. Let's say that you live in the city, and across from you is a building 60 feet high. You can get permission to put antennas on the roof of the obstructing building, but there's no power there. You can't run a cable across the street, and you can't build a tower tall enough to get over the building. In this case, we have a 100 foot path from the passive repeater to your house (approximately .02 mile). Our free space loss for this path is –70 dB and the connector-to-connector loss is –28 dB. Assuming that the originating station is still 4 miles away, our total connector-to-connector loss is 102 dB. Now our +23 dBm transmitter gets a very respectable –79-dBm signal to the receiver. Yay! we can get our full 11 Mb/s speed and still have an 8 dB fade margin.

So in certain circumstances, a passive repeater can give you great results. It works best when the two path lengths are vastly different. The absolute poorest result occurs when the obstruction is in the middle of the path. In this case, you have to use an active repeater to get the signal through.

—*Ron Wickersham*

HACK #79 Determining Antenna Gain

Figure out the approximate gain of your home brew antenna—without a spectrum analyzer.

After building one of the many antennas in this chapter, or perhaps designing one of your own, you will inevitably wonder just how much gain your antenna provides. While an ideal testing rig would include a spectrum analyzer and lab conditions, most people can't afford to bring such resources to bear on their little antenna project. Fortunately, informal gain tests are simple to perform, given some simple tools and a little patience.

Here is one method for estimating gain. While your results might not be as accurate as those provided by a "real" radio lab, it can give you a fair estimate of how well your equipment performs, for very little cost.

What you'll need:

- Two radio cards of the same manufacturer and firmware revision, as well as external antenna connectors (Lucent/Orinoco/Proxim cards, or Prism II cards like the Senao/EnGenius work well)
- Two laptops

- The antenna to be tested
- Two antennas of known gain (preferably low gain and somewhat directional, like sector antennas)
- Two tripods, mounts, and pigtails for the above antennas
- A large, flat outdoor space free of obstacles
- A notebook
- A friend, and a means of communicating with that friend (such as cell phones or FRS radios)

Connect an antenna to one of the cards, and using a program like Net-Stumbler [Hack #21], run a simple site survey. Walk around the area a bit, and look for an unused (or lightly used) channel. Once you decide on a channel, quit NetStumbler and return to the other laptop. With the two laptops close to each other, set up an Ad-Hoc network on that channel. Don't worry about your IP configuration, just set both machines to the same ESSID and channel. If you are using a Prism II card, you might prefer to use one laptop in Host AP mode [Hack #57] instead.

If you are using an Orinoco card on a Windows machine, open the "Site Monitor" utility in the client driver, on both machines. If you are running Linux, I recommend using Wavemon [Hack #33] on both machines. Otherwise, open the client monitoring tool that came with your card. In my experience, the Orinoco Site Monitor or wavemon on Linux are the preferred tools for monitoring signal strength in real time, as they update quickly and keep a history for you. Don't use a network scanner like NetStumbler, as it has been known to get confused when performing simple signal strength tests. While still close together, verify that the two laptops can monitor each other with no problems. It is much easier to debug configuration problems now than when you are far away from your friend later.

When you are satisfied that everything is working properly, you are ready to head out into the field. Set up the tripods and mounts about 300 feet or so apart. Be sure that your tripods are at least 5 feet high, to clear the 0.6 Fresnel zone. The *Fresnel* (pronounced "fray-NELL") *zone* refers to the shape of a wave as it leaves the antenna, expanding in a circular direction as it travels. It is well illustrated by the diagram at *http://www.ydi.com/deployinfo/ad-fresnel-zone.php*. Using antennas of known gain on both sides, plug in your laptop and see what kind of signal you can find. With your friend keeping his end steady, slowly rotate your antenna until you achieve the highest possible gain between the two points. Now, lock down your side, and let your friend rotate his end until he achieves the highest gain. Work slowly, and keep in constant communication with your friend at the other end, until you agree on the best possible position for both antennas. Be sure that both of you take your hands off of the antenna before taking a reading.

Once you are satisfied that the antennas are well aligned, make a note of the received signal and noise from both sides. Let the entire rig rest a couple of minutes, and see if the signal fluctuates at all. If it does, you might be encountering unexpected noise on the band, so you might try a different channel.

When you are happy with your link, it is time to try out your new antenna. Without moving the other end, carefully replace one antenna with the antenna to be tested. Ideally, you should use the same pigtail and feed line to eliminate the possibility of variations in the cabling. While watching the signal strength meter, slowly rotate the antenna until the highest possible gain is achieved. Again, let the entire system rest for a moment or two. When the link looks stable, record the received signal and nose from both sides.

The difference between both readings, plus the gain of the antenna that was traded out, is the approximate gain of your home brew antenna. For example, suppose you first measured a signal of −56 dBm using a 10 dBi sector. When you swapped it out for a circular waveguide, your signal strength jumped to −50 dBm. The difference between the readings (6 dBm) plus the gain of the known antenna (10 dBi) equals the approximate gain of the waveguide, which is approximately 16 dBi.

You can also compute the difference in noise readings to see an approximate estimation of how well the antenna rejects noise from the path. With noise, a lower signal is better. Remember that you are dealing with negative numbers, so a noise reading of −100dBm is actually *better* than −90dBm. Likewise, since you want *more* signal, a reading of −50 dBm is much better than −56 dBm.

One critical point that isn't measured in this sort of test is *Standing Wave Ratio* (SWR). This is a measurement of how much signal is being reflected back into your radio from the antenna, and tells whether your antenna is well matched to the frequency your radio is transmitting on. Unfortunately, I know of no good method for determining the SWR of very low power cards at 2.4 GHz without using expensive equipment. Fortunately, as these radios put out only a few milliwatts, there is little chance that your radio will actually be damaged by a mismatched antenna. It just won't work very well.

Once your antennas are aligned in a setup like this, you can test as many home brew designs as you like. Just be sure to keep the other end steady, and take everything one step at a time. Make a note of everything you observe as you go, and keep the number of variables to a minimum. While this method might not be as accurate as a spectrum analyzer, it is a very cost-effective way of getting an estimation of how your antenna design actually performs.

## CHAPTER SIX

Long Distance Links

Hacks #80–85

The stated average range of a piece of consumer 802.11b equipment is 300 to 1,500 feet. Of course, this estimate is what is printed on the side of the box, and the number is chosen to be somewhere between actual technical constraints and the marketing department's agenda—and should therefore be taken with the standard issue grain of salt. What the side of the box doesn't tell you is that radio range isn't something "built into" a product, but is in fact the same for all wireless devices: potentially infinite, but bounded by transmitter power, antenna gain, clean line of sight, and relative noise in the environment.

While the intended range might just be a couple of hundred feet, wireless aficionados everywhere have proven that it is possible to use the 802.11 family of devices to build reliable data links of 10 miles or more. The hacks in this chapter expose some of the important details you need to keep in mind, as well as techniques you can use to make your long distance projects possible.

HACK #80 Establishing Line of Sight

Use these methods to quickly tell if a long distance wireless shot is possible.

Wireless networks operate at microwave frequencies and, as such, work much better when the client's antenna can see the AP's antenna, with nothing but air between. Over short distances (within a few hundred feet), wireless networks can tolerate a few objects in the way. But as you try to push your signal further, having clean Line Of Sight (LOS) is absolutely critical.

How can you tell if a given point has LOS to another point several miles away? The short answer is that without actually having a look, you can't. If the far end is more than a couple of miles away, it becomes difficult to tell, even with a high-powered telescope. But using these techniques, you can make an educated guess as to what is at least within the realm of possibility.

Using a GPS to Log Prospective LAT/LONG/ALT

When visiting a potential node site, it's a good idea to bring along an accurate GPS. It can log not only the (more or less) precise latitude and longitude, but also the altitude of the site. After collecting points, you can pull them into your topographical software and plot them. For example, the Topo! package from National Geographic (*http://maps.nationalgeographic. com/topo/*) allows you to easily mark up a topographical map and analyze arbitrary points and routes. Draw routes between any two points to figure out how the land lies between them. This gives you an easy visual reference for a given shot, as shown in the cross section provided by Topo! in Figure 6-1.

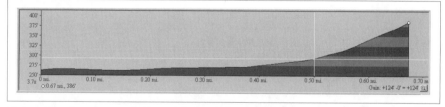

Figure 6-1. A cross-section "lay of the land" between two points.

Keep in mind that, although the Topo! software has surveyed geological data, it won't have tree or building information. You can get a general idea of how cluttered an area is, but you won't really know until you try the shot. Using the overhead view in conjunction with the cross section, you can not only weed out the obvious negatives (as in Figure 6-2), but also find potential work-arounds.

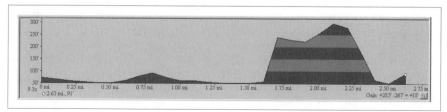

Figure 6-2. A long distance nightmare with no chance of a decent shot.

Using the overhead view to locate key repeater points can be fun. Find out where the good sites are, and try contacting the people at those points. More often than not, people are willing to work with local community groups to provide free access (particularly if they don't have to do much besides provide electricity, and can get free high-speed access besides.)

Plotting the Points on a 3D Map

A couple of software packages from DeLorme (Topo USA and 3-D Topo-Quads, available at *http://www.delorme.com/*) have the ability to create 3D renderings of a topological region, complete with data markers and labels (Figure 6-3). While it's a cool feature and is rather compelling in presentations, it has limited practical value beyond helping to visualize the surrounding terrain.

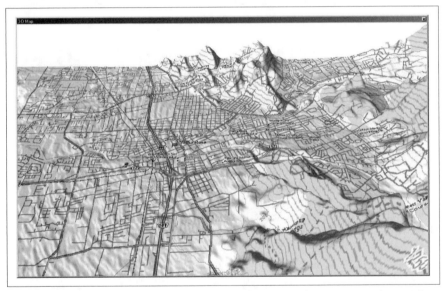

Figure 6-3. DeLorme's TopoUSA gives you a 3D rendering of any topo region, complete with data points.

Generally speaking, the more data points you collect, the more impressive your visual presentation will be.

Once your points are plotted on a map, you can very quickly determine which sites are worth developing. If you can't get direct line of sight to a place you'd like, take a look at the surrounding geography and see whether you can find another way. If you can't go through, you'll have to go over or around. Software topo maps can make finding the "bank shots" much easier.

Remember that these tools will show you the lay of the land but don't provide data on ground clutter, such as trees and buildings. The tools aren't perfect, but they can give you an idea of what you have to work with when building a large wireless network.

HACK #81 Calculating the Link Budget

Figure out whether a long distance link is even possible before you buy any equipment.

How far will it go? That's a very good question. It depends on all sorts of factors, including the power output and sensitivity of your card, quality of your cable, connectors and antenna, intervening clutter and noise, and even weather patterns (on long distance links). While it's impossible to precisely take all of these variables into account, you can make a good estimate before buying any hardware. The following describes a simple way to build an estimate, referred to as the *link budget*.

First, figure out how much loss the signal will incur in the space between the two sites. This is called the *path loss*. One common formula for estimating path loss at 2.4 GHz is:

```
L = 20 log(d) + 20 log(f) + 36.6
```

where L is the loss in dB, d is the distance in miles, and f is the frequency in Megahertz.

So, suppose you wanted to set up a five-mile link between two points, using channel 6 (2.437 GHz):

```
L = 20 log(5) + 20 log(2437) + 36.6
L = (20 * 0.69) + (20 * 3.38) + 36.6
L = 13.8 + 67.6 + 36.6
L = 118
```

At five miles, with no obstacles in between, you will lose 118 db of signal between the two points. Our link must tolerate that much loss (plus a bit extra to account for weather and miscellaneous interference) or it will be unreliable.

If you don't want to bother calculating path loss on your own, you can use Table 6-1 to get a rough estimate. This table was computed with the above formula and rounded up.

Table 6-1. *Approximate free space path loss at 2.412GHz*

Distance (in miles)	Loss (in dB) @ 2.412GHz (ch. 1)
0.5	98
1	104
2	110
3	114
4	116
5	118
7	121
10	124
15	128
20	130
25	132
30	134

Now that you have the free space path loss, add up all of your gains (radios + antennas + amplifiers) and subtract your losses (cable length, connectors, lightning arrestors, and miscellaneous other losses). Let's assume you are using Orinoco Silver cards (15 dBm) and no amplifiers, with a 12 dBi sector on one side, and a 15 dBi yagi on the other. I assume you're using 1 meter of LMR 400 and a lightning arrestor on each side, allowing a 0.25 dB loss for each connector, and 1 dB for each pigtail. Since all of the units are in dB, we can use simple addition and subtraction:

```
Site A:
Radio - Pigtail - Arrestor - Connector - Cable - Connector + Antenna
 15   -   1    -  1.25   -   .25   -  .22  -   .25    +   12  = 24.03
Plus Site B:
 15   -   1    -  1.25   -   .25   -  .22  -   .25    +   15  = 27.03
Equals: 51.06 total gain
```

Now, subtract the path loss from that total:

```
51.06  - 118 = -66.94
```

There you have the perceived signal level at either end of the link: −66.94 dBm. But is it enough for communications? Look up the receiver sensitivity specs for the Orinoco Silver card to see how much signal it needs. You can look it up in the radio card documentation, or consult the handy table in "Client Capability Reference Chart" [Hack #65].

Consulting the table, it appears that the Orinoco Silver has a receive sensitivity of −82 dBm at 11 Mbps. As we are providing a signal of −66.94 dBm, we have a "fudge factor" of 15.06 db (82 − 66.94 = 15.06). Theoretically, this usually works at 11 Mbps (in good weather), and should have no problem at all syncing at 5.5 Mbps. The radios should automatically sense when the link becomes unreliable, and re-sync at the fastest possible speed.

Typically, a margin of error of 20 db or so is safe enough to account for normal intervening weather patterns. Using more powerful radios (such as the Cisco 350 at 20 dBm, or the EnGenius/Senao at 23 dBm), more sensitive radios (again, like the Cisco 350 or EnGenius/Senao), or higher-gain antennas would help shore up this connection to 11 Mbps. Using higher-gain cards in conjunction with high-gain dishes makes it possible to extend your range well beyond 25 miles, but be sure to observe the FCC limits on power and gain.

Online tools like Green Bay Professional Packet Radio's *Wireless Network Link Analysis* can give you a good ballpark estimate on what it will take to make your link possible. Check out their excellent resources at *http://www. gbonline.com/~multiplx/wireless/page09.html.*

HACK #82 Aligning Antennas at Long Distances

By working methodically and communicating well, you can easily bring up wireless links several miles apart.

The farther apart your points are, the harder it is to aim your antennas. At distances up to five miles or so, this is rarely a problem. Just so long as you have enough total gain to overcome the path loss, which you should have calculated by now [Hack #81]. At greater distances, getting the antennas pointed directly at each other can be quite tricky. Here is a list of techniques that might help you get your dishes pointed where they need to be:

- Use mobile phones or FRS/GMRS radios [Hack #9] to maintain communications between the two points while you're aiming the antennas. It helps to have at least two people at each end (one to manipulate the antenna, and another to coordinate with the other end). Radios often work much better in areas where mobile phone coverage is spotty.

- Set up all of your network settings ahead of time, so there aren't any variables once you get to the remote site. Check all gear, ping each box, and even transfer a file or two to be sure that your equipment works at close range. You don't want to question it later if you have problems getting the link going.

- Use a tool like the Wavemon [Hack #33] or Kismet [Hack #31], or a good built-in client [Hack #20] to show the signal strength and noise readings in real time. This kind of tool is your best friend, short of an actual spectrum analyzer.

- Work on one end of the link at a time, slowly changing one variable at a time, until you see the maximum signal strength and lowest noise at each end of the link.

- If you have one handy (and your link budget permits it), first try an omni or sector antenna on one end of the link. Once you find the other end of the link, replace it with your dish or yagi and tune it in. Typically, the higher gain the antenna, the shorter the beam width, and therefore, the harder it is to aim.

- Sweep slowly, and don't be afraid to go beyond the best perceived signal. Most antennas have smaller side lobes that appear as false positives. Keep moving until you find the main lobe. It should stand out significantly from the others, once you find it.

- Many times, particularly with offset dish antennas and yagi antennas, the antenna appears to be aimed too low or far to the left or right of the other end of the link. This is normal. Don't worry about how it looks, worry about finding the greatest possible signal.

- Do NOT touch the actual antenna while taking a reading. Resting your hand on the antenna interferes with the radiation pattern, and drains your signal very quickly. Take your readings with all hands clear of the equipment.

- Don't forget to compare horizontal and vertical polarization. Try the antennas in both positions, and use the one that shows the lowest noise.

- Once your link is in place, consider using WEP to discourage others from attempting to connect to it. If you want to provide wireless access at either endpoint, set up another gateway, preferably with caching services (such as caching DNS and a transparent web proxy, like Squid). This helps reduce the amount of traffic that goes over the long link, cuts down on network collisions, and generally makes more efficient use of the link.

It can take all day to properly align antennas at a great distance, but it can also be fun, with the right group of people. Just take your time, think about what you're doing, and be sure to leave time at the end of the day to celebrate!

Slow Down to Speed Up

HACK
#83   On a flaky link, talking slowly can actually speed up data transfers.

The speed at which a radio can communicate with another depends on how much signal is available. In order to maintain communications as the available signal fades, the radios need to transmit data at a slower rate. Normally, the radios attempt to work out the available signal on their own and automatically select the fastest possible speed for communications. But in fringe areas with a barely adequate signal, packets may be needlessly lost while the radios continually renegotiate the link speed.

For example, suppose you have a long distance point-to-point link made of Orinoco radios. The received signal at each end varies between –83 and –80 dBm. The threshold for an Orinoco to flip from 11 Mbps to 5.5 Mbps is –82 dBm, so the radios spend at least part of their time negotiating the best speed. Operating on a borderline signal level like this leads to excessive retransmissions that can seriously degrade performance.

If you can't add more antenna gain or reposition your equipment to achieve enough signal for your link, consider forcing your card to sync at a lower rate. This will mean fewer retries, and can be substantially faster than using a continually flip-flopping link. Each driver has its own method for setting the link speed. In Linux, set the link speed with *iwconfig*:

```
pebble~# iwconfig eth0 rate 2M
```

This forces the radio to always sync at 2 Mbps, even if other speeds are available. You can also set a particular speed as a ceiling, and allow the card to automatically scale to any slower speed, but go no faster. For example, you might use this on the example link above:

```
pebble~# iwconfig eth0 rate 5.5M auto
```

Using the auto directive this way tells the driver to allow speeds up to 5.5 Mbps, and to run slower if necessary, but will never try to sync at anything faster. To restore the card to full auto scaling, just specify auto by itself:

```
pebble~# iwconfig eth0 rate auto
```

Cards can generally reach much further at 1 Mbps than they can at 11 Mbps. There is a difference of 12 dB between the 1 Mbps and 11 Mbps ratings of the Orinoco card—that's four times the potential distance just by dropping the data rate! On a marginal link, it is usually worth sacrificing an attempt at speed to achieve a more efficient link. If you absolutely need to go faster, find a way to get more signal between the two points.

HACK #84 Taking Advantage of Antenna Polarization

Use electromagnetic polarization to avoid noise from other antennas in the same spectrum.

One extremely important property of electromagnetic waves to consider is *polarization*. An electromagnetic wave is actually comprised of two simultaneous and inseparable fields: the electrical field and the magnetic field. These two fields are perpendicular to each other, and both are perpendicular to the direction in which the wave propagates.

An antenna must be oriented to match the polarization of the incoming energy, or it will only receive a small portion of it. Practically speaking, this means that antennas with matching polarization will see each other well, while antennas with opposite polarization will hardly see each other at all.

Both horizontally and vertically polarized antennas are common, but in some exotic antennas, circular (clockwise or counter-clockwise) polarization is possible. The polarization of the antenna on each end of a link must match, or the radios will have trouble talking to each other. Omnis and sectors are generally vertically polarized, although horizontally polarized variations do exist (see "Slotted Waveguides" [Hack #77] for an example of a do-it-yourself horizontally polarized omni). Yagis and dishes can be mounted vertically or horizontally, depending on the application.

On a long distance point-to-point link, be sure to try both horizontal and vertical polarization to see which incurs the lowest noise. Simply try the link one way, then rotate both dishes 90 degrees and try it again. You can tell the polarization of most antennas by the position of their driven element (the part connected to the center conductor of your antenna feed). The polarization of a dish is indicated by the position of the front element, not the rear reflector, so an oval dish that points "up and down" is probably mounted in horizontal polarization, and therefore won't be able to talk very well to a vertically polarized omni. Sectors and other sealed antennas typically indicate their polarization on the back of the antenna.

You can use polarization to your advantage to use multiple radios on a single point-to-point link. For example, you can run two parallel links on the same channel, one with vertical and one with horizontal polarization. If separated by a few feet, two dishes can operate quite happily on the same channel without substantially interfering with each other, and provide twice the bandwidth using the same channel.

HACK #85   Map the Wireless Landscape with NoCat Maps

Manage many wireless nodes with this open source mapping project.

In addition to commercial tools like Topo! and the DeLorme map software [Hack #80], there are a number of freely available mapping solutions that make use of public GIS data. While there is a huge amount of data available about the surface of our planet, most of the tools used to query and view the data are far from simple.

The NoCat Map project combines two powerful GIS programs to build a sophisticated but easy-to-use node database. It is built on MapServ (*http://mapserver.gis.umn.edu/*) and Grass (*http://grass.itc.it/*), and is available at *http://maps.nocat.net/*. NoCat Maps integrates the data and rendering functionality of MapServ and Grass with a simple node database, and attempts to provide useful data and visualization from the result. Users can add data for their own equipment, including latitude, longitude, altitude, and contact information. If this data isn't known ahead of time, it can make an approximate guess from the user's mailing address.

This data can then be queried and compared to other nodes in the database to find likely point-to-point links. You can then select a node from the database and view the likeliest links in a simple table, as shown in Figure 6-4.

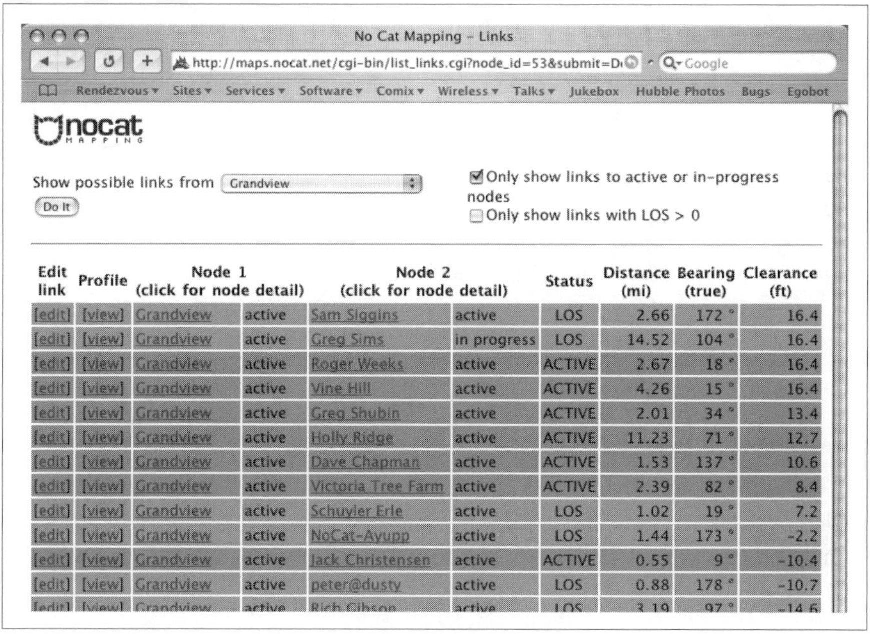

Figure 6-4. View likely point-to-point links at a glance.

Since the position of each node is known, the distance and bearing can easily be calculated. By consulting the GIS data for the land elevation between the two nodes, a minimum clearance can also be estimated. This can be shown graphically by clicking on the "View Profile" link.

Figure 6-5 shows the profile of a possible link between two points. Note that just as with other tools that rely on GIS data, this shows the lay of the land without any indication of ground clutter (buildings, trees, etc.). This is good enough to go on for a rough estimate, and is especially helpful for eliminating definite impossibilities (Figure 6-6).

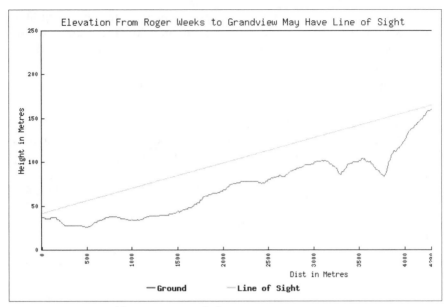

Figure 6-5. One possible point-to-point link.

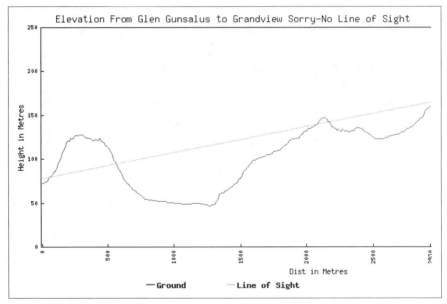

Figure 6-6. This is not the link you are looking for. Move along.

NoCat Maps is a work in progress, and currently supports only data for Sonoma County, CA. However, the source code is freely available, as are the data sets for just about every location in the U.S. If you are looking for an inexpensive method for managing a large number of outdoor point-to-point links, this software could be just what you want.

## CHAPTER SEVEN

Wireless Security

Hacks #86–100

When it comes to wireless networking, there is no such thing as physical security. You might be able to lock down the physical network infrastructure of a business or other facility, but radio waves pass through walls, carrying your network data with them. Don't delude yourself by thinking that a low-powered access point won't reach much further than your parking lot. Remember that although you may not see your network using a laptop outside your building, someone with a large enough antenna can likely read your network traffic from a mile or more away. I have personally seen a simple 24 dBi dish detect hundreds of wireless networks from the top of Queen Anne hill in Seattle. These were networks with SSIDs like "Linksys" and "default," which obviously were coming from low-end, consumer-grade access points without any external antennas. I certainly couldn't have made a reliable network link to them, but I could have passively logged their traffic from miles away quite easily. Short of wrapping your entire building with a metal screen to build an effective Faraday cage, you should expect the signal of your APs to leak out well beyond your immediate vicinity.

This chapter is devoted to workable methods for controlling access to your wireless network. A control mechanism could be something as simple as a WEP key, or as complex as a captive web portal with a RADIUS backend. We will also look at several ways you can protect your own data when using other wireless networks, even if those networks are completely public and open.

HACK #86 Making the Best of WEP

While not the answer to every wireless security need, WEP can still be effective if used properly.

The 802.11b specification provides a form of encryption called Wired Equivalent Privacy (WEP). It operates on the Media Access Control (MAC) layer, which is part of the Data Link layer of the OSI model. When using WEP, only clients that know the "secret key" can associate with an Access Point or Peer-to-Peer Group. Anyone without the key may be able to see network traffic, but every frame is encrypted. The specification employs a 40-bit shared-key RC4 PRNG algorithm from RSA Data Security. Virtually all cards that speak 802.11b support this encryption standard.

Although hardware encryption sounds like a good idea, the implementation in 802.11b is far from perfect. First of all, the encryption provided happens at the link layer, not at the application layer. This means that your communications are protected up to the gateway, but no further. Once it hits the wire, your packets are sent in the clear. Worse than that, every other legitimate wireless client that has the key can read your packets with impunity, since the key is shared across all clients. You can try it for yourself. On a network using WEP, simply run a packet sniffer such as *tcpdump* [Hack #37] or Ethereal [Hack #38] on your laptop and watch your neighbor's packets just fly by.

40- Versus 64- Versus 104- Versus 128-bit WEP

Why do the various card manufacturers quote so many different key lengths? The original 802.11b specification defined a 40-bit user-specified key. This key is combined with a 24-bit *Initialization Vector* (the IV), a random number that is part of the WEP algorithm. Together, this yields 64 bits of "key," although the IV is actually sent in the clear!

Likewise, a 104-bit WEP is used with the IV to yield 128 bits of "key." This is why user-defined keys are 5 characters long (5 characters × 8 bits/character = 40 bits) or 13 characters long (13 characters × 8 bits/character = 104 bits). The user doesn't define the IV; it is part of the WEP algorithm (and is generally implemented as 24 random bits.)

Naturally, more bits sounds more secure to the consumer, so some manufacturers choose to list the larger number as the "key length." Unfortunately for WEP, more bits do not necessarily mean significantly greater security.

Many manufacturers have implemented their own proprietary extensions to WEP, including 104-bit keys and dynamic key management. Unfortunately, as they are not defined by the 802.11b standard, there is no guarantee that cards from different manufacturers that use these extensions will interoperate.

To throw more kerosene on the burning WEP tire mound, a team of cryptographers at the University of California at Berkeley (among others; see the references at the end of this section) has identified weaknesses in the way WEP is implemented, effectively making the number of bits used in the encryption key irrelevant. With all of these problems, why is WEP still supported by manufacturers? And what good is it for securing your network?

WEP was not designed to be the ultimate "killer" security feature (nor can anything seriously claim to be). Its acronym makes the intention clear: *wired equivalent protection.* In other words, the aim behind WEP is to provide no greater protection than you would have when you physically plug into your Ethernet network. Keep in mind that in a wired Ethernet setting, there is no encryption provided by the protocol at all.

WEP provides an easy, generally effective, interoperable deterrent to unauthorized access. Given the choice between an open access point with all of the defaults in place and a network running 40-bit WEP, the casual user running NetStumbler [Hack #21] will choose to investigate the open network every time. While definitely not beyond the reach of a determined network cracker, a well-chosen WEP key is still just too much of a pain for the average War Driver to deal with. To make the best use of WEP, consider the following guidelines:

Use a nonobvious key. Dictionary attacks against a WEP key are executed much more quickly and easily than a full-blown AirSnort session. Make sure that your key doesn't use a simple word, even if you obfuscate it further with l33t h4x0r sP33k. Believe me, network crackers know how to speak it better than you do. Throw in a couple of symbols, or better yet, use a Hex key with nonprintable characters.

Use the longest key that your hardware supports. If all of your wireless network hardware supports 104-bit WEP, use it. But keep in mind that many devices do not support 104-bit WEP, and those that do may not interoperate well.

Change keys often. Current WEP key attacks depend on either a dictionary attack or the collection of large amounts of data to deduce the key. The more often you change the key being used, the more difficult a potential cracker's job will be. Unfortunately, this might not be feasible for a network with a large user base, as you would be faced with the classic key distribution problem.

Use WEP in combination with other security features. If you happen to have a network that uses hardware of the same manufacturer, you might be able to take advantage of proprietary extensions to shore up WEP. For example, Cisco equipment supports rapid WEP key rotation and dynamic keying using 802.1x. If all of your clients can take advantage of these extensions, then use them. Unfortunately, as we will see in "Dispel the Myth of Wireless Security" [Hack #87], using other standard features like "closed" networks and MAC filters really does little to improve network security.

Consider WEP a deterrent, not a guarantee. Remember that it is unlikely that WEP alone will keep out the most determined attackers. When building a security policy, be sure to consider your likeliest threats, and weigh them against the benefits and restrictions of your implementation. The threat model for a wireless network on dial-up in a house in the middle of the woods looks very different from that of an AP on the internal LAN at a law firm downtown. Consider the risks and benefits of your wireless network, and configure it accordingly.

Consider not using WEP at all. This chapter is full of practical implementations that neatly sidestep the whole question of WEP security by introducing strong application-layer encryption. Consider doing away with WEP altogether in favor of strong authentication and encryption.

See Also

- Your 802.11 Wireless Network has No Clothes (*http://www.cs.umd.edu/ ~waa/wireless.pdf*) by Arbaugh, Shankar, and Wan, University of Maryland, March 30, 2001.

- Weaknesses in the Key Scheduling Algorithm of RC4 (*http://www. crypto.com/papers/others/rc4_ksaproc.ps*) by Fluhrer, Mantin and Shamir, July 25, 2001.

- Using the Fluhrer, Mantin, and Shamir Attack to Break WEP (*http:// www.cs.rice.edu/~astubble/wep/*) AT&T Labs Technical Report by Stubblefield, Ioannidis, and Rubin, August 21, 2001.

- Security of the WEP algorithm (*http://www.isaac.cs.berkeley.edu/isaac/ wep-faq.html*) by Borisov, Goldberg, and Wagner, UC Berkeley, April 1, 2001.

Dispel the Myth of Wireless Security
#87   Find out for yourself just how "secure" your standard wireless network really is.

Despite a few good online articles and countless alarmist news items decrying parasitic War Drivers and War Chalkers contributing to the moral decay of the country, a surprising number of people still install wireless equipment with all of the defaults enabled. There are a huge number of access points in use today that unintentionally advertise a default SSID, bridge directly to an Ethernet network, and use no encryption whatsoever (or a WEP key left on the factory setting, and therefore easily deduced).

But even if all standard precautions are in place, how much "security" do wireless access points actually provide? Having heard all sorts of widely varying estimates and assumptions from people who should be able to make an educated guess, I finally decided to see for myself what it would take to circumvent the security of my own standard 802.11b network.

The Test Environment

Since my "production" wireless network is actually an open node on Seattle Wireless, I decided to put together a temporary lab network consisting of the following:

- A "Graphite" AirPort
- An iMac with an AirPort card running OS X
- An iBook with an AirPort card running the Debian Linux distribution

In order to make the test as difficult as possible, I decided to create a "closed" network (that doesn't broadcast the SSID), enable WEP, and implement a MAC address filter. The AirPort was set to the SSID *stealthy*, with the unlikely deduced WEP key of *t8$Gc*. I added a MAC address filter that allowed only the AirPort card in the iMac to connect to it, and I also set the AirPort to channel 1 (the only unused channel in my immediate area). The Ethernet on the AirPort was connected to my local house network and configured to use NAT.

After resetting the Airport, I verified that I couldn't detect the *stealthy* SSID from either the iMac or the iBook. I then connected to the AirPort with the iMac, specifying the network name and WEP key explicitly. I got a DHCP lease of 10.0.1.2, and verified that I could in fact browse the Web. To be sure that the MAC filter was working properly, I also verified that I could not associate with the AirPort from the iBook, even using the proper WEP key and SSID. I then set the iMac to flood ping the AirPort, in order to generate a large amount of wireless traffic:

```
rob@imac:~$ sudo ping -f 10.0.1.1
```

Now everything was in place to test this configuration with the iBook.

Step 1. Detect the Network

Of course, the first step was to detect the network's presence. This was easily accomplished with Kismet **[Hack #31]**. As you can see in Figure 7-1, the *stealthy* network was detected immediately.

Note that the network would be detected instantly (provided that someone was actually using it), regardless of whether I had called it *stealthy* or something original and tricky like *kpX284W_m*. Obfuscating the SSID of your network does *nothing* to enhance the security of your wireless network, regardless of whether you broadcast beacons. For the record, I started Kismet at 18:23, at which point it began logging all 802.11 frames that it

```
┌─Network List──(Autofit)─────────────────────────────────────────┐┌─Info─┐
│    Name                         T W Ch Packts Flags IP Range     ││Ntwrks│
│  ! <stealthy>                   A Y 01   9615       0.0.0.0       ││     1│
│                                                                  ││Pckets│
│                                                                  ││  9615│
│                                                                  ││Cryptd│
│                                                                  ││  8996│
│                                                                  ││ Weak │
│                                                                  ││     1│
│                                                                  ││Noise │
│                                                                  ││     0│
│                                                                  ││Discrd│
│                                                                  ││     0│
│                                                                  ││Pkts/s│
│                                                                  ││   376│
│                                                                  ││      │
│                                                                  ││Elapsd│
│                                                                  │└000104┘
├─Status───────────────────────────────────────────────────────────────────┤
│                                                                           │
│  Found SSID "stealthy" for cloaked network BSSID 00:02:2D:27:D9:22        │
│  Connected to Kismet server version 2.8.1 build 20030126205324 on localhost:2│
└─Battery: AC 100% 0h0m0s──────────────────────────────────────────────────┘
```

Figure 7-1. A "stealthy" network detected.

encountered. Now that I knew the channel and SSID of the target network, it was time to move to the next step.

Step 2. Find a Valid MAC Address

I know of two ways to find valid MAC addresses for a given network. You could associate with the AP and run an IP layer network sniffer such as Ethereal **[Hack #38]** or *tcpdump* **[Hack #37]**. This is, of course, the hard way, particularly if you already have Kismet handy.

The easy way is to select the network you are interested in (press **ss** to sort by SSID, and arrow down to it if necessary) and then view the associated clients (press **c**). Presto, you have a list of MAC addresses for clients that are using the network, and presumably are on the permitted MAC table. Wireless clients send their MAC address in the clear, regardless of whether the AP requires WEP.

These steps took just a few seconds (it actually took me longer to run the screen grab utility than to execute the attacks). Now came the tricky part: cracking the WEP key.

Step 3. Crack the WEP Key

It is entirely possible to have AirSnort crack an 802.11 stream in real time. In my meager testing, I have found this to be fairly unstable using Debian on an iBook. Rather than risk a crash in the middle of my test, I decided to just run it against the pcap dump that Kismet creates automatically. I opened the dump file immediately, and then checked its progress every 10 minutes or so.

As you can see in Figure 7-2, AirSnort was successful in finding the WEP key (*t8$Gc*) after only 3.4 million packets.

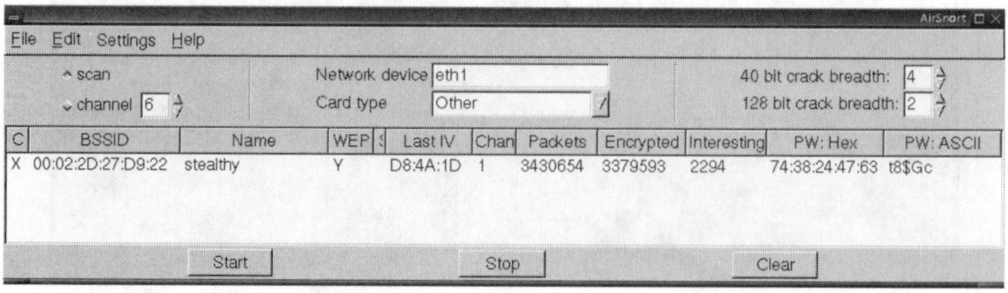

Figure 7-2. *WEP key found.*

I stopped Kismet, and noted the time. It was now 19:50. 1 hour and 27 minutes had passed, and Kismet had accumulated only 490,796,602 bytes (that's less than 490 MB, or considerably less than a single CD ISO). I think this was a particularly lucky run, as many people have reported having to log a couple of gigabytes of data before AirSnort could guess the key.

Now armed with the correct SSID, a valid MAC address, and the WEP key, I could actually attempt to access the wireless network. Note that until now, absolutely no information has been transmitted by the iBook, making detection of this attack a practical impossibility.

Step 4. Logging In

After quitting Kismet and taking the wireless card out of monitor mode, I configured the iBook to use the proper network parameters:

```
root@ibook:~# ifconfig eth1 hw ether 00:30:65:1E:81:9B
root@ibook:~# iwconfig eth1 key 's:t8$Gc'
root@ibook:~# iwconfig eth1 essid stealthy
```

Ah, but what IP address information should I use? Up until now, I hadn't looked at any IP layer traffic. Kismet could not reveal the IP range, because it didn't have the WEP key. At this point, I could have started up Ethereal and looked at the captured *pcap dump* [Hack #39], but it was much simpler to view the network data in real time using *tcpdump* [Hack #37] like so:

```
root@ibook:~# tcpdump -n -i eth1
19:52:08.995104 10.0.1.2 > 10.0.1.1: icmp: echo request
19:52:08.996412 10.0.1.1 > 10.0.1.2: icmp: echo reply
19:52:08.997961 10.0.1.2 > 10.0.1.1: icmp: echo request
19:52:08.999220 10.0.1.1 > 10.0.1.2: icmp: echo reply
```

```
19:52:09.000581 10.0.1.2 > 10.0.1.1: icmp: echo request
19:52:09.003162 10.0.1.1 > 10.0.1.2: icmp: echo reply
^C
```

Since the ping flood was still running, I quickly hit Control-C to kill *tcp-dump*. Using *tcpdump* with the −n switch, IP addresses that are actively in use on the network are revealed. Based on this information, it is possible to infer that the *stealthy* network is using 10.0.1.x, it is most likely using a class C or class A netmask, and 10.0.1.1 is probably a good guess at the default router. Had this been an actual real-world network, it would have been trivial to find the default router and local DNS servers by looking at actual network traffic in Ethereal.

Rather than step on the IP address being used by the iMac (10.0.1.2), I decided to pick a different address altogether. If this would work, it should allow the iMac and iBook to coexist on the network without too much interference.

```
root@ibook:~# ifconfig eth1 10.0.1.3 netmask 255.255.255.0 broadcast 10.0.1.
255
root@ibook:~# route add default gw 10.0.1.1
root@ibook:~# ping -c2 yahoo.com
PING yahoo.com (66.218.71.198): 56 data bytes
64 bytes from 66.218.71.198: icmp_seq=0 ttl=242 time=32.5 ms
64 bytes from 66.218.71.198: icmp_seq=1 ttl=242 time=33.2 ms

--- yahoo.com ping statistics ---
2 packets transmitted, 2 packets received, 0% packet loss
round-trip min/avg/max = 32.5/32.8/33.2 ms
```

As you can see, I was able to ping *yahoo.com* (and had full network access from that point on). Given the correct SSID, WEP key, and a valid MAC address, the AirPort could not distinguish me from the iMac and therefore could do nothing to keep me out. Note that while the AirPort can't tell the difference, a program such as arpwatch [Hack #100] can detect many sorts of MAC address shenanigans, but only if the AirPort is configured as a bridge. Since it is set up as a NAT in this configuration (as many APs are by default), the sharing of MAC addresses between clients is completely invisible to the rest of the network.

Post Mortem

I hope this little experiment gives you some idea of what you are up against when relying on the built-in security measures of 802.11b. Using inexpensive hardware and freely available tools, a typical Wi-Fi network can be easily cracked in a mere hour and a half (although it will probably take a bit longer on average, depending on how busy the network is, potentially offset by a bit of luck).

What does this mean for wireless security? Should we run screaming to our system administrators and toss the whole lot into the garbage? Of course not. This whole exercise is presented to drive home this point: if you are concerned about wireless security, you must use strong application-layer encryption and authentication. Much of the rest of this chapter details other freely available tools that you can use to protect your network and your wireless users against these attacks.

Cracking WEP with AirSnort: The Easy Way
#88   Use a dictionary attack to test the security of your WEP key.

While widely publicized for its ability to crack a WEP key in real time by attacking weaknesses in the implementation, AirSnort requires a potentially large amount of data to be gathered before the attack is successful. AirSnort also comes with a largely unknown utility that will perform a dictionary attack on a relatively tiny sampling of network traffic.

Using the aptly named *decrypt* utility, you can attempt to decrypt a WEP stream by trying a list of potential candidates from a word list. This attack can be carried out in a matter of minutes, rather than the hours that would be required to collect the large traffic samples needed to interpolate a WEP key.

To use the *decrypt* utility, you first need a packet dump from a utility that can capture raw 802.11 frames (such as Kismet **[Hack #31]**). You will also need a list of suitable candidates, namely words that are either 5 or 13 characters long (for 40-bit or 104-bit WEP respectively). Invoke the utility like this:

```
# decrypt -f /usr/dict/words -m 00:02:2D:27:D9:22 -e encrypted.dump -d ↵
out.dump
Found key: Hex - 61:6c:6f:68:61, ASCII - "aloha"
```

Notice that you also need to specify the BSSID of the network you wish to attempt to decrypt. In this case, the BSSID is the same as the MAC address of the AP, but can be set to virtually anything. You can obtain this field from the Info pane inside Kismet when capturing the data **[Hack #31]**. If successful, the decrypt utility displays the WEP key, decrypts the entire stream (specified by the -e switch), and saves it to a file of your choice (specified by the -d switch).

This output file is suitable for import into any standard packet-analysis tool, such as *tcpdump* (**[Hack #37]**) or Ethereal **[Hack #39]**.

Of course, this attack succeeds only if the WEP key actually appears in your list of words to try. Unix password crackers have developed utilities over the years that will not only try words from the dictionary, but will try common (and even unusual) variations on these words until a match is found. The use of these tools is left as an exercise to whatever demented individuals find it worth their while to do so.

Again, the point of this hack isn't to encourage you to go around breaking into people's networks, but to stress the importance of strong encryption and proper network configuration. It is just plain foolish to expect WEP to answer all of your security needs when tools like AirSnort so easily demonstrate its inherent weaknesses.

You can download AirSnort from *http://airsnort.shmoo.com/*. There is also a wealth of information there about passive monitoring, WEP implementations, and wireless security in general.

HACK #89 NoCatAuth Captive Portal

Provide cryptographically sound access control using only a web browser.

NoCatAuth is an open source implementation of a *captive portal*. The idea behind a captive portal is fairly straightforward. When a user behind a captive portal attempts to browse to any web page, they are redirected to a page with a login prompt as well as information about the wireless network they are connected to. If the gateway consults with a central authority to determine the identity of the connected wireless user, once satisfied, it then relaxes its firewall rules accordingly. Until the user logs in, no other network traffic is permitted to pass through the gateway.

Rather than rely on the built-in security features of 802.11b, the network is configured with no WEP and as an open network. The AP is also in bridged mode and connected via a crossover cable to an Ethernet card on a Linux router. It is then up to the router to issue DHCP leases, throttle bandwidth, and permit access to other networks.

Written in Perl and C, NoCatAuth takes care of the dirty work of implementing the portal itself. It presents the user with a login prompt, consults a MySQL database (or other authentication source) to look up user credentials, and securely notifies the wireless gateway of the user's status. On the gateway side, the software manages local connections, sets bandwidth throttling and firewall rules, and times out old logins after a user-specified time limit. The software is freely available and released under the GPL.

We are designing the system so that trust is ultimately preserved: the gateways and end users need trust only the Auth system, which is secured with a registered SSL certificate. Passwords are never given to the wireless gateway (thus protecting the users from "bad guy" node owners), and gateway rules are only modified by a cryptographically signed message from the Auth system (protecting the gateway from users or upstream sites trying to spoof the Auth system).

We provide for three possible classes of wireless user: Public Class, Co-op Class, and Owner Class:

Public Class

> This kind of user would be someone who knows nothing about the local wireless network, and simply is looking for access to the Internet. This class is granted very little bandwidth, and users are restricted in what services they can access by the use of firewall rules. The Public Class user is given the opportunity to learn more about who is providing the wireless service and how they can get in touch with the local group (and ultimately get more access). They do not have personal logins, but must still authenticate by manually skipping the login process—hence the term "catch and release."

Co-op Class

> This class consists of users with pre-arranged login information. The rules for membership should be determined by the local community groups and are configured in the central Auth system database. This class is typically granted much greater bandwidth and access to ports, as users can now be held accountable for their own actions.

Owner Class

> This is much the same as the Co-op Class, but is reserved for the owner of a given node and anyone else to whom they want to grant access. The Owner Class pre-empts traffic from all other classes and has free use of all network resources.

The typical connection process is shown in Figure 7-3.

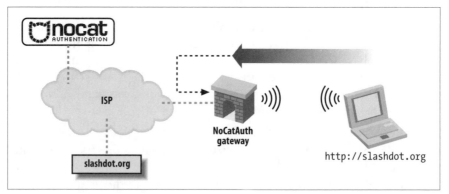

Figure 7-3. The user's web traffic is "captured" by the gateway.

A roaming user associates with the AP and is immediately issued a DHCP lease. All access beyond contacting the Authentication Service is denied by default. When the user tries to browse the Web, she is immediately redirected to the gateway service, which then redirects her to the Auth system's

SSL login page (after appending a random token and some other information to the URL line). This process is completely transparent to the user, as shown in Figure 7-4.

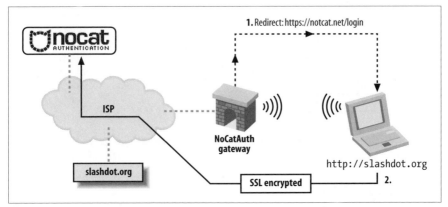

Figure 7-4. The user is redirected to an SSL-encrypted page on the Authentication Server.

The user is then presented with three choices: log in with their pre-arranged login information, click on a link to find out more about membership, or click the *Skip Login* button.

Once the user has either logged in correctly or skipped the process, the Auth system then creates an outcome message, signs it with PGP, and sends it back to the wireless gateway, as shown in Figure 7-5. The gateway has a copy of the Authentication Service's public PGP key, and can verify the authenticity of the message. Since part of the data included in the response is the random token that the gateway originally issued to the client, it makes it very difficult to fake out the gateway with a "replay attack." The digital signature prevents the possibility of other machines posing as the Authentication Service and sending bogus messages to the wireless gateway.

Now, if all has gone well for the user, the wireless gateway modifies its firewall rules to grant further access, and redirects the user back to the site to which they were originally trying to browse—see Figure 7-6.

In order to keep the connection open, a small window is opened on the client side (via JavaScript) that refreshes the login page every few minutes. Once the user moves out of range or quits his browser, the connection is reset and requires another manual login.

The requirements on the gateway side are minimal (the system was designed to run under Linux 2.4, on a 486 with 16 Mb RAM). The Authentication Service is designed to be administered by a group that maintains its user database in whatever way they see fit. It can easily be configured to provide

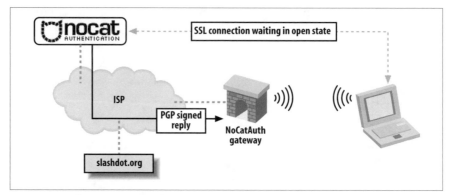

Figure 7-5. The user presents their credentials to the Authentication Service, which then notifies the gateway.

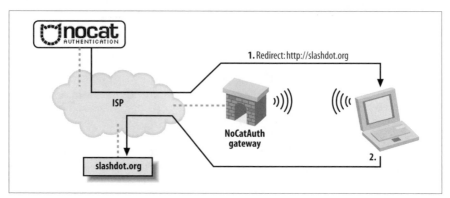

Figure 7-6. The user is redirected to their original site, and goes about their merry way.

"Members Only" access, so rather than use a graded, class-based mechanism, users are either granted full access or none at all.

The NoCatAuth system is under active development and has a variety of new features. "Passive" mode now allows operation without the connect-back phase (to allow installation behind a NAT firewall). There are also many additional backend authentication methods, including PAM, RADIUS, TACACS+, and even IMAP. The gateways can be configured to throttle inbound and outbound traffic to a specified rate, as well as filter ports, protocols, services, and anything else that *iptables* can track. If you use the Pebble distribution [Hack #53], it comes with the NoCat gateway pre-configured. You can always get the latest version of NoCatAuth from *http://nocat.net/*.

NoCatSplash and Cheshire

If you need a simple "splash screen" for your wireless users, try either of these simple captive portals.

Some people find that Perl is too heavy of a requirement for their gateway hardware, making it impractical to use NoCatAuth. If you are only looking for a "click here to continue" sort of splash page (without the full authentication mechanism), you may be interested in NoCatSplash. It is a port of NoCatAuth entirely rewritten in C. Its requirements are quite small, but it supports only simple open mode portal functionality. The current version works under Linux, and portability to BSD and other systems is planned for the near future.

To install NoCatSplash, download the current CVS tree or just grab the archive available at *http://nocat.net/download/NoCatSplash/*. Unpack the archive, navigate to *NoCatSplash-nightly/*, and install it with a simple:

```
rob@florian:~/NoCatSplash-nightly$ ./configure; make; make install
```

This installs *splashd* to */usr/local/sbin/*, and puts the *nocat.conf* configuration file in */usr/local/etc/*. Edit the *nocat.conf* file to your tastes, taking note to set the ExternalDevice, InternalDevice, LocalNetwork, and DNSAddr options to fit your network layout. See the comments in the configuration file for details.

Start the portal by running *splashd* as root:

```
root@florian:~# /usr/local/sbin/splashd &
```

NoCatSplash uses the same firewall scripts as NoCatAuth to do the actual firewall manipulation. It installs these scripts to */usr/local/libexec/nocat/*, making it simple to customize your firewall rules if you need to. With *splashd* running, any users whose traffic originates on InternalDevice will be captured and shown the splash page defined in *nocat.conf*. The default *html* files for the splash page are kept in */usr/local/share/nocat/htdocs/*, but can be kept wherever you like by setting the DocumentRoot in *nocat.conf*.

Another possible alternative to NoCatAuth is Cheshire, a captive portal written completely in shell script. It is available at *http://nocat.net/download/cheshire/*. The goal of Cheshire is to provide the smallest possible captive portal, suitable for use with very tiny Linux installations. Without decent networking functions of its own, Cheshire needs a couple of helper apps to do the dirty work of actual networking. Notably, it needs the *getpeername* utility from NetPipes (*http://freshmeat.net/projects/netpipes/*). It also needs the *faucet* utility from the same package, or it can use the system's *inetd* if you have one installed.

Apart from this, standard system tools such as sed, awk, and cron are all you need. Cheshire works fine under the very lightweight ash shell. If you want to serve graphics on your splash page, and your gateway has a slow CPU, you will probably be happiest with a "real" web server rather than using Cheshire itself. I find that khttpd (the Kernel space http server available in Linux 2.4) works very well for this job, and is very tiny.

To install Cheshire, extract the archive into */usr/local/cheshire/*. Edit the *cheshire.conf* file in this directory to your liking, and launch the script using faucet like this:

```
root@gateway:~# faucet 5280 --in --out --daemon /usr/local/cheshire/bin/grin
```

If you would rather not use faucet, you can run Cheshire out of your inetd. Add the port as a service in */etc/services* by appending a line like this:

```
cheshire              5280/tcp
```

Add Cheshire itself to your */etc/inetd.conf* with this line:

```
cheshire  stream  tcp  nowait  root  /usr/local/cheshire/bin/grin
```

Finally, you will probably want to boot your users out ever so often, to force them to see the splash page again. Use the system cron to accomplish this. I run it once a day at 4:00 in the morning. Put a line like this in the crontab for root:

```
0 4 * * *      /usr/local/cheshire/bin/grin -R
```

While Cheshire and NoCatSplash might not be as feature rich as NoCat-Auth, their requirements are very simple. They can be ideal for situations where you simply want to give people an idea of whose network they are using, especially if the capabilities of your wireless gateway are limited.

HACK #91 Squid Proxy over SSH

Secure your web traffic from prying eyes—and improve performance in the process.

squid is normally used as an HTTP-accelerator. It is a large, well-managed, and full-featured caching HTTP proxy that is finding its way into many commercial web platforms. Since it performs all of its magic on a single TCP port, it is an ideal candidate for use with an SSH tunnel. This not only helps to secure your web browser when using wireless networks, but also potentially makes your browser run even faster. Best of all, squid is open source and freely available from *http://www.squid-cache.org/*.

First, choose a server on which to host your squid cache. Typically, this will be a Linux or BSD machine on your local wired network—although squid also runs in Windows, under Cygwin (*http://www.cygwin.com/*). You want to have a fast connection to your cache, so choosing a squid cache at the other end of a dial-up connection is probably a bad idea (unless you enjoy simulating what the Internet was like in 1995). On a home network, this is typically the same machine you use as a firewall or DNS server. Fortunately, squid isn't very demanding when it supports only a few simultaneous users, so it can happily share a box that runs other services.

It is beyond the scope of this hack to include full squid installation instructions, but configuration isn't especially difficult. Just be sure to check your access rules and set a password for the management interface. If you have trouble getting it to run, check out Jennifer Vesperman's "Installing and Configuring Squid" at *http://linux.oreillynet.com/pub/a/linux/2001/07/26/ squid.html*.

When squid is installed and running, it binds to TCP port 3128 by default. Once you have it running, you should test it manually by setting your HTTP proxy to the server. For example, suppose your server is running on *mysquid.house* (assuming that you are running the TLD of *.house* **[Hack #56]**). In Mozilla, go to *Preferences → Advanced → Proxies*, as in Figure 7-7.

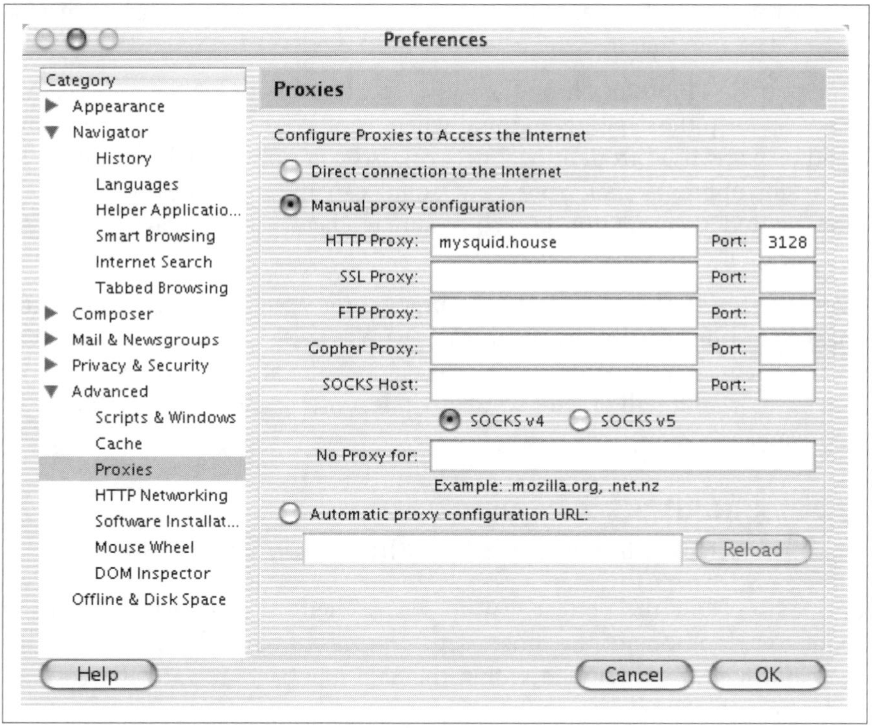

Figure 7-7. Test your squid using the HTTP Proxy field in Mozilla.

Enter "mysquid.house" as the HTTP Proxy host, and "3128" for the port. Click OK, and try to load any web page. You should immediately see the page you requested. If you see an "Access Denied" error, look over the *http_access* lines in your *squid.conf*, and restart squid if necessary.

Once you are satisfied that you have a happy squid, then you need only to forward your connection to it over SSH. Set up a local listener on port 3128, forwarding to mysquid.house:3128 like this:

```
rob@caligula:~$ ssh -L3128:localhost:3128 mysquid.house -f -N
```

This will set up an SSH tunnel and fork into the background automatically. Next, change the HTTP Proxy host in your browser to localhost, and reload your page. As long as your SSH tunnel is running, your web traffic will be encrypted all the way to *mysquid.house*, where it is decrypted and sent on to the Internet.

The biggest advantage of technique (compared to using the SSH SOCKS 4 proxy [Hack #92]) is that virtually all browsers support the use of HTTP proxies, while not every browser supports SOCKS 4. Also, if you are using OS X, there is support for HTTP proxies built into the OS itself. This means that every properly written application will use your proxy settings transparently. I'll go into that in more detail later [Hack #97].

Note that HTTP proxies have the same difficulties with DNS as a SOCKS 4 proxy, so keep those points in mind when using your proxy. Typically, your squid proxy is used from a local network, so you don't usually run into the DNS schizophrenia issue. But your squid can theoretically run anywhere (even behind a remote firewall), so be sure to check out the notes on DNS in that hack.

Running squid takes a little bit of preparation, but can both secure and accelerate your web traffic when using wireless. Of course, squid will support as many simultaneous wireless users as you care to throw at it, so be sure to set it up for all of your regular wireless users, and keep your web traffic private.

HACK #92   SSH SOCKS 4 Proxy

Protect your web traffic using the basic VPN functionality built into SSH itself.

In the search for the perfect way to secure their wireless networks, many people overlook one of the most useful features of SSH: the -D switch. This simple little switch is buried within the SSH manpage, toward the bottom, and is described next.

-D port

> Specifies a local "dynamic" application-level port forwarding. This works by allocating a socket to listen to port on the local side, and whenever a connection is made to this port, the connection is forwarded over the secure channel, and the application protocol is then used to determine where to connect to from the remote machine. Currently the SOCKS 4 protocol is supported, and SSH will act as a SOCKS 4 server. Only root can forward privileged ports. Dynamic port forwardings can also be specified in the configuration file.

This turns out to be an insanely useful feature if you have software that is capable of using a SOCKS 4 proxy. It effectively gives you an instant encrypted proxy server to any machine that you can SSH to. It does this without the need for further software, either on your laptop or on the remote server.

Just as with SSH port forwarding **[Hack #93]**, the -D switch binds to the specified local port and encrypts any traffic to that port, sends it down the tunnel, and decrypts it on the other side. For example, to set up a SOCKS 4 proxy from local port 8080 to *remote* from your wireless laptop, type the following:

```
rob@caligula:~$ ssh -D 8080 remote
```

That's all there is to it. Now you simply specify `localhost:8080` as the SOCKS 4 proxy in your application, and all connections made by that application will be sent down the encrypted tunnel. For example, to set your SOCKS proxy in Mozilla, go to *Preferences → Advanced → Proxies*, as shown in Figure 7-8.

Select *Manual proxy configuration*, then type in localhost as the SOCKS host. Enter the port number that you passed to the -D switch, and be sure to check the SOCKS 4 button.

Click *OK*, and you're finished. All of the traffic that Mozilla generates is now encrypted, and appears to originate from the remote machine that you logged into with SSH. Anyone listening to your wireless traffic now sees a large volume of encrypted SSH traffic, but your actual data is well protected.

About DNS

One important point to keep in mind is that SOCKS 4 has no native support for DNS traffic. This has two important side effects to keep in mind when using it to secure your wireless transmissions:

- DNS lookups are still sent in the clear. This means that anyone listening in can still see the names of sites that you browse to, although the actual URLs and data are obscured. This is rarely a security risk, but it is worth keeping in mind.

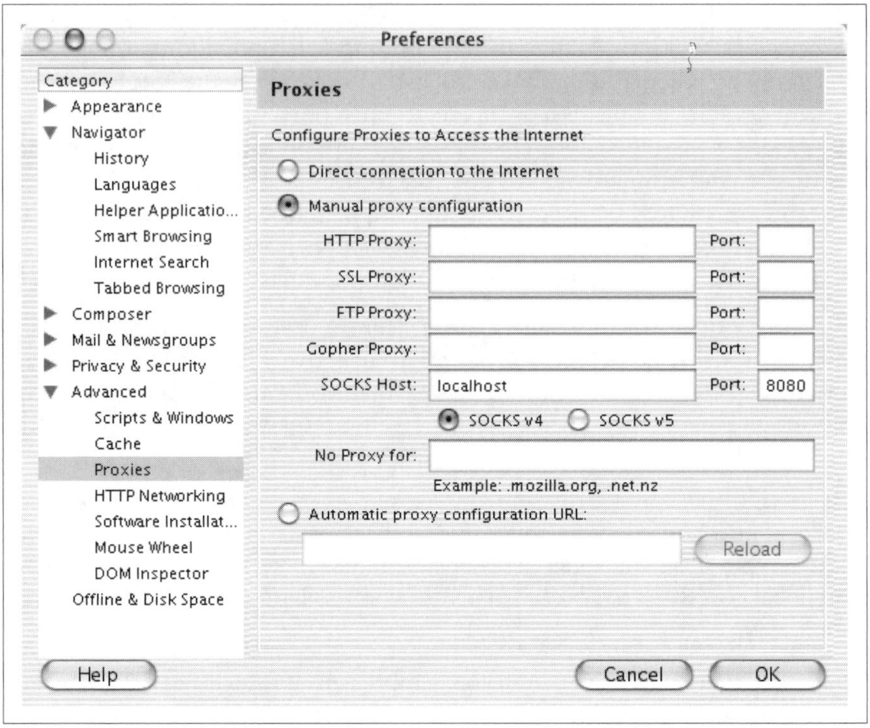

Figure 7-8. Proxy settings in Mozilla.

- You are still using a local DNS server, but your traffic originates from the remote end of the proxy. This can have interesting (and undesirable) side effects when attempting to access private network resources.

To illustrate the subtle problems that this can cause, consider a typical corporate network with a web server called *intranet.mybusiness.com*. This web server uses the private address 192.168.1.10, but is accessible from the Internet through the use of a forwarding firewall. The DNS server for *intranet.mybusiness.com* normally responds with different IP addresses depending on where the request comes from, perhaps using the views functionality in BIND 9. When coming from the Internet, you would normally access *intranet.mybusiness.com* with the IP address 208.201.239.36, which is actually the IP address of the outside of the corporate firewall.

Now suppose that you are using the SOCKS proxy example just shown, and *remote* is actually a machine behind the corporate firewall. Your local DNS server returns 208.201.239.36 as the IP address for *intranet.mybusiness.com* (since you are looking up the name from outside the firewall). But the HTTP request actually comes from *remote*, and attempts to go to 208.201.239.36. Many times, this is forbidden by the firewall rules, as internal users are supposed to access the intranet by its internal IP address, 192.168.1.10. How can you work around this DNS schizophrenia?

One simple method to avoid this trouble is to make use of a local hosts file on your laptop. Add an entry like this to */etc/hosts* (or the equivalent on your operating system):

```
192.168.1.10    intranet.mybusiness.com
```

Likewise, you can list any number of hosts that are only reachable from the inside of your corporate firewall. When you attempt to browse to one of those sites, the local hosts file is consulted before DNS, so the private IP address is used. Since this request is actually made from *remote*, it finds its way to the internal server with no trouble. Likewise, responses arrive back at the SOCKS proxy on *remote*, are encrypted and forwarded over your SSH tunnel, and appear in your browser as if they came in from the Internet.

SOCKS 5 support is planned for an upcoming version of SSH, which will also make tunneled DNS resolution possible. This is particularly exciting for OS X users, as there is support in the OS for SOCKS 5 proxies. Once SSH supports SOCKS 5, every native OS X application will automatically be able to take advantage of encrypting SSH socks proxies. In the meantime, we'll just have to settle for encrypted HTTP proxies [Hack #91].

H A C K #93 Forwarding Ports over SSH

Keep network traffic to arbitrary ports secure with SSH port forwarding.

In addition to providing remote shell access and command execution, OpenSSH can also forward arbitrary TCP ports to the other end of your connection. This can be extremely handy for protecting email, web, or any other traffic that you need to keep private (at least, all the way to the other end of the tunnel).

SSH accomplishes local forwarding by binding to a local port, performing encryption, sending the encrypted data to the remote end of the SSH connection, then decrypting it and sending it to the remote host and port you specify. Start an SSH tunnel with the -L switch (short for Local):

```
root@laptop:~# ssh -f -N -L110:mailhost:110 -l user mailhost
```

Naturally, substitute *user* with your username, and *mailhost* with your mail server's name or IP address. Note that you will have to be root on *laptop* for this example, since you'll be binding to a privileged port (110, the POP port). You should also disable any locally running POP daemon (look in */etc/inetd.conf*) or it will get in the way.

Now to encrypt all of your POP traffic, configure your mail client to connect to *localhost* port 110. It will happily talk to *mailhost* as if it were connected directly, except that the entire conversation will be encrypted.

The -f forks SSH into the background, and -N tells it not to actually run a command on the remote end (just do the forwarding). If your SSH server supports it, try the -C switch to turn on compression—this can significantly improve the time it takes to download your email.

You can specify as many -L lines as you like when establishing the connection. To also forward outbound email traffic, try this:

```
root@laptop:~# ssh -f -N -L110:mailhost:110 -L25:mailhost:25 -l user
mailhost
```

Set your outbound email host to *localhost*, and your email traffic will be encrypted as far as *mailhost*. This generally is only useful if the email is bound for an internal host, or if you can't trust your local network connection (as is the case with most wireless networks). Obviously, once your email leaves *mailhost*, it will be transmitted in the clear, unless you've encrypted the message with a tool like PGP or GPG.

If you're already logged into a remote host, and need to forward a port quickly, try this:

1. Press ENTER.

2. Type **~C**.

3. You should be at an ssh> prompt. Enter the -L line as you would from the command line.

For example:

```
rob@catlin:~$
rob@catlin:~$ ~C (it doesn't echo)
ssh> -L8080:localhost:80
Forwarding port.
```

Your current shell then forwards local port 8000 to *catlin*'s port 80, as if you had entered it in the first place.

You can also allow other (remote) clients to connect to your forwarded port with the -g switch. If you're logged in to a remote gateway that serves as a NAT for a private network, then a command like this:

```
rob@gateway:~$ ssh -f -g -N -L8000:localhost:80 10.42.4.6
```

forwards all connections from gateway's port 8000 to internal host 10.42.4.6's port 80. If the gateway has a live Internet address, anyone from the Net is allowed to connect to the web server on 10.42.4.6 as if it were running on port 8000 of the gateway.

One last point worth mentioning: the forwarded host doesn't have to be *localhost*; it can be any host that the machine you're connecting to can access directly. For example, to forward local port 5150 to a web server somewhere on an internal network, try this:

```
rob@remote:~$ ssh -f -N -L5150:intranet.insider.nocat:80 gateway.nocat.net
```

Assuming that you're running a TLD **[Hack #56]** of *.nocat*, and that *gateway. nocat.net* also has a connection to the private *.nocat* network, all traffic to 5150 of *remote* is obligingly forwarded to *intranet.insider.nocat:80*. The address *intranet.insider.nocat* doesn't have to resolve in DNS to *remote*; it isn't looked up until the connection is made to *gateway.nocat.net*, and then it's *gateway* that does the lookup. To securely browse that site from *remote*, try connecting to *http://localhost:5150/*.

Although SSH also has functionality for acting as a SOCKS 4 proxy (with the -D switch **[Hack #92]**), it just isn't well suited for routing all network traffic to the other end of a tunnel. You can use a real encapsulating tunnel such as vtun **[Hack #98]** in conjunction with SSH to forward *everything*.

SSH is an incredibly flexible tool, with much more functionality than I can cover here. See the references below for more fun things you can do with SSH.

See Also

- man ssh
- *SSH, The Secure Shell: The Definitive Guide* (*http://www.oreilly.com/ catalog/sshtdg/*) by Daniel J. Barrett and Richard Silverman (O'Reilly)

Quick Logins with SSH Client Keys

HACK #94

Using SSH keys instead of password authentication to speed up and automate logins.

When you're an admin on more than a few machines, being able to navigate quickly to a shell on any given server is critical. Having to type **ssh** *my.server. com* (followed by a password) is not only tedious, but it also breaks your concentration. Suddenly having to shift from "where's the problem?" to "getting there," and back to "what's all this, then?" has led more than one admin to premature senility. It promotes the digital equivalent of "why did I come into this room, anyway?" (and the problem is only made worse by */usr/games/ fortune*!).

At any rate, more effort spent logging into a machine means less effort spent solving problems. Recent versions of SSH offer a secure alternative to endlessly entering a password: *public key exchange*.

For these examples, I assume that you're using OpenSSHv3.4p1 or later. To use public keys with an SSH server, you'll first need to generate a public/private key pair:

```
$ ssh-keygen -t rsa
```

You can also use -t dsa for DSA keys, or -t rsa1 if you're using Protocol v1. And shame on you if you are using v1! Upgrade to v2 as soon as you can!

After you enter the above command, you should see something like this:

```
Generating public/private rsa key pair.
Enter file in which to save the key (/home/rob/.ssh/id_rsa):
```

Just press Enter there. It will then ask you for a passphrase; just press Enter twice (but read the Security note below). Here's what the results should look like:

```
Enter passphrase (empty for no passphrase):
Enter same passphrase again:
Your identification has been saved in /home/rob/.ssh/id_rsa.
Your public key has been saved in /home/rob/.ssh/id_rsa.pub.
The key fingerprint is:
a6:5c:c3:eb:18:94:0b:06:a1:a6:29:58:fa:80:0a:bc rob@localhost
```

This created two files: *~/.ssh/id_rsa* and *~/.ssh/id_rsa.pub*. To use this key-pair on a server, try this:

```
$ ssh server "mkdir .ssh; chmod 0700 .ssh"
$ scp .ssh/id_rsa.pub server:.ssh/authorized_keys2
```

Of course, substitute your server name for *server*. It should ask for your password both times. Now, simply ssh *server* and it should log you in automatically, without a password. And yes, it will use your shiny new public key for scp, too.

If this didn't work for you, check your file permissions on both *~/.ssh/** and *server:~/.ssh/**. Your private key (*id_rsa*) should be 0600 (and be present only on your local machine), and everything else should be 0655 or better.

Terrific. So you can now SSH to any machine quickly and with a minimum of fuss. Is it possible to make it even quicker to connect to machines you frequently touch? You bet [Hack #95].

Security Concerns

Some consider the use of public keys a potential security risk. After all, one has only to steal a copy of your private key to obtain access to your servers. While this is true, the same is certainly true of passwords.

Ask yourself, how many times a day do you enter a password to gain shell access to a machine (or scp a file)? How frequently is it the same password on many (or all) of those machines? Have you ever used that password in a way that might be questionable (on a web site, on a personal machine that isn't quite up to date, or possibly with an SSH client on a machine that you don't directly control)? If any of these possibilities sound familiar, then consider that an SSH key in the same setting would make it virtually impossible for an attacker to later gain unauthorized access (providing, of course, that you keep your private key safe).

Another way to balance ease of use with security is to use a passphrase on your key, but use the SSH agent to manage your keys for you. When you start the agent, it will ask you for your passphrase once, and will cache it until you kill the agent. Some people even go as far as to store their SSH keys on removable media (like a USB key chain) and take their keys with them wherever they go. However you choose to use SSH keys, you'll almost certainly find that they're a very useful alternative to traditional passwords.

"Turbo-Mode" SSH Logins
Even faster logins from the command line.

If you've just come from the previous two hacks, you've only seen half of the solution! Even with client keys, you still have to needlessly type **SSH server** every time you want to SSH in. Back in the dark, insecure, unenlightened days of rsh, there was an obscure feature that I happened to love, which hasn't (yet) been ported to SSH. It used to be possible to symlink *usr/bin/rsh* to a file of the same name as your server. rsh was smart enough to realize that if it wasn't called as rsh, that it should rsh to whatever name it was called as.

Of course, this is trivial to implement in shell. Create a file called *SSH-to* with these two lines in it:

```
#!/bin/sh
ssh `basename $0` $*
```

(Those are backticks around basename $0.) Now put that in your PATH (if ~/ *bin* doesn't exist or isn't in your PATH already, it should be) and set up symlinks to all of your favorite servers to it:

```
$ cd bin
$ ln -s ssh-to server1
$ ln -s ssh-to server2
$ ln -s ssh-to server3
```

Now, to SSH to server1 (assuming you've copied your public key over as just described), simply type **server1** and you'll magically end up with a shell on server1, without typing **ssh**, and without entering your password. That

$* at the end allows you to run arbitrary commands in a single line (instead of spawning a shell), like this:

```
server1 uptime
```

This will simply show the uptime, number of users, and load average on server1, then exit. Wrap it in a for loop and iterate over a list of servers to get a pinpoint status of all of your machines.

I believe that this is the quickest way to use SSH, short of setting up single character aliases to do it for you (which is excessively hackish, unmaintainable, and unnecessary, although it does seem to impress some people):

```
$ alias a='ssh alice'
$ alias b='ssh bob'
$ alias e='ssh eve'
...
```

At any rate, SSH has many options that make it a very flexible tool for securely navigating between any number of servers. Now if we can just find a way to make it log in and actually fix the machine for you, we'd have a *real* hack.

HACK #96   OpenSSH on Windows Using Cygwin

Use any of the powerful OpenSSH hacks in this chapter on a Windows box.

So you've read all the nifty cool hacks so far using OpenSSH, but you're a Windows guy or gal who hasn't (yet) taken the plunge into the world of Linux. That's okay! You can still take advantage of the power of OpenSSH on your Windows box by using a tool called Cygwin.

As the Cygwin web site explains:

Cygwin is a Linux-like environment for Windows. It consists of two parts:

A DLL (cygwin1.dll) which acts as a Linux emulation layer providing substantial Linux API functionality.

A collection of tools, which provide Linux look and feel.

This powerful and free package allows you to run many free software packages in Linux, all without leaving the safety and comfort of your Windows environment.

Installation

The software can be downloaded from *http://www.cygwin.com/*. To install Cygwin, run *setup.exe* and then select the Linux tools you want to install. These will be downloaded from the Internet and installed automatically. Using *setup.exe*, you can also choose to download only the install files, or to install them from a local directory. For the purposes of this hack, I assume that you are installing directly from the Internet.

In the first dialog box, choose an installation directory, installation type, and default text file type. Unless you need to change any of these options, just stick with the defaults for now. In the second dialog box, choose a directory where the software packages will be downloaded. This is useful to remember if you're going to be doing multiple installs. Third, you need to choose an Internet connection type. If you're inside a corporate network, you may need to consult with someone on these settings. Generally a direct connection works if you are a home user.

Lastly, you need to choose a download site. There are a whole range of sites listed, located all around the world. Choose the site that is roughly closest to your country.

setup.exe will then download the next portion of the setup program, and you will be prompted to Select Packages, as shown in Figure 7-9.

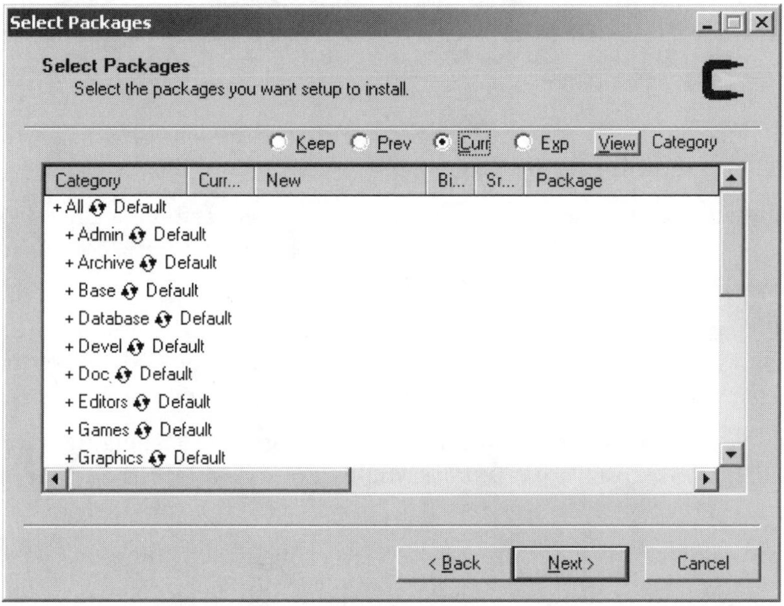

Figure 7-9. Cygwin Install Packages screen.

There are a large number of software packages that Cygwin can install for you. To add OpenSSH as an installed software package, navigate to the Net category. Click on the plus sign next to Net and scroll down until you find the line that lists OpenSSH, as shown in Figure 7-10.

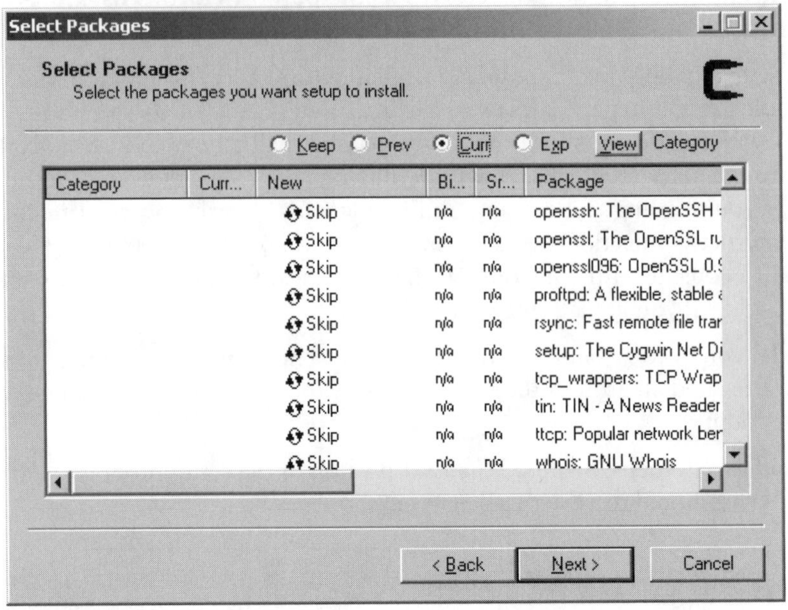

Figure 7-10. Locate openssh.

Click once on the word "Skip" on the line that shows *openssh*. You will see the change shown in Figure 7-11.

Note that when you selected *openssh*, *openssl* is also automatically selected. This is because *openssh* relies on the encryption routines contained in *openssl*.

One more package you will need to install, particularly if you want the sshd daemon to run as a service in Windows 2000 or Windows XP, is *cygrunsrv*. This package can be found in the Admin category, as shown in Figure 7-12.

Click *Next*, and Cygwin will begin downloading and installing the selected packages. Once installation is done, you'll have Cygwin icons on your desktop and in the Start menu.

To get things properly set up, you need to change a few things in your System Environment. In Windows 2000 and Windows XP, right-click on *My Computer* and choose *Properties*. Click on the *Advanced* tab and then select *Environment Variables*. Find the variable for Path and double-click on it. At the end of the path, add a semicolon and the full path to the installed Cygwin (*C:\cygwin\bin* by default, unless you changed it when you installed it). Also add a new variable by clicking on *New*. The variable name is CYGWIN. The variable value should be ntsec tty.

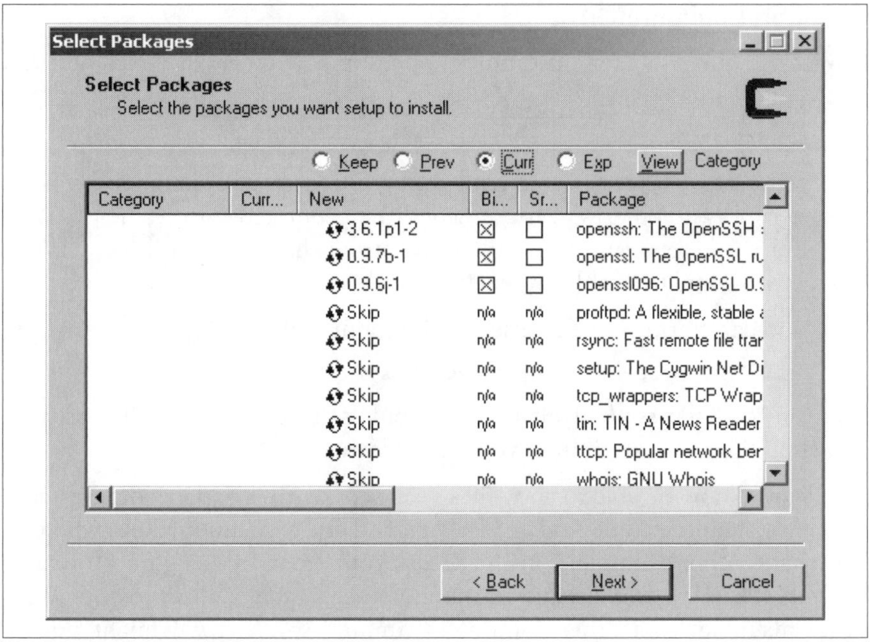

Figure 7-11. Select openssh.

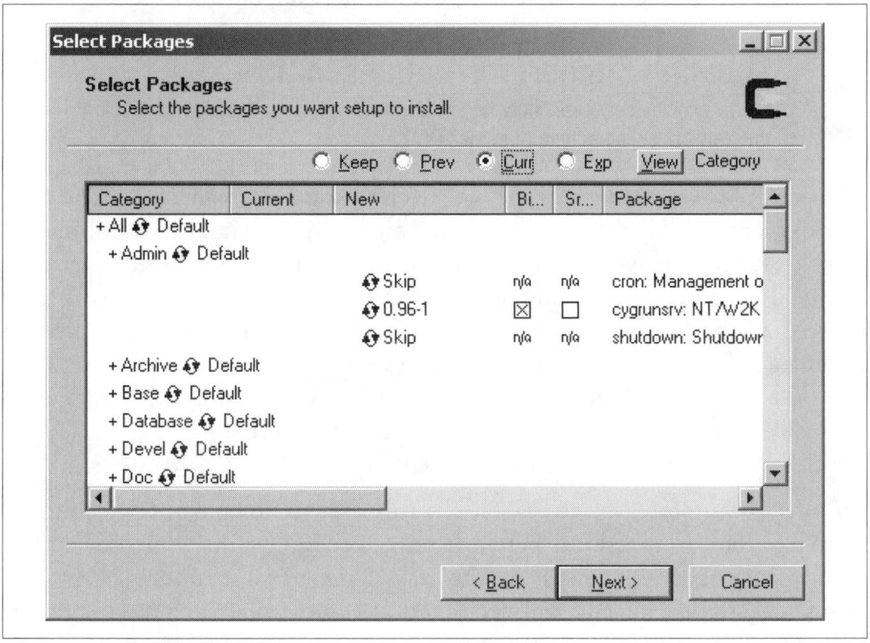

Figure 7-12. Select cygrunsrv

OpenSSH Configuration

To get the openssh daemon running, open up a Cygwin bash shell and run this:

```
Administrator@notebook ~$ ssh-host-config -y
```

This generates *ssh* keys and an *sshd* config file for your system, and sets up *sshd* to run as a Windows service. You'll be prompted for a value of CYG-WIN for *sshd* at startup. Enter the same string that you used for the CYG-WIN environment variable: ntsec tty.

Now you can start up *sshd* as a service by running this command:

```
Administrator@notebook ~$ cygrunsrv -S sshd
```

You can test your *sshd* installation by typing ssh localhost. If all goes well, you should be able to log in to your own machine.

You should now be able to copy files with scp, set up key dependencies, and use all of the other time saving SSH tips and tricks mentioned elsewhere in this chapter. For example, you can secure your email by using port forwarding [Hack #93]. With *sshd* up and running, you can even connect to your Windows machine from other computers running *ssh*. Cygwin might not be quite as powerful as a complete Linux installation, but it allows you to use many important free software packages without even having to reboot.

Location Support for Tunnels in OS X

HACK #97

Easily choose between encrypted and unencrypted communications using the Network Location feature in Mac OS X.

It is possible [Hack #91] to encrypt your web traffic by passing it over an SSH tunnel to an HTTP proxy. While you might think that you would always want to keep your web traffic encrypted, there are cases where it just isn't practical to do so. For example, if you are using a wireless network that makes use of a captive portal (such as NoCatAuth) that redirects the user to a web page before granting network access, then your tunnel will fail to connect. Of course, after you have authenticated, your tunnel will work as it normally would. But you need to connect to the authentication service "in the clear" in order to present your credentials.

Another common reason to disable the tunnel is to download large volumes of public data from a local network resource. Rather than force all of the data to be encrypted, routed all the way down to your tunnel server, and ultimately sent back again and decrypted, it is probably much more efficient to connect directly and download it in the clear. Ask yourself the question, "does it really matter if people on the local wireless know that I'm downloading a Debian ISO from a local mirror?"

While in most operating systems you would have to change the preferences of your browser in order to choose not to use the proxy, OS X has a much more elegant solution. There is a very flexible network configuration system built into the OS that allows for independent settings of every network interface, and storing as many of these settings as you like. It is called the Network Location feature, and is accessible at all times from the Apple menu (Figure 7-13).

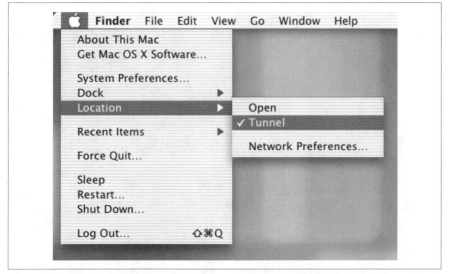

Figure 7-13. Easily jump from one network configuration to another.

OS X ships with a default location called "Automatic". I find it useful to remove this location, and create a couple of specific new locations: "Open" and "Tunnel".

Open *Network Preferences*, either from the Apple menu or in *System Preferences*. On the *Location* drop-down box, select *New Location...* and create a location called *Open*. This is the location you would use when you don't need to use the encrypted tunnel. When you are happy with these settings, create another location called *Tunnel* (as in Figure 7-14). Select the AirPort interface, and click the *Proxies* tab. Check the *Web Proxy* (HTTP) box, and add 127.0.0.1 as the hostname and 3128 as the port number.

I also find it useful to add a proxy bypass for the *.local* domain, so that the proxy isn't used when accessing local Rendezvous sites (although why Apple doesn't do this by default, I'll never know).

Click *Apply Now*, and you're all done. You can now choose whether to use the encrypted proxy by simply selecting your Location from the Apple

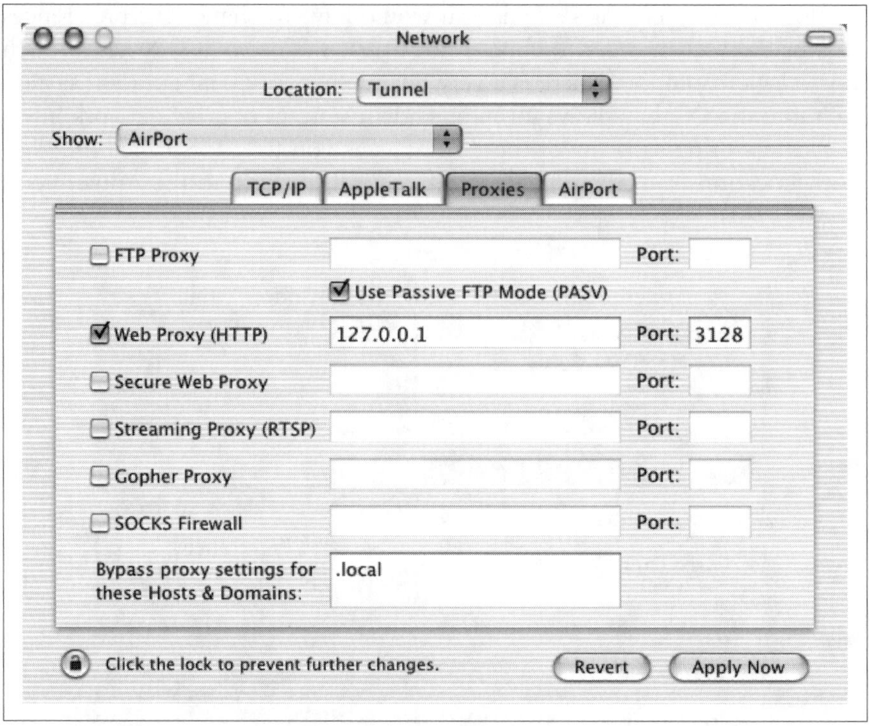

Figure 7-14. *Create an encrypted location called Tunnel.*

menu. It takes a moment or two for the changes to take, as the interfaces are actually brought down and back up (and so they need to request a new DHCP lease, register the changes with any running programs, etc.). Don't forget to start your SSH tunnel [Hack #91] before trying to use the Tunnel location.

One word of caution about the bypass settings, and network proxy settings in general: The bypass box seems only to allow for one top-level domain, but does allow any number of subdomains or hostnames. Unfortunately, they are completely ignored by some applications (notably Mozilla and iTunes). At least at the time of this writing (OS X 10.2.6), you need to specify separate settings for your proxies in Mozilla, and disable proxy settings altogether when using iTunes with remote streams if they get in the way.

HACK   Using vtun over SSH
#98   Connect two networks together using vtun and a single SSH connection.

vtun is a user space tunnel server, allowing entire networks to be tunneled to each other using the tun universal tunnel kernel driver. Using an encrypted tunnel such as vtun allows roaming wireless clients to secure all of their IP traffic using strong encryption. It currently runs under Linux, BSD, and Mac OS X. These examples assume that you are using Linux.

The procedure described next will allow a host with a private IP address (10.42.4.6) to bring up a new tunnel interface with a real, live routed IP address (208.201.239.33) that works as expected, as if the private network weren't even there. Do this by bringing up the tunnel, dropping the default route, then adding a new default route via the other end of the tunnel.

To begin with, here is the (pretunneled) configuration of the network:

```
root@client:~# ifconfig eth2
eth2 Link encap:Ethernet HWaddr 00:02:2D:2A:27:EA
inet addr:10.42.3.2 Bcast:10.42.3.63 Mask:255.255.255.192
UP BROADCAST RUNNING MULTICAST MTU:1500 Metric:1
RX packets:662 errors:0 dropped:0 overruns:0 frame:0
TX packets:733 errors:0 dropped:0 overruns:0 carrier:0
collisions:0 txqueuelen:100
RX bytes:105616 (103.1 Kb) TX bytes:74259 (72.5 Kb)
Interrupt:3 Base address:0x100

root@client:~# route
Kernel IP routing table
Destination Gateway Genmask Flags Metric Ref Use Iface
10.42.3.0 * 255.255.255.192 U 0 0 0 eth2
loopback * 255.0.0.0 U 0 0 0 lo
default 10.42.3.1 0.0.0.0 UG 0 0 0 eth2
```

As you can see, the local network is 10.42.3.0/26, the IP is 10.42.3.2, and the default gateway is 10.42.3.1. This gateway provides network address translation (NAT) to the Internet. Here's what the path looks like to *yahoo.com*:

```
root@client:~# traceroute -n yahoo.com
traceroute to yahoo.com (64.58.79.230), 30 hops max, 40 byte packets
1 10.42.3.1 2.848 ms 2.304 ms 2.915 ms
2 209.204.179.1 16.654 ms 16.052 ms 19.224 ms
3 208.201.224.194 20.112 ms 20.863 ms 18.238 ms
4 208.201.224.5 213.466 ms 338.259 ms 357.7 ms
5 206.24.221.217 20.743 ms 23.504 ms 24.192 ms
6 206.24.210.62 22.379 ms 30.948 ms 54.475 ms
7 206.24.226.104 94.263 ms 94.192 ms 91.825 ms
8 206.24.238.61 97.107 ms 91.005 ms 91.133 ms
9 206.24.238.26 95.443 ms 98.846 ms 100.055 ms
10 216.109.66.7 92.133 ms 97.419 ms 94.22 ms
11 216.33.98.19 99.491 ms 94.661 ms 100.002 ms
12 216.35.210.126 97.945 ms 93.608 ms 95.347 ms
13 64.58.77.41 98.607 ms 99.588 ms 97.816 ms
```

In this example, we are connecting to a tunnel server on the Internet at 208.201.239.5. It has two spare live IP addresses (208.201.239.32 and 208.201.239.33) to be used for tunneling. We'll refer to that machine as the server, and our local machine as the client.

Now, let's get the tunnel running. To begin with, load the tun driver on both machines:

```
# modprobe tun
```

It is worth noting that the tun driver will sometimes fail if the kernel version on the server and client don't match. For best results, use a recent kernel (and the same version, e.g., 2.4.20) on both machines.

On the *server* machine, save this file to */usr/local/etc/vtund.conf*:

```
options {
port 5000;
ifconfig /sbin/ifconfig;
route /sbin/route;
syslog auth;
}

default {
compress no;
speed 0;
}

home {
type tun;
proto tcp;
stat yes;
keepalive yes;

pass sHHH; # Password is REQUIRED.

up {
ifconfig "%% 208.201.239.32 pointopoint 208.201.239.33";

program /sbin/arp "-Ds 208.201.239.33 %% pub";
program /sbin/arp "-Ds 208.201.239.33 eth0 pub";

route "add -net 10.42.0.0/16 gw 208.201.239.33";
};

down {
program /sbin/arp "-d 208.201.239.33 -i %%";
program /sbin/arp "-d 208.201.239.33 -i eth0";

route "del -net 10.42.0.0/16 gw 208.201.239.33";
};
}
```

Launch the vtund server like so:

```
root@server:~# vtund -s
```

Now, you'll need a *vtund.conf* file for the client side. Try this one, again in */usr/local/etc/vtund.conf*:

```
options {
port 5000;
ifconfig /sbin/ifconfig;
route /sbin/route;
}

default {
compress no;
speed 0;
}

home {
type tun;
proto tcp;
keepalive yes;

pass sHHH; # Password is REQUIRED.

up {
ifconfig "%% 208.201.239.33 pointopoint 208.201.239.32 arp";

route "add 208.201.239.5 gw 10.42.3.1";
route "del default";
route "add default gw 208.201.239.32";

};

down {
route "del default";
route "del 208.201.239.5 gw 10.42.3.1";
route "add default gw 10.42.3.1";
};
}
```

Finally, run this command on the client:

```
root@client:~# vtund -p home server
```

Presto! You now not only have a tunnel up between *client* and *server*, but also have added a new default route via the other end of the tunnel. Take a look at what happens when we traceroute to *yahoo.com* with the tunnel in place:

```
root@client:~# traceroute -n yahoo.com
traceroute to yahoo.com (64.58.79.230), 30 hops max, 40 byte packets
1 208.201.239.32 24.368 ms 28.019 ms 19.114 ms
2 208.201.239.1 21.677 ms 22.644 ms 23.489 ms
3 208.201.224.194 20.41 ms 22.997 ms 23.788 ms
4 208.201.224.5 26.496 ms 23.8 ms 25.752 ms
5 206.24.221.217 26.174 ms 28.077 ms 26.344 ms
```

```
 6  206.24.210.62 26.484 ms 27.851 ms 25.015 ms
 7  206.24.226.103 104.22 ms 114.278 ms 108.575 ms
 8  206.24.238.57 99.978 ms 99.028 ms 100.976 ms
 9  206.24.238.26 103.749 ms 101.416 ms 101.09 ms
10  216.109.66.132 102.426 ms 104.222 ms 98.675 ms
11  216.33.98.19 99.985 ms 99.618 ms 103.827 ms
12  216.35.210.126 104.075 ms 103.247 ms 106.398 ms
13  64.58.77.41 107.219 ms 106.285 ms 101.169 ms
```

This means that any server processes running on *client* are now fully available to the Internet, at IP address 208.201.239.33. This has happened all without making a single change (e.g., port forwarding) on the gateway 10.42.3.1.

Here's what the new tunnel interface looks like on the client:

```
root@client:~# ifconfig tun0
tun0 Link encap:Point-to-Point Protocol
inet addr:208.201.239.33 P-t-P:208.201.239.32 Mask:255.255.255.255
UP POINTOPOINT RUNNING MULTICAST MTU:1500 Metric:1
RX packets:39 errors:0 dropped:0 overruns:0 frame:0
TX packets:39 errors:0 dropped:0 overruns:0 carrier:0
collisions:0 txqueuelen:10
RX bytes:2220 (2.1 Kb) TX bytes:1560 (1.5 Kb)
```

and here's the updated routing table—note that we still need to keep a host route to the tunnel server's IP address via our old default gateway; otherwise, the tunnel traffic couldn't get out:

```
root@client:~# route
Kernel IP routing table
Destination Gateway Genmask Flags Metric Ref Use Iface
208.201.239.5 10.42.3.1 255.255.255.255 UGH 0 0 0 eth2
208.201.239.32 * 255.255.255.255 UH 0 0 0 tun0
10.42.3.0 * 255.255.255.192 U 0 0 0 eth2
10.42.4.0 * 255.255.255.192 U 0 0 0 eth0
loopback * 255.0.0.0 U 0 0 0 lo
default 208.201.239.32 0.0.0.0 UG 0 0 0 tun0
```

To bring down the tunnel, simply kill the vtund process on *client*. This restores all network settings back to their original state.

This method works fine, if you trust vtun to use strong encryption and to be free from remote exploits. Personally, I don't think you can be too paranoid when it comes to machines connected to the Internet. To use vtun over SSH (and therefore rely on the strong authentication and encryption that SSH provides), simply forward port 5000 on *client* to the same port on *server*. Give this a try:

```
root@client:~# ssh -f -N -c blowfish -C -L5000:localhost:5000 server
root@client:~# vtund -p home localhost
root@client:~# traceroute -n yahoo.com
traceroute to yahoo.com (64.58.79.230), 30 hops max, 40 byte packets
1 208.201.239.32 24.715 ms 31.713 ms 29.519 ms
```

```
 2 208.201.239.1 28.389 ms 36.247 ms 28.879 ms
 3 208.201.224.194 48.777 ms 28.602 ms 44.024 ms
 4 208.201.224.5 38.788 ms 35.608 ms 35.72 ms
 5 206.24.221.217 37.729 ms 38.821 ms 43.489 ms
 6 206.24.210.62 39.577 ms 43.784 ms 34.711 ms
 7 206.24.226.103 110.761 ms 111.246 ms 117.15 ms
 8 206.24.238.57 112.569 ms 113.2 ms 111.773 ms
 9 206.24.238.26 111.466 ms 123.051 ms 118.58 ms
10 216.109.66.132 113.79 ms 119.143 ms 109.934 ms
11 216.33.98.19 111.948 ms 117.959 ms 122.269 ms
12 216.35.210.126 113.472 ms 111.129 ms 118.079 ms
13 64.58.77.41 110.923 ms 110.733 ms 115.22 ms
```

In order to discourage connections to vtund on port 5000 of the server, add a net filter rule to drop connections from the outside world:

```
root@server:~# iptables -A INPUT -t filter -i eth0 -p tcp --dport 5000 ↵
-j DROP
```

This allows local connections to get through (since they use loopback), and therefore requires an SSH tunnel to *server* before accepting a connection.

As you can see, this can be an extremely handy tool to have around. In addition to giving live IP addresses to machines behind a NAT, you can effectively connect any two networks together if you can obtain a single SSH connection between them (originating from either direction).

If your head is swimming from this *vtund.conf* configuration, or if you're feeling lazy and don't want to figure out what to change when setting up your own client's *vtund.conf* file, take a look at the automatic *vtund.conf* generator [Hack #99].

Tips and Tricks

While that should be enough information to get vtund up and running on your system, here are a couple of additional points to keep in mind.

- The session name (*home* in the preceding example) must match on the client *and* the server sides, or you'll get an ambiguous "server disconnected" message.

- The same goes for the password field in the *vtund.conf* file on both sides. It must be present *and* match on both sides, or the connection won't work.

- If you're having trouble connecting, make sure you're using the same kernel version on both sides, and that the server is up and running (try telnet server 5000 from the client side to verify that the server is happy).

- Try the direct method first, then get SSH working once you are happy with your *vtund.conf* settings.

If you're still having trouble, check */etc/syslog.conf* to see where your auth facility messages are going, and watch that log on both the client and server when trying to connect. It can be tricky getting vtun running the first time, but once it is properly configured, it works like a charm.

Automatic vtund.conf Generator

Generate a vtund.conf on the fly to match changing network conditions.

If you've just come from the previous hack [Hack #98], then this script will generate a working *vtund.conf* for the client side automatically.

If you haven't read the previous hack (or if you've never used vtun), then go back and read it before attempting to grok this bit of Perl. Essentially, it attempts to take the guesswork out of changing the routing table around on the client side by autodetecting the default gateway, and building the *vtund.conf* accordingly.

To configure the script, take a look at the *Configuration* section. The first line of $Config contains the addresses, port, and secret that we used in the vtun hack. The second is there simply as an example of how to add more.

To run the script, either call it as vtundconf home, or set $TunnelName to the one you want to default to. Better yet, make symlinks to the script like this:

```
#ln -s vtundconf home
#ln -s vtundconf tunnel2
```

then generate the appropriate *vtund.conf* by calling the symlink directly:

```
#vtundconf home > /usr/local/etc/vtund.conf
```

You might be wondering why anyone would go to all of the trouble to make a script to generate a *vtund.conf* in the first place. Once you get the settings right, you'll never have to change them, right?

Well, usually that is the case. But consider the case of a Linux laptop that uses many different networks in the course of the day (say, a DSL line at home, Ethernet at work, and maybe a wireless connection at the local coffee shop). By running vtundconf once at each location, you will have a working configuration instantly, even if your IP and gateway is assigned by DHCP. This makes it easy to get up and running quickly with a live, routable IP address, regardless of the local network topology.

Incidentally, vtun currently runs well on Linux, FreeBSD, OS X, Solaris, and others.

The Code

Save this file as *vtundconf*, and run it each time you use a new wireless network to generate an appropriate *vtund.conf* for you on the fly:

```perl
#!/usr/bin/perl -w

# vtund wrapper in need of a better name.
#
# (c)2002 Schuyler Erle & Rob Flickenger
#
################ CONFIGURATION

# If TunnelName is blank, the wrapper will look at @ARGV or $0.
#
# Config is TunnelName, LocalIP, RemoteIP, TunnelHost, TunnelPort, Secret
#
my $TunnelName = "";
my $Config     = q{
  home     208.201.239.33 208.201.239.32 208.201.239.5  5000  sHHH
  tunnel2  10.0.1.100      10.0.1.1       192.168.1.4    6001  foobar
};

################ MAIN PROGRAM BEGINS HERE

use POSIX 'tmpnam';
use IO::File;
use File::Basename;
use strict;

# Where to find things...
#
$ENV{PATH}  = "/bin:/usr/bin:/usr/local/bin:/sbin:/usr/sbin:/usr/local/↵
sbin";
my $IP_Match = '((?:\d{1,3}\.){3}\d{1,3})';       # match xxx.xxx.xxx.xxx
my $Ifconfig = "ifconfig -a";
my $Netstat  = "netstat -rn";
my $Vtund    = "/bin/echo";
my $Debug    = 1;

# Load the template from the data section.
#
my $template = join( "", );

# Open a temp file -- adapted from Perl Cookbook, 1st Ed., sec. 7.5.
#
my ( $file, $name ) = ("", "");
$name = tmpnam( )
  until $file = IO::File->new( $name, O_RDWR|O_CREAT|O_EXCL );
END { unlink( $name ) or warn "Can't remove temporary file $name!\n"; }

# If no TunnelName is specified, use the first thing on the command line,
# or if there isn't one, the basename of the script.
```

```
# This allows users to symlink different tunnel names to the same script.
#
$TunnelName ||= shift(@ARGV) || basename($0);
die "Can't determine tunnel config to use!\n" unless $TunnelName;

# Parse config.
#
my ($LocalIP, $RemoteIP, $TunnelHost, $TunnelPort, $Secret);
for (split(/\r*\n+/, $Config)) {
  my ($conf, @vars) = grep( $_ ne "", split( /\s+/ ));
  next if not $conf or $conf =~ /^\s*#/o; # skip blank lines, comments
  if ($conf eq $TunnelName) {
    ($LocalIP, $RemoteIP, $TunnelHost, $TunnelPort, $Secret) = @vars;
    last;
  }
}

die "Can't determine configuration for TunnelName '$TunnelName'!\n"
  unless $RemoteIP and $TunnelHost and $TunnelPort;

# Find the default gateway.
#
my ( $GatewayIP, $ExternalDevice );

for (qx{ $Netstat }) {
  # In both Linux and BSD, the gateway is the next thing on the line,
  # and the interface is the last.
  #
  if ( /^(?:0.0.0.0|default)\s+(\S+)\s+.*?(\S+)\s*$/o ) {
    $GatewayIP = $1;
    $ExternalDevice = $2;
    last;
  }
}

die "Can't determine default gateway!\n" unless $GatewayIP and
$ExternalDevice;

# Figure out the LocalIP and LocalNetwork.
#
my ( $LocalNetwork );
my ( $iface, $addr, $up, $network, $mask ) = "";

sub compute_netmask {
  ($addr, $mask) = @_;
  # We have to mask $addr with $mask because linux /sbin/route
  # complains if the network address doesn't match the netmask.
  #
  my @ip = split( /\./, $addr );
  my @mask = split( /\./, $mask );
  $ip[$_] = ($ip[$_] + 0) & ($mask[$_] + 0) for (0..$#ip);
  $addr = join(".", @ip);
  return $addr;
```

```
}

for (qx{ $Ifconfig }) {
  last unless defined $_;

  # If we got a new device, stash the previous one (if any).
  if ( /^([^\s:]+)/o ) {
    if ( $iface eq $ExternalDevice and $network and $up ) {
      $LocalNetwork = $network;
      last;
    }
    $iface = $1;
    $up = 0;
  }

  # Get the network mask for the current interface.
  if ( /addr:$IP_Match.*?mask:$IP_Match/io ) {
    # Linux style ifconfig.
    compute_netmask($1, $2);
    $network = "$addr netmask $mask";
  } elsif ( /inet $IP_Match.*?mask 0x([a-f0-9]{8})/io ) {
    # BSD style ifconfig.
    ($addr, $mask) = ($1, $2);
    $mask = join(".", map( hex $_, $mask =~ /(..)/gs ));
    compute_netmask($addr, $mask);
    $network = "$addr/$mask";
  }

  # Ignore interfaces that are loopback devices or aren't up.
  $iface = "" if /\bLOOPBACK\b/o;
  $up++    if /\bUP\b/o;
}

die "Can't determine local IP address!\n" unless $LocalIP and $LocalNetwork;

# Set OS dependent variables.
#
my ( $GW, $NET, $PTP );
if ( $^O eq "linux" ) {
  $GW = "gw"; $PTP = "pointopoint"; $NET = "-net";
} else {
  $GW = $PTP = $NET = "";
}

# Parse the config template.
#
$template =~ s/(\$\w+)/$1/gee;

# Write the temp file and execute vtund.
#
if ($Debug) {
  print $template;
} else {
  print $file $template;
```

```
    close $file;
    system("$Vtund $name");
}

__DATA__

options {
    port $TunnelPort;
    ifconfig /sbin/ifconfig;
    route /sbin/route;
}

default {
    compress no;
    speed 0;
}

# 'mytunnel' should really be `basename $0` or some such
# for automagic config selection
$TunnelName {
    type tun;
    proto tcp;
    keepalive yes;

    pass $Secret;

    up {
     ifconfig "%% $LocalIP $PTP $RemoteIP arp";
     route "add $TunnelHost $GW $GatewayIP";
     route "delete default";
     route "add default $GW $RemoteIP";
     route "add $NET $LocalNetwork $GW $GatewayIP";
    };

    down {
     ifconfig "%% down";
     route "delete default";
     route "delete $TunnelHost $GW $GatewayIP";
     route "delete $NET $LocalNetwork";
     route "add default $GW $GatewayIP";
    };
}
```

HACK 100 Tracking Wireless Users with arpwatch

Automatically keep a database of MAC address to IP address mappings.

MAC address filters are easily circumvented using commonly available
tools—see "Dispel the Myth of Wireless Security" [Hack #87]. If your APs are
bridged to the Ethernet segment, there are a couple of utilities you can use to
look for people fiddling with their MAC addresses. One such tool is
arpwatch, available from *http://www-nrg.ee.lbl.gov/nrg.html*.

---

arpwatch runs as a daemon on any machine, and keeps track of the MAC address/IP address pairs as ARP replies pass through the network. When it notices something out of the ordinary, it logs the activity to syslog, as well as sends an email to the address of your choice. Aside from looking for suspicious activity, this also gives you a nice log of every new user on your wireless network. This can be fun to watch over time, particularly if you are running an open wireless network.

After you unpack the arpwatch archive, take a look at *addresses.h*. This is where the email address is set, so be sure to update it before you compile arpwatch. Set WATCHER to whatever you like (the default is "root," which sends it to root at the machine that is running arpwatch).

You should be able to build and install the binaries with the usual commands:

```
root@florian:~/arpwatch-2.1a11# ./configure; make; make install
```

Unfortunately, this doesn't install all of the necessary pieces. In particular, arpwatch expects */usr/local/arpwatch* to exist by default and to contain the *arp.dat* database file. It also looks in this directory for an Ethernet OUI to manufacturer a list to give more informative information about the machines it sees. Check out "Finding Radio Manufacturers by MAC Address" [Hack #27] for more details about the OUI portion of MAC addresses. Create the necessary directory and files with the following commands:

```
root@florian:~/arpwatch-2.1a11# mkdir /usr/local/arpwatch
root@florian:~/arpwatch-2.1a11# cp ethercodes.dat /usr/local/arpwatch
root@florian:~/arpwatch-2.1a11# touch /usr/local/arpwatch/arp.dat
```

Finally, if you have sufficient space, I highly recommend installing the man pages as well:

```
root@florian:~/arpwatch-2.1a11# cp *.8 /usr/local/man/man8
```

Now you can start arpwatch as a daemon. Specify the interface you would like to watch with the -i switch.

```
root@florian:~# arpwatch -i eth0
```

This should start arpwatch as a daemon. If it doesn't seem to be running, it will log any problems to syslog, so take a look at your system logs (particularly */var/log/messages* and */var/log/syslog*).

Now, as machines ARP for each other on the network, arpwatch keeps track of them. Every time there is new activity, you should get an email that looks something like this:

```
From: arpwatch@florian.rob.swn (Arpwatch)
Date: Mon Jun 23, 2003  2:16:51  PM US/Pacific
To: root@florian.rob.swn
Subject: new station (dhcp-68)
```

```
       hostname: dhcp-68
     ip address: 10.15.6.68
ethernet address: 0:30:65:03:e7:8a
 ethernet vendor: APPLE COMPUTER, INC.
      timestamp: Monday, June 23, 2003 14:16:51 -0700
```

You will be notified by email whenever a new client is detected, when an already logged MAC address is seen in use with a new IP address, and when the MAC address associated with a particular IP changes. There are a number of legitimate reasons why IP-to-MAC address mappings may change (particularly if you are running a busy network with an insufficient number of available DHCP leases). Regardless of the cause, arpwatch keeps a nice historical log of the traffic it sees, which can be valuable when tracking down potential miscreants. Since arpwatch logs to syslog as well as email, you can easily generate reports or graphs by processing these logs whenever you like.

While arpwatch faithfully logs everything it sees, it doesn't actually take any corrective action on its own. If you need an automated method for reacting to suspicious ARP or other activity on your network, take a look at Snort (*http://www.snort.org/*).

It is possible to provide secure wireless services, but only by fully understanding the protocol's strengths and weaknesses and applying a liberal amount of application layer encryption. I hope that this chapter has made you more aware of the common pitfalls, and has armed you with some valuable tools for keeping your wireless networks secure and fun to use.

Deep Dish Parabolic Reflector Template

Figure A-1 is the template for the Deep Dish Parabolic Reflector [Hack #70].

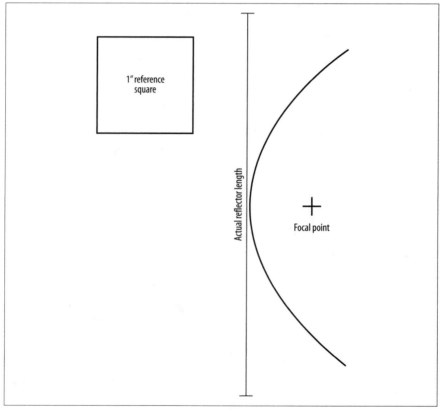

Figure A-1. Reflector template

Index

We'd like to hear your suggestions for improving our indexes. Send email to *index@oreilly.com*.

convert utility (Image Magick), 28
cryptography
    strong application layer
        encryption, 90
    WEP encryption (see WEP
        encryption)
curl network utility, 69
Cygwin, 244–248
    installing, 244–247
    OpenSSH configuration, 248
cylindrical waveguide antennas, 158

D

data and voice applications, Bluetooth
    suitability for, 8
Data Link layer (OSI model), 221
data rates
    802.11b equipment, 4
    802.11g, 6
    low data throughput with 900
        MHz, 10
    low throughput with Bluetooth, 8
    Powerline Ethernet, 17
data services, mobile network (see
    mobile data networks)
Debian-based Pebble, using as wireless
    access point, 134
decrypt utility, 228
deep dish cylindrical reflector (see
    parabolic dish antennas)
default gateway, pinging to troubleshoot
    connectivity, 64
DeLorme (Topo USA and 3-D
    TopoQuads), 210
Dev FS, running on Linux kernel, 148
device pairing, 33, 41
    RFCOMM interface, binding to
        dial-up networking device, 34
DHCP
    configuring IP address for
        AirPort, 116
    configuring service on AirPort, 117
        bridging and, 118
    leases, troubleshooting, 63
    WET11, problems with, 110
dhcpd, configuring for AirPort
    Linux, 113
dialup, configuring for AirPort APs, 116
Dial-up Networking (DUN) profile,
    Bluetooth, 32

dictionary attacks against a WEP
    key, 222
dipole antennas, 176
directionality of antennas, 155, 182
    parabolic dishes, 159
    slotted waveguides
        highly directional, 198
        omnidirectional, 197
    unidirectional waveguide
        antennas, 197
    waveguide feed with Primestar
        dish, 187
dishes
    parabolic dish antennas, 159
        mesh vs. solid reflectors, 159
    recycled satellite dishes, using for
        antennas, 184–187, 187–190
    satellite and DSS, conversion to 2.4
        GHz dishes, 159
    (see also antennas; parabolic dish
        antennas)
distances, free space path losses for, 212
DIY AP running Linux, 84
DNS
    multicast service advertisements, 70
    name resolution, troubleshooting, 64
    SSH Socks 4 proxy and, 237–239
do-it-yourself antennas (see under
    antennas)
DriftNet (image grabber for X11), 89
DSL Reports' Speed test, 90
DSS dish mount (recycled), using, 169
DSSS (Direct Sequence Spread
    Spectrum), 1
    802.11, compatibility with
        802.11b/g, 2
    802.11g, backwards compatibility
        with 802.11b radios, 6
dual-band access points (802.11a), 3
DUN (Dial-up Networking) profile,
    Bluetooth, 32

E

EAP (Extensible Authentication
    Protocol), 15
eavesdropping on wireless networks
    DriftNet tool, 89
    EtherPEG tool, 88
    MAC filering and, 147

Colophon

Our look is the result of reader comments, our own experimentation, and feedback from distribution channels. Distinctive covers complement our distinctive approach to technical topics, breathing personality and life into potentially dry subjects.

The tool on the cover of *Wireless Hacks* is a wire cutter/pliers combo tool. It is typically used to cut or trim a piece of wire, and can bend it into an appropriate shape. In a pinch, it can also strip the insulation from heavy gauge wire, although a wire stripper is really the proper tool for that job. Its insulated handle provides a small measure of protection from electricity, but when using a wire cutter, be sure to first disconnect power from the wire you are cutting. Always wear eye protection when using a cutting device of any kind.

Mary Brady was the production editor and the copyeditor for *Wireless Hacks*. Colleen Gorman was the proofreader. Brian Sawyer and Claire Cloutier provided quality control. Matt Hutchinson and James Quill provided production support. Ellen Troutman-Zaig wrote the index.

Emma Colby designed the cover of this book, based on a series design by Edie Freedman. The cover image is a photograph from the Stockbyte WorkTools CD. Emma Colby produced the cover layout with QuarkXPress 4.1 using Adobe's Helvetica Neue and ITC Garamond fonts.

David Futato designed the interior layout. This book was converted by Julie Hawks to FrameMaker 5.5.6 with a format conversion tool created by Erik Ray, Jason McIntosh, Neil Walls, and Mike Sierra that uses Perl and XML technologies. The text font is Linotype Birka; the heading font is Adobe Helvetica Neue Condensed; and the code font is LucasFont's TheSans Mono Condensed. The illustrations that appear in the book were produced by Robert Romano and Jessamyn Read using Macromedia FreeHand 9 and Adobe Photoshop 6. This colophon was written by Rob Flickenger.